JULIETTE ROSSANT

SUPER CHEF

THE MAKING OF THE GREAT MODERN RESTAURANT EMPIRES

Free Press
New York London Toronto Sydney

FREE PRESS
A Division of Simon & Schuster, Inc.
1230 Avenue of the Americas
New York, NY 10020

Designed by Karolina Harris

Manufactured in the United States of America

10 9 8 7 6 5 4 3 2 1

Library of Congress Cataloging-in-Publication Data Control Number: 200443210

ISBN 978-1-4165-6841-4

For information regarding special discounts for bulk purchases,
please contact Simon & Schuster Special Sales at
1-800-456-6798 or business@simonandschuster.com

For my husband,
sine qua non

Contents

List of Photographs

Note from the Author

How many times have reporters asked Wolfgang Puck about his caviar-and-salmon pizza? A million. How many times has he been asked how he managed to open Chinois on Main only a year after Spago Hollywood, or how he raised twice the money much less managed more than one restaurant for the first time in his life? Just about never.

To watch a chef's face transform from dread at the millionth request for the same worn-out story of how such-and-such a dish came about to the excited realization in their eyes that they were at last being asked about their new business empires, that was a never-ending delight. I had the pleasure of hearing their tales, and it is their wonder and adventure that I have tried to impart in this book, rather than focus on hot food or cold commerce.

To the chefs who are the subjects profiled in this book—the main ingredients—I am grateful. While great financial rewards have come to them, they have also come at great risks and costs not limited to the financial variety. They lead the way for others and create models for future careers. They remain vulnerable artists, and they have been open and vulnerable to me.

This book is by no means all flattery and praise, and each of you chefs who have bravely allowed me to walk briefly along your very special, individual roads without benefit of your knowing what I would write, I thank: Wolfgang, Charlie, Todd, Mary Sue, Susan, and Tom. If I have been critical of you at times in this book, my critiques arise first and foremost from unabashed admiration for the unique genius that drives each of you. Your genius far outweighs any criticism of a mere writer who has only briefly had the privilege of sharing part of your lives; I am merely trying to share your tales with those who have not witnessed your efforts. Thanks also to the wonderful colleagues around you.

To all readers, the chefs about whom I wrote own privately held companies, so in all cases financial figures were available to me only on such occasions as they were told to me by a Super Chef or an associate. In no case have I had benefit of a clear-cut financial picture such as an annual report with a balance sheet of assets and liabilities. This was the same situation I faced at *Forbes* when writing the Celebrity Chefs column for the "Celebrity 100" issue and the Middle East section for the global "Billionaires list." The lack of financial snapshots only challenged me to sift more carefully through other information I gathered.

Thanks go to Leslie Jones, Philip Rappaport (now at Bantam Books), and very specially Liz Stein and Martha Levin of Simon & Schuster's Free Press, who gave me opportunity and guidance; Gloria Loomis of the Watkins Loomis Literary Agency; and Ellen Geiger of Curtis Brown Ltd.

Thanks to Tim Forbes and *Forbes* magazine, especially editor Peter Newcomb for assigning me the Celebrity Chefs column of the "Celebrity 100" issue. Natalie Cannestra has helped me above and beyond duty, always. Tom Easton, now of *The Economist,* and Marc Ballon, now of the *Jewish Journal of Greater Los Angeles,* have always been inspiring and enthusiastic supporters.

Julia Collins not only gave good advice and warm support but also inspiration with her own brave and wonderfully written book, *My Father's War.* Jen Mitchell provided superb transcriptions. To Silvia Elias and her family I am maternally grateful.

Deepest thanks goes to my family. My mother Colette nourished my love of food and writing. My father James encouraged my curiosity and determination. I cherish my childhood memories of helping my sister Marianne make paté, my sister Cecile make sushi, and my brother Tomas eat his pasta creations. Cousin John of *Business Week* helped me get started as a journalist. My in-laws extended homes and help with love. My husband has been a constant companion and help; his expertise in management consulting, his business acuity, and his knowledge of Media and Entertainment all coupled with common sense have given me great insight into what Super Chefs have become and into what they may further evolve.

My son ate his first adult foods all on one magnificent day: lunch care of Michael Mina at Aqua in San Francisco and dinner care of executive chef Mark Purdy at Charlie Palmer's Dry Creek Kitchen. Such a propitious entry into food has given me high hopes (and immediately inspired another book).

If you get your ego involved in your business, then you fuck up for sure.

—WOLFGANG PUCK

I didn't have mentors who taught me the business. It's the school of hard knocks: they don't teach you this in school.

—CHARLIE PALMER

This is a trial-and-error thing. There's no 101 course on how to expand a restaurant business.

—TODD ENGLISH

In retrospect, there were plenty of things that were tough, and I think that's what drove people like me and Susan, Barbara Tropp and Joyce Goldstein and Lidia Bastianich and Anne Rosenzweig. Those people owned their own restaurants because being in the system with men just never felt equal and fair, so it's like "I'm going to be my own boss—that's how I'm going to deal with this!"

—MARY SUE MILLIKEN (WITH SUSAN FENIGER)

We talked about what we wanted to do, more from a business viewpoint and not from a food or wine or service standpoint—more from what we thought was missing in the restaurant business, what we thought the hospitality industry should be doing, what we thought was the way to go about running a restaurant.

—TOM COLICCHIO

SUPER CHEF

INTRODUCTION

> The ability to recall a taste sensation, which I think of as "taste memory," is a God-given talent, akin to perfect pitch, which makes your life richer if you possess it. If you aren't born with it, you can never seem to acquire it. . . . And naturally good chefs and cooks must depend upon memory when they season or when they are combining subtle flavors to create a new sauce or dish.
>
> —James Beard, *Delights and Prejudices* (1964)

How *does* one become a Super Chef? First, James Beard advised, one needs "taste memory." Such memory starts in childhood. Wolfgang Puck's mother was a pastry chef. Charlie Palmer learned to cook in high school. Todd English claims his Italian grandmother inspired him. Mary Sue Milliken and Susan Feniger both credit their mothers for sparking their appreciation. Tom Colicchio grew up in a Neapolitan family in New Jersey who treated meals as an integral part of family ritual and even had an uncle who sold fresh vegetables.

Some chefs study formally at organized schools; others pass on school and simply work. Tom Colicchio never "studied"—other than read, re-read, and then read again Jacques Pépin's *La Technique* while he apprenticed. Wolfgang Puck won an Austrian national culinary championship after only three years of gastronomical studies at the technical school in Villach, where he started at the age of 14. Todd English graduated from the Culinary Institute of America (CIA) at the top end of his class. Charlie Palmer and Susan Feniger are also CIA graduates; Mary Sue Milliken graduated from Washburne Culinary Institute in Chicago.

Schooling only helps prepare for placement; apprenticeship is the most important part not only of learning but also of becoming recognized and of advancing. With the Austrian national prize in his pocket, Wolfgang Puck worked for six years in France before becoming an executive chef in Indianapolis, and he worked in a undistinguished downtown Los Angeles restaurant before getting his big break from Patrick Terrail at Ma Maison. Fresh from the CIA, Charlie Palmer landed a full-time job at La Côte Basque but also took on unpaid work off-hours at La Petite Marmite and La Chantilly before he got his break at the River Café. Both Mary Sue Milliken and Susan Feniger worked at Le Perroquet in Chicago after they finished school, and both apprenticed in France (L'Olympe and L'Oasis, separately) before launching their partnership at City Café.

When a cook has proven him- or herself at every station in the kitchen, knows each step of preparation for every dish on the menu, and can produce every dish perfectly and repeatedly, that cook can become a *sous chef* ("under chef") and eventually a chef. A chef who shows talent for the creation of new sauces and dishes—a signature—has become a great chef.

Typically, such great chefs work for others (a restaurateur or another chef) and then open their own restaurant. Opening up a restaurant is no light matter. Describing their move from the eleven-table City Café to their own 5,000-square-foot City Restaurant in Los Angeles in 1984, Mary Sue Milliken confessed:

> We didn't know much about business at all, and that's one of the real stumbling blocks for chefs. You know, you're really focused on Food, you're really, really passionate—
>
> —and then there's never a good time, added Susan Feniger, and no one really likes it that much—
>
> —for learning about business and all the things that go hand-in-hand with business: how to run it, the ups and downs, how to imagine the future, how to control costs, how to increase sales, none of that.

Managing not one but many restaurants in more than one geographic location is just where becoming a Super Chef first becomes a distant glimmer. To take that quantum leap, a chef must show aptitude for other professions, such as restaurateur and entrepreneur, financier, realtor, and media star. Some of it can be learned—but when and how, when a rising chef has already spent most of his or her adult life so far just learning to become a chef? Culinary schools have only recently begun to teach some of these other skills.

People who made the leap between 1980 and 2000 from owning their first restaurant to forming an empire have been extraordinary leaders indeed. They are phenomena, and this change in cookery has been nothing less than phenomenonal. The question is, will Super Chefs last?

CONSIDER four earlier French chefs whose careers had deep impacts on these Super Chef phenomena: Antonin Carême, Auguste Escoffier, André Soltner, and Ferdinand Point.

Though *haute cuisine* (high cooking as opposed to *cuisine bourgeoise* or home cooking) is recognized as having begun under François Pierre de la Varenne (1615–1678), as Anne Willan described in *Great Cooks and Their Recipes,* it was less than two centuries ago that the father of *haute cuisine,* Marie-Antoine (Antonin) Carême (1784–1833), wrote his crucial five-volume *L'art de la cuisine française au dix-neuvième siècle.* Among his many achievements, Carême codified the French sauces handed down from La Varenne: *espagnole, vélouté, allemande,* and *béchamel.* Of equal importance, however, he was one of the last master chefs in private service, and his employers included France's preeminent diplomat Charles Maurice de Talleyrand-Perigord, Russia's Czar Alexander I, England's King George IV, and France's Baron James de Rothschild.

Georges-Auguste Escoffier (1846–1935) is generally recognized as "the chef of kings and the king of chefs." Among his many accomplishments, he institutionalized *service à la russe,* organized restaurant menus and restaurant kitchens, and recorded recipes for chefs. Escoffier sent out over 2,000 chefs he had trained to promote French food and French products around the world. His personal concern for the welfare of his colleagues raised the status of cooking as a profession. He worked for César Ritz, "the king of hoteliers and hotelier of kings," who created the Savoy and Carleton hotels in London and the Ritz in Paris, the jewels of a hotel empire.

Escoffier was one of the first chefs to gain celebrity on the order of that enjoyed by actors or politicians of his day, though he did not own an interest in the Ritz Development Company, whose kitchen brigades he organized. He dabbled with his own product lines of Spécialités Escoffier, but he remained a chef always and was never interested in developing businesses himself; he sold out his shares in Spécialités Escoffier within a decade. Under Escoffier and Ritz, great chefs became famous for their work in public restaurants: Escoffier mapped out the restaurant industry for the twentieth century.

André Soltner (born 1932) was the chef of Lutèce in New York from 1961 and owner from 1972. He sold it in 1994, just as Super Chefs were coming into their own. For over three decades, Lutèce was considered the single best restaurant in America and Soltner the most celebrated chef. In 1968, he became the first French chef outside France to win the *Meilleur Ouvrier de France,* the highest French recognition for chefs. Honors in just the past decade include the French *Chevalier de la Légion d'Honneur* and the James Beard Foundation Lifetime Achievement Award. He still teaches at the French Culinary Institute in New York. Soltner had no empire but he did have Lutèce, "the repository of the gracious ways of our inherited past," as Seymour Britchky wrote in *The Lutèce Cookbook.*

Just as Soltner carried Escoffier's torch to new heights as the most famous chef-restaurateur in America, back in France the apprentices of Ferdinand Point (1897–1955) were challenging the rigidity surrounding Escoffier's *haute cuisine* recipes with their own *nouvelle cuisine.* Point's apprentices, such as Paul Bocuse, became internationally famous: in the 1970s, Bocuse started an empire from Disney's Epcot Center to restaurants in Tokyo and Melbourne. Still, none of those French chefs ever penetrated deeply into that singularly large and lucrative market called America, and so their empires never reached the size of their later, American-based colleagues.

Nevertheless, *nouvelle cuisine* and its rebel chefs shook an America already convulsed by a health food craze. Their cookbooks abounded. Their chefs toured America. American culinary schools started teaching *nouvelle cuisine,* so that at the CIA in the late 1970s Charlie Palmer studied classical, Escoffier-influenced recipes and less than five years later Todd English was immersed in an American take on *nouvelle cuisine.*

THESE rebels of *nouvelle cuisine* opened the door for the rise of American regional cuisine, just as the media in America were becoming widely food conscious. While Bocuse and contemporaries (Louis Outhier, Roger Vergé, Paul Haeberlin, Michel Guérard, Henri Chapel, Pierre Troisgros, and Alain Senderens) trained and inspired the coming generation in America that would include Super Chefs, the American public was coming to appreciate fine food. Newspapers led by the *New York Times* began running special restaurant, dining, and food sections, and journalists who specialized in food became famous themselves: Pierre Franey, Craig Claiborne, R. W. Apple, Jr., and most recently Ruth Reichl to name journalists at *The New York Times* alone.

Television rode right behind print. By the second of her four-decade reign, Julia Child had become a household name, famous enough to inspire a Dan Akroyd impersonation on *Saturday Night Live* in 1978. Child spawned a troop of like-minded chef educators for decades, including Jacques Pépin and Martin Yan, as well as early entertainers, such as the Galloping Gourmet. It was their enduring success on PBS channels that opened the door for the Food Network with Emeril Lagasse and Sara Moulton, not to forget Martha Stewart. Unlike the Super Chefs, however, Child herself never owned a restaurant, nor have many of the Food Network stars owned either restaurants or restaurant empires. However, Child championed chefs with professional organizations like the James Beard Foundation (whose award is the culinary equivalent of an Oscar), the American Institute of Wine and Food (AIWF), and the International Association of Cooking Professionals (IACP).

Lastly, major technology changes enabled chefs to expand their empires: transportation, communications, refrigeration, packaging, and education. In the world of food, the "global village" had two levels of impact. On the first, the ingredients of regional cuisines became physically accessible most everywhere. On the second, and in contrast, a chef no longer needed to be present physically in any specific restaurant thanks to mobile telephony and the Internet.

Another essential ingredient that made Super Chefs possible was money. The American economic boom of the 1980s and 1990s meant not only that capital was available for such risky ventures as fine dining restaurants but also that more and more people had income to dispose upon the delights of expensive restaurants. In fact, customers were often attracted to investing in their own "trophy" restaurants. As Phil Colicchio explained of his decision to invest in his cousin Tom's restaurants, "Is it fun and cool to bring your friends and clients to your restaurant, that happens to be the best new restaurant in the country? It's way cool!"

From this combination of ingredients and intertwined experiences, the phenomenon of Super Chefs arose.

A NUMBER of ingredients go into making Super Chefs. Their businesses reach geographically outside one city and beyond restaurants into other businesses. They are celebrated for their cooking talents and bedazzling, media-savvy ways. They manage large businesses, building brand names and personal wealth unheard of before among chefs. Their business empires are enduring.

Why were these six chefs profiled and not others? Drawing a single model of the successful Super Chef is not possible, but the adventures of these six Super Chefs captured important variations. Their careers offered some of the best stories, tales of success, disaster, and rebuilding, of contrasting culinary styles and business styles, of geographies and backgrounds.

Wolfgang Puck is the wealthiest Super Chef, and as the longest survivor he has simply done the most. Charlie Palmer has become an investor in restaurant real estate, in other chefs' restaurants, in a host of supply companies, and in hotels. Todd English, while trying to rival Puck, is finding himself breaking new ground in non-food and non-kitchen products. Mary Sue Milliken and Susan Feniger, more than just representing a rising percentage of women chefs, have wrestled most honestly with the issue of staying true to their art. Tom Colicchio represents rising Super Chefs as they play catch-up by accelerating through the expansion cycle.

"Raw talent is not enough," Mary Sue Milliken said. "The biggest ingredient for a chef to be successful is to wear all the hats at a certain level. You don't have to be a great CFO, but you have to be a great leader. You have to be a leader to your CFO. You have to be a leader to your cooks in the kitchen. And actually a lot of great chefs are not great leaders. They are so creative, but they alienate people. They can only grow to a certain point because people think they are assholes."

Most chefs who reach Super Chef level are well liked, hardworking, and irrepressibly optimistic people who have grown emotionally and intellectually as their companies have faltered and flourished. Though they all started in a profession that is largely manual, they are intellectually impressive and innately driven. Their adventures also help answer important questions: how are Super Chefs affecting the food, restaurant, and other newly encompassed industries, and how are they shaping the careers of future chefs?

Courtesy of the Food Network

1 WOLFGANG PUCK

"Get place and wealth, if possible, with grace;
if not, by any means get wealth and place."
—Alexander Pope, *Imitations of Horace* (1738).

ON an October evening in 2002, cool, electric-blue lights marked the entrance to Hangar 8 at the Santa Monica Airport. Just outside the hangar, a huge crowd of fancy suits, BMW dealers from the U.S., Canada, and New Zealand, had gathered for the release of BMW's latest model, the Z-4. Arriving alone and on time was the evening's only announced celebrity, Wolfgang Puck, whose company was catering the 750 guests.

It was hard to find Wolfgang. At celebrity events like the Oscar parties he has a spotlight on him: here, the diminutive Puck, dressed in chef's whites, blended into the sea of milling waiters. The event organizer singled him out among the crowds as he greeted BMW's VIP dealers. A dealer's wife asked him what if anything on the night's menu was on the Weight Watchers® diet she was following. "Everything!" he answered with a grin.

Wolf bustled over to the main preparation area behind the hangar for a first inspection. A line of waiters lingered to collect trays of potstickers and other *hors d'oeurvres* while Puck gave last-minute orders to his cooks. Ten minutes later, he was walking through two nearby auxiliary kitchens and then conferred on the side of the event space with catering vice president Kevin Charbonneau for an update. The evening's food featured all of his fine dining restaurants in Los Angeles: Spago, Chinois, Granita, and Vert.

Appetizers were served before BMW's presentation, an assortment of Wolfgang Puck pizzas and light dishes from Chinois including a "walkabout" chicken salad with bean sprouts, crushed peanuts, and ginger-lemongrass dressing in a take-out container with chopsticks. The pizza quickly grew cold in the outdoor space and the chicken salad tasted mostly of cabbage, but the car dealers threw themselves at the fare with vigor.

Guests packed the hangar for the corporate presentation, which included the second season of BMW's digital film series *The Hire*. As the last film finished, the screen rolled up to reveal seven silver Z-4s streaming toward the guests. When the lead car halted at the hangar entrance, out stepped the surprise star of the evening, the Godfather of Soul himself.

James Brown moved directly onto the stage, already decked with a full band and chorus, and swung straight into a set that led with Sex Machine: "Get up, get on up and then shake your money maker." There was a semblance of shuffling to the beat, a faint hint of swaying in the stodgy audience. "Money maker"—they understood that part.

Wolfgang stood at the back of the hangar, grinning and grooving happily by himself as he waited patiently for a short stint at the microphone to address his guests and invite them back outside the hangar for dinner.

The moment never came. Despite all efforts at timeliness, the presentation had run too long. When James Brown finished his set, he walked straight off stage, and BMW herded their guests directly outside for dinner.

Later, after most of the crowd had filled their first plates, Wolfgang took his turn to sit behind the wheel of one of the seven silver Z-4s. He hobnobbed for another hour. Then about quarter of ten he left—quietly and alone. Another event was about to start that evening at Spago Beverly Hills that required his presence. Another busy night was just starting.

WOLFGANG Johann Puck was born in 1949, in a small village near the thirteenth-century town of St. Veit an der Glan, Austria. His stepfather was a coal miner who followed work around the country, so Wolfgang grew up largely under the influence of his pastry chef mother and grandmother. Against his stepfather's wishes, he set out to become a chef at the age of 14. He managed to enter the technical school in the nearby city of Villach and won an Austrian national contest in cooking. Upon graduation in 1966 at the age of 17, he left Austria for France.

Among the French restaurants where he apprenticed, two of the most famous and most influential upon him were L'Ostau de Baumanière under Raymond Thuilier and Café Maxim, where he worked with a French colleague, Guy LeRoy. Wolfgang was a hard worker, recalled Thuilier's grandson Jean-André Charial, now himself chef and proprietor of Baumanière. "He was very good because after one year my grandfather asked him to be a chef at the other restaurant we owned."

In 1973, Wolfgang and Guy LeRoy left Paris for America. Wolf found a job as executive chef at La Tour in Indianapolis, but soon Guy and he left for Los Angeles. The two of them roughed it out at a restaurant in the downtown Arco Towers until first Guy and then Wolfgang were offered jobs by restaurateur Patrick Terrail at Ma Maison in 1975.

The eclectic restaurant had Astroturf on the floors and resembled a beach bungalow, but until Wolfgang got there it had not been known for its cuisine. When Mark Peel (later executive chef and co-owner of Campanile in Los Angeles) arrived at Ma Maison in the midseventies to begin his career by peeling vegetables, Wolfgang was low-key and Guy LeRoy was "highly spirited and gregarious—and temperamental." The menu was straight from their days at Baumanière—"but it was new for Los Angeles, more evolved." Over time, Wolfgang began to create his own dishes.

"There is no doubt that our outlandish Friday lunches gave the restaurant its Hollywood cachet," wrote Terrail in his book *A Taste of Hollywood*. "Ma Maison became the place to go for Friday lunch to celebrate conquering or surviving the week. . . . One time, we counted 52 Rolls Royces in our parking lot. . . . But the Friday lunches were really known for all the beautiful women who came out in droves—Cheryl Tiegs, Tawny Little, Morgan Fairchild, Jane Seymour . . . and the well tended made fashion statements that ranged from sophisticated and subtle to blatantly sexual. . . . We used to ring the bell for the most outrageous female outfit."

Other regulars included Orson Welles, Elizabeth Taylor, Frank Sinatra, Jacqueline Bisset, Dudley Moore, Suzanne Somers, Peter Falk, Michael Caine, Burt Reynolds, Stevie Wonder, Suzanne Pleshette, Woody Allen, and Ed McMahon. In 1977, star-chasing *People* magazine reported a studio executive's observation that, "If someone dropped a bomb on this place, it would paralyze the entire entertainment industry."

Another important element of Ma Maison was its cooking school, Ma Cuisine. Judy Gethers, whose family owned Ratner's delicatessen in New York, ran it. Terrail brought in visiting chefs, such as Louis Outhier, Roger Vergé, and Julia Child.

Terrail also catered private parties and events at Hollywood studios, particularly MGM, where he knew the president, Dan Melnick. Thanks to the MGM connection, Ma Maison catered a dinner at the Cannes Film Festival 1976 for *That's Entertainment, Part II,* featuring all American food and the following year opened a restaurant there solely for the film festival.

In 1975, Wolfgang invited an old Paris flame, Marie France, to join him in Los Angeles. Six months later they were married, and Guy LeRoy moved out. In 1979, Marie France left Wolfgang for another man.

It was the height of disco, and a few months after his divorce Wolfgang met Barbara Lazaroff at a discotheque. Next morning, she appeared at Ma Maison for a cooking lesson. They paired up soon afterward—Barbara with her famous satin jacket that read "I'm not Wolfgang Puck's girlfriend; he's my boyfriend." Thus began Puck-Lazaroff, perhaps the most spectacular, successful, and influential partnership since Auguste Escoffier teamed up with César Ritz.

In 1981, just before Spago opened, Patrick Terrail wrote, "If Escoffier is remembered as the 'chef of kings and the king of chefs,' Wolfgang Puck is 'chef to the stars and a star of the chefs.' " In that case, Barbara is his agent, his Lew Wasserman, his Swifty Lazar, his Mike Ovitz. Terrail wrote further, "The only reason we're [Puck and Terrail] no longer together today is very simple: I'm just not as good a restaurant partner as his wife Barbara. . . . Wolf has the creativeness, and she has the style."

During the seventies, America's first Super Chef Jeremiah Tower had joined Alice Waters at Chez Panisse. As he describes in *California Dish,* Tower was the first to cook "California Cuisine" on a fateful evening in October 1976 with his "Northern California Regional Dinner." Perhaps more importantly, in 1974 Tower had also launched the heart of the casual fine dining revolution with his "panisse" pizzas, using "California goat cheese and Sonoma beefsteak tomatoes." As Barbara pointed out, both Alice and Wolf knew these pizzas from southern France, where they had both sampled them before. Wolf's favorite was Chez Gu et Fils, only an hour away from L'Ostau de Baumanière.

Puck and Lazaroff picked up on many of the same trends as Tower and Waters and successfully blended them to create a leading force in fine dining that left the competition behind for many, many years.

THERE were numerous stories about the launching of Spago.

The original name of Spago was "Mt. Vesuvio," the brainchild of Wolfgang and the *maître d'* at Ma Maison, Henri Labadie. Hollywood music composer Giorgio Moroder contributed the name "Spago" meaning "a string with no beginning and no end," a play on the Italian word spaghetti. Others said the word was just a humble Neapolitan slang word for the same. "It was supposed to be a pizza and pasta joint," said Mark Peel, Spago's first chef, who claims to have brought the pizzas to Spago along with the pizza oven builder's telephone number when he came back to Wolfgang after a stint at Chez Panisse.

One afternoon—the only time in those days when Wolfgang and Barbara used to get together, between his lunch and dinner shifts—Wolf told her, "You know, I always thought I wanted to put one of those pizza ovens out in a restaurant, but I guess the fire department wouldn't let us." Barbara did not take the remark lying down (as they were). Instead, she rolled over and called the fire department. "Look, it will be sort of like a fireplace," she told a fire inspector. "We'll build counters in front of it." Later, she confided, "I was making it up as I went along." To see the oven from the door, Barbara had to take out a load-bearing wall and install columns; the oven went in the column line.

Initially, Spago was going to be a two-in-one restaurant, with dining upstairs and a bistro downstairs, "fun for everyday." The food was to be more Provençal-Italian than the French food at Ma Maison. Initially, Wolfgang was not planning to leave Ma Maison; by 1981, he had about 10 percent ownership.

The problem was that Terrail wanted the same deal at Wolfgang's restaurant. Wolfgang said, "No, this is my idea. I found the money. I found the location. You want to walk in and have the majority ownership?" Terrail wanted 51 percent. "Patrick said, then you have to leave. I said, no, forget it, then I am going to do that myself." Unfortunately, it leaked out that he was leaving to open his own restaurant. "Everyone came to me and said, 'When are you going to open your restaurant? We all want to come.'" All this was going on in Terrail's restaurant, and he would not tolerate it. "Naturally, he fired me and told me to leave," Wolfgang said, right away.

So, Wolfgang and Barbara decided to open the restaurant together. First, they raised over $400,000 among 29 limited partners at $15,000 each, 22 of whom were Ma Maison customers. When that effort didn't raise enough cash, Wolfgang and one Ma Maison customer, a dentist named Don Salk, cosigned a bank loan. The site they had found was the old Kavkaz restaurant on Sunset Boulevard.

Barbara was in charge of Spago's shoestring construction. Mark Peel designed Spago's kitchen, based on spatial and mechanical drawing classes he had taken in school, as well as practical experience. "Barbara's idea to have theatrical lighting is borrowed from upstairs at Chez Panisse—the layout is the same," he said. While he waited for Spago to be built, Wolfgang wrote the first of several cookbooks, *Wolfgang Puck's Modern French Cooking for the American Kitchen,* with a forward by his mentor Raymond Thuilier.

Only a week before the opening, Wolfgang jotted down the menu in pen on a white pad on four sheets of paper: appetizers, pasta, pizza, main courses. Like Mozart writing music, Puck wrote the menu without a single cross-out. Peel kept the four pages, each one framed, and gave them to Wolfgang on Spago's twentieth anniversary. Peel dared add one thing to the maestro's list, angel hair pasta with goat cheese.

"We hammered the last nail in at 4:00 p.m.," Peel said. "When we opened at 6:00 p.m., we had the menus taped in front of us." They had never made any of the food before.

On January 16, 1982, Spago opened to the public. The lineup on opening night consisted of Wolfgang on grill, Kazuto Matsusaka in the pantry, Nancy Silverton and Mary Bergin in pastry, and Mark Peel on pasta.

"When we opened Spago, nobody tried out the menu," Wolfgang said. "I knew Nancy was a good pastry chef. Kazuto was good at making salads—he worked with me at Ma Maison, and Mark worked with me at Ma Maison. We just opened, and then I looked around, and then next thing the restaurant is full. Then I thought, 'We're in the shit for sure!' "

A few years later, it was much the same. "In those days, it was so crazy," said another Puck protegée Ann Gingrass. "I was on the grill. He [Wolf] wanted to make all customers happy. He would come with a huge *paillarde* to cover the grill. I would have to clear out so he could cook. I had to learn to not let those things bother me." Puck would cook off-menu for his important guests.

Ma Maison and other movie star customers came pouring in, including actors Sean Connery, Sidney Poitier, Michael Caine, Peter Falk, Victoria Principal, and Cher. The restaurant lured a who's who of Hollywood elite and was famous for the number of limousines in the parking lot, just as Ma Maison had been.

Within its first six months, Spago had replaced Ma Maison in *People* magazine as the nationally famous haunt of Hollywood stars. "Until recently, top honors went to Ma Maison, Patrick Terrail's French eatery on the fringe of Beverly Hills. The new challenger is, of all things, a pizzeria, plunked down on once fashionable Sunset Strip. Its owner—oh, perfidy!—is none other than Wolfgang Puck, 32, former head chef at Ma Maison."

By 1983, the fame of Spago, "where the pizza itself has celebrity status," had reached across the country and was picked up in papers like *The Washington Post.* Wolfgang grossed a million dollars and expanded seating from 100 to 135 with a heated tent. Spago was running at 250 covers a night.

Spago was important for its exhibition kitchen. Nevertheless, Barbara's design of the restaurant broke the mold of fine dining, because it had an uncomplicated, casual design that utilized cheap patio furniture, art by local artists, and an exposed beam ceiling. The kitchen, almost directly opposite from the door, allowed Wolfgang to interact with any guest who walked in.

"The big, open kitchen was not used prior [to Spago] in upscale dining establishments, though it was common in fast food restaurants," said designer Adam Tihany, who later designed other Spago restaurants. "From most everywhere you could see the kitchen. The kitchen was very integral, full-size wall, and Wolfgang as a persona behind and in front of the wall, creating this dynamic and exciting relationship between chef and customers. It was a huge PR stunt. You needed a certain kind of person to do it. His energy and concepts were ground breaking." With theatrical spotlights on Puck, he could be seen from almost anywhere in the restaurant and, just as important, the customers could see each other.

The open kitchen was, however, a challenge for the chefs who worked in it. Even though many guests came to Spago to be seen by others, they looked at the chefs also. "It's like being in a window display," recalled Lissa Doumani, a Spago alumna now co-chef and co-owner of Terra in Napa with her husband Hiro Sone, another Spago alumnus. "You have to remember not to scratch your nose. You have to turn around and hit the deck if you cough. You are in a fishbowl. You have to keep that in mind, and it takes a lot of work."

The simple patio furniture and Barbara's often exotic clothing made for a new kind of relaxed ambience. Barbara was largely responsible for the feel of the front of the house. "Barbara went to the flower market twice a week, spending $1,000 a shot for flower arrangements at Spago," said

Lissa Doumani. "They were unbelievably huge arrangements. No one had ever seen this before. This was exotic to the ninth degree, just the ginger plants that hung, the use of colors in the chairs, fabric on the bar, the floor. She created an atmosphere of excitement and interest and energy—the same with music. There was a rollicking atmosphere." It was a scene, and Wolfgang had the Hollywood clients who fit right in, people who wanted to be seen.

Henri Labadie, the *maître d'*, also helped to create the reputation that Spago was hard to get into and well worth it for those who did. Wolfgang, with prodding from others, eventually fired Henri who was rumored to accept bribes for entrance.

Booking a table at Spago was also legendary, but less known was the office line previously used by a dominatrix named "Madame Isis." Peel installed an extension of that line at the pizza station so he and Wolfgang would not have to go all the way to the office to answer. During prep hours in the daytime, Nancy Silverton and Mary Bergin would prepare pastry at the pizza station. Often, Nancy and Mary would answer in the name of Madame Isis to keep the name alive—these calls were staff favorites. There was also a bathroom overlooking the parking lot, and occasionally wild events transpired there with the shades left open.

Management at the beginning of Spago was just as haphazard as the opening itself. Wolfgang's operating principle was simple. "You have to make more money than you spend; otherwise you don't stay in business." He hired a friend's girlfriend to handle both the books and the phones, part-time. She quit in tears. The phones were always lit but rarely answered. After about two weeks, Spago shifted to COD payment to vendors, because they could not keep the invoices straight.

Finally, five months after Spago opened, Wolfgang brought in Tom Kaplan. They had only known each other a few months. With a degree in art history from Bowdoin College, Kaplan had been working while establishing his California residency for business school as a manager at Croissant USA. Two weeks after he joined, Terrail and Wolfgang bought the place out. Terrail went on a trip, and Kaplan got to know Wolfgang. Two months later, Wolfgang left to start Spago. Kaplan stayed a few more months under Terrail's wing and then came to a crossroads. He could go on to business school, have Terrail send him to hotel school, or let Wolfgang put him straight into business itself at Spago. Kaplan protested that he knew no accounting, but Wolfgang was insistent that he take over the front of the house and back office.

Kaplan was innately organized, but "the place was in shambles," he said. "They had *no idea* they were going to be that busy." He worked day and night—and when it was organized enough, he checked himself into a hospital. When he checked out of the hospital, Tom hired a bookkeeper and an assistant. Another longtime Puck associate, Jannis Swerman, joined Kaplan on the floor about the same time, the first of many great colleagues.

A FEW months after the original Spago opened in 1982, word of its phenomenal success reached Tokyo. A group of Japanese businessmen approached Wolfgang for a copy of Spago in Tokyo. When Wolfgang refused, they went ahead and built a carbon copy, right down to hiring a hostess who resembled Barbara. Wolfgang had no recourse, because he had not trademarked the name "Spago." The Japanese, on the other hand, could not get the food right. They approached him a second time, and Wolfgang made a licensing deal under a new company, Trattoria Spago, Inc. (TSI). He sent over a team of chefs to help train their cooks.

Scarcely a year after the successful opening of the original Spago, in 1983 Wolfgang opened his second fine dining restaurant, Chinois on Main. Some of his customers in Spago had a space on Main Street in Santa Monica and wanted a second Spago in the spot. At the time, there were virtually no fine dining restaurants in that section of Santa Monica. Michael McCarty's Michael's and Piero Selvaggio's Valentino's were some distance away. Puck was already itching for another culinary challenge and had chefs Richard Krause and Kazuto Matsusaka ready to move into the new restaurant, featuring Chinese cuisine influenced by French.

Again, Barbara designed the new restaurant. Rather than mimic the extremely inexpensive design she did for Spago, Barbara went all out and created her own homage to Chinese art. Plates were custom-made, the art was exquisite antiques, and the exhibition kitchen was top of the line.

"It was very expensive to build Chinois for us: half the size for twice the price of Spago," Wolfgang said. "It was money well spent, looking back, but when you don't have it, it's a problem."

Chinois cost more, but of all their restaurants before and since, it is the only one that has not changed in the 20 years since it was designed, Barbara asserted. "It was ahead of its *Zeitgeist,* and it's still timely and not dated. When we talk about money issues, one should consider durability." At one point, they ran out of money. They raised more, but it put construction on hold for months.

With two restaurants 15 miles apart in two different cities, Wolfgang could not control both at the same time and needed strong management. He already had Tom Kaplan at Spago, so he made fellow Austrian Micky Kanolzer general manager at Chinois. Still, he needed more staff.

Ordering kitchen equipment from a wholesaler, Tom had met and befriended Bella Lantsman, a bookkeeper. Before Chinois had opened, Kaplan asked her to become the new bookkeeper there. Bella struggled with the decision: she felt she owed her employer, who had given her her first job. Her employer realized that Bella had a better future with Wolfgang and gave his blessing for her to accept the new job. In 1989, when Kanolzer moved to another, newer Puck restaurant, Bella became general manager.

The first year and a half, Chinois on Main was buried in debt, despite the success of the restaurant. As usual with his early deals, Wolfgang owned at least 51 percent of the restaurant. He considered selling Chinois several times.

For Kanolzer, too, Chinois was a trying experience. "We were packed from day one, even though we were six months late with the opening," Kanolzer said. "It was always high maintenance for the restaurant, all these little details: Barbara treated it more like a museum. If there was a little scratch here, she went ballistic. It wasn't easy to maintain." Still, conceded Kanolzer, Chinois on Main remains packed to this day, and "Barbara did do a good job."

In Wolfgang's career, Chinois has been more important than Spago, because it marks the real beginning of his career as restaurateur and entrepreneur.

> That was really the defining moment, when you have to give up control. Not completely, but a little bit. So that's when I had to decide—Mark Peel is going to be in charge at Spago, and I'm going to be in both restaurants. So, for close to three months, I spent much more time at Chinois than Spago. I used to be at Chinois until nine o'clock at night and then go to Spago, but

all of a sudden, I was in a different position. Before, at Spago, I boned the beef and lamb, I cut the fish, I went to market, I did everything.

Wolfgang Puck was no longer just a celebrity chef: he had begun the transformation into a Super Chef. Barbara was by his side, making sure it happened. In September 1983, they married privately. The following year, they had a public wedding that only Robin Leach's *Lifestyles of the Rich and Famous* could encompass. In 1986, Wolfgang began to appear on ABC's *Good Morning America* and his second book, *The Wolfgang Puck Cookbook,* was published.

BY 1989, Wolfgang was ready to open his third restaurant, Postrio in San Francisco. The Kimpton Group had started a trend of hotels opening up celebrity chef–run restaurants with their restaurant Masa's, headed by Masataka Kobayashi. Founder and then chairman Bill Kimpton, along with Tom La Tour, current president and CEO, turned to Wolfgang to open up a restaurant in the Prescott Hotel.

The deal was unusual. According to La Tour, "All the deals are different, but Postrio was trailblazing, with a small fee and a piece of the upside, that is, the back-end interest. If it were successful, he would get a piece of the action, and if the restaurant were sold he would get a piece of the action."

Kimpton hotels are almost all nonunion, and the Prescott is in a large city that could support the cost of a celebrity chef. The restaurant drew customers from locals but was a benefit directly for the hotel. "The restaurant can support higher room rates, so the Prescott Hotel has done better than its peers because Postrio is located in the hotel," La Tour said.

Wolfgang's other interest in opening in San Francisco was that the husband and wife team of David and Ann Gingrass were hoping to move to northern California, and Wolfgang wanted to keep them on his team. The initial plan was to open a second Spago in the hotel. Soon they all realized that there was a lot of resistance to Los Angeles chefs coming to San Francisco, so they changed the name to Postrio, referring to the restaurant's location on Post Street and the trio of Wolfgang, Ann, and David.

Nevertheless, the restaurant was essentially a copy of Spago with a few classics drawn from the San Francisco Bay area and an emphasis on locally sourced ingredients. "The idea was a little bit of San Francisco,

Chinatown, Little Italy, and some traditional things," Ann Gingrass said, "to make sure it worked." Kimpton employed Ann and David, but Wolfgang directed them. The kitchen was responsible for breakfast, lunch, dinner, and room service for the hotel.

IN 1990 Wolfgang opened Eureka in Los Angeles, which was both a restaurant and a brewery. The Los Angeles Brewing Company was already under construction when the owners approached Wolfgang. They were chronically out of money, but by linking a restaurant and the brewery together and raising funds from many of Wolfgang's Spago customers, they were able to open both.

The success of the project depended, however, on the brewery's distributing beer in retail outlets, not just the restaurant. A big fan of beer and sausages, Micky Kanolzer, already six years at Chinois, jumped at the chance to run Eureka. The restaurant was big, with 200 seats, but filled easily with people from nearby movie studios. Also, the restaurant was cheaper than others in fine dining, with entrees at $14–20, although it was still a serious restaurant.

Wolfgang knew nothing about brewing beer and did not interfere with the beer making. The beer was good in the restaurant, but something happened in the bottling process. The beer turned cloudy in the bottles distributed in stores. Customers would come into Eureka with a six-pack asking for their money back, even though it wasn't the restaurant that had sold them the beer.

Kanolzer tried to suggest that the brewers add vitamin B to the beer, a natural preservative, which would prevent the beer from clouding when exposed to temperature changes, but they refused. They were adhering strictly to German *Reinheitsgebot* (brewing purity law), dating back to 1516.

"I knew it was getting tough," Kanolzer said. "People came by and said, 'Are you going to close down?' It was difficult to imagine, since the restaurant was packed."

Wolfgang turned to experts in the field to try to save Eureka. The Los Angeles Brewing Company had filed for bankruptcy protection on a $1 million debt, 10 percent of which was Wolfgang's. Puck attempted to separate the beer business from the restaurant and have it handed over to the Boston Beer Company, which would pay Eureka a royalty.

Wolfgang had contacted Jim Koch, head of Boston Beer. Koch said, "This is savable, a very good brewery. It's probably too big, and it's not all that well run." Koch decided that he was interested in running the brewery and, after meeting with Wolfgang and Barbara, decided he could do business with them. He brought his CFO and accountant to examine the company and put together a joint venture proposal.

"It was a common problem, easily fixable," Koch explained. "It is a technically difficult thing to correctly bottle a good beer. Good beer is like fresh bread. You can't let it sit on the shelf for six months. You have to bottle it right. The brew house, bottling line, tanks—you have to do a good job in all three. Someone with the skills for running a brewery wouldn't have had the problems they had."

Wolfgang made sure his staff was paid before the company went into bankruptcy. Chef Jody Denton moved to Mark Miller's Red Sage Grill in Washington, D.C., soon to become a presidential favorite at the nearby White House. Wolfgang told Kanolzer that they would reopen soon. "Wolfgang was getting frustrated. He was in with a lot of personal money. He lost quite a bit, $1 million or more, and others went into that thing because Wolf was a part of it."

Negotiations with the landlord fell through. Koch offered all he could. "The landlord didn't want to renew the lease. We said, 'We will pay the back rent. We will assume everything in a new lease.' He turned out to be uncooperative or to have other ideas."

The restaurant closed in May 1992, after 23 months.

IN 1991, Wolfgang opened another fine dining restaurant, Granita, in Malibu. This beach community was inhabited by many of his movie star customers in Los Angeles. Granita, or Italian ice, was Wolfgang's Italian-inspired restaurant.

The location was risky. Malibu did not have any fine dining restaurants at the time because most of the wealthy crowd was seasonal. Spago regulars urged Wolfgang to open up there anyway, and these customers became investors in the new restaurant.

The restaurant, though in a beach community famous for cliff-hugging bungalows, was not on the beach. Granita nests in the Malibu Colony Plaza, an outdoor shopping center. To compensate for the lack of beachfront view of the Pacific, Barbara created a sea within. As she had done at

Courtesy of the Wolfgang Puck Collection

INTERIOR OF GRANITA

Chinois, Barbara went all out on Granita's décor, hiring artisans to create a lavish set with coral aquariums, undersea motifs, and tiles. The *Los Angeles Times* commented, "Every surface is patterned in a kaleidoscope of colors so dizzying that some people prefer to sit outside, where they can focus on the food."

Construction was a nightmare. The price was set too low, at $1 million, roughly the same as Barbara had spent on the much smaller Chinois. The original owner refused to let them use the septic system (Malibu had no sewage pipelines), so Barbara had to arrange for a second, separate septic system, which required tearing up the parking lot. Then, she had to clear the wood-burning oven and the fireplace with the coastal commission. Some neighbors protested against the complex. On top of all this, she was pregnant. As a last straw, while she and Wolf were on a cruise with her parents and his, they discovered that approval had not come from the City of Malibu because the city had lost their plans six months earlier. They had to rush the papers in, because within a week the city was putting a stop to new restaurants. "As Wolf said, I got more faxes than the captain" of their cruise. All the while, she was building Eureka and putting in appearances at Spago and Chinois. For a time, she stopped all construction on Granita and shifted to Eureka.

By coming to Malibu, noted the *Los Angeles Times,* "Puck is in effect providing them the convenience of their own Puckateria. This may explain why Granita lacks the distinct culinary personality of Spago (pizza and pasta), Chinois (Chinese) and Eureka (beer and sausage). Granita—call it Wolfgang's One-Stop—serves a little of all three."

For some years Granita lost money, Tom Kaplan admitted. The L.A. riots a year after Granita's opening did not help matters for Granita or any other restaurant in the Los Angeles area. Further, what Wolfgang and Barbara had not considered was the "intensity" of Malibu's seasonality. "Mud slides and road closures—that was new!" Kaplan said. Nor had they anticipated the effects of coastal weather. "You could have a Friday night where you had 250 reservations," Kaplan explained, "and then the rain comes and you lose the weekend." The restaurant remains open to this day and has been making money for years, even if the investment has still not been paid off.

To shore up sales, in late 1993 Wolfgang made a deal with Visa, publicly dropping American Express in return for advertising for Granita.

In a newspaper ad that ran in the *Los Angeles Times,* the *San Francisco Chronicle, Daily Variety,* and the *Hollywood Reporter* in January 1994, American Express suggested that customers consider thousands of other fine restaurants in the Los Angeles area that gladly welcome American Express. AmEx continued the battle, offering frequent restaurant-goers a one-time $25 reward if they used their American Express cards in a local restaurant.

In retrospect, Kaplan said, Granita was simply bigger than need be, but the concept created a showcase for another aspect of Wolfgang's cuisine—and rising protégés. Granita opened with an all-Spago chef cast led by Joseph Manzare. It was a springboard for Lee Hefter, who first became executive chef at Granita before going on to Spago Hollywood and then Spago Beverly Hills. Then in 1997 Jennifer Naylor took the helm.

Naylor came from the restaurant family who owned the Tiny's restaurant chain in Los Angeles. Inspired by the success of Mary Sue Milliken and Susan Feniger's City Restaurant, she pursued fine dining. She spent time at Eureka and several other of Wolfgang's restaurants. Wolfgang also sent her on *stages,* most importantly one with Italy's only three-star woman chef of the time, Nadia Santini of Restaurante dal Pescatore in Mantua. Wolfgang moved her back to Granita as executive chef, where she remains to date, happily creating her own dishes inspired by Wolfgang and Nadia.

WOLFGANG'S stepfather was an amateur boxer, and they used to go to Caesars Palace in Las Vegas for boxing matches. Until the 1990s, Las Vegas was a wasteland in terms of fine food. Casinos and hotels served grub plentifully, by the buffet plateful. All that changed when Wolfgang opened Spago Las Vegas in December 1992.

Caesars Palace was hit hard by the newer, flashier Mirage next door, whose volcanoes and tigers were luring once-loyal customers in droves. Caesars Palace had already approached Wolfgang to do a Spago in Lake Tahoe but had rejected the proposal Wolf came back with. Then, independently, real estate developer Sheldon Gordon approached Caesars with a retail shopping concept.

According to Tom Kaplan, the idea for the Forum Shops at Caesars was to combine a shopping mall and a restaurant mall with a one-way, moving sidewalk leading from the exit of the Mirage. "People would come from the Mirage, and then they couldn't get out," Kaplan said. "At the time, nobody thought it was smart. 'Shopping in Vegas? Forget about it!' they said."

Gordon enlisted the help of the Simon Property Group, experts in mall development, and finally convinced Caesars that the shopping mall would work. Then Gordon started approaching Wolfgang to add a Spago as the anchor restaurant, but each time Wolfgang refused. Finally, during one attempt to woo him, Wolfgang sent Tom Kaplan in his stead. Kaplan showed Gordon the proposal they had prepared for Caesars in Lake Tahoe, and Gordon accepted. Kaplan was surprised. "I think he really needed the name Spago to continue on to bring on other stores. Once Spago decided to come, Gucci said OK."

According to the terms, Wolfgang and Gordon would each own 50 percent. Wolfgang then sold part of his shares to other investors. Though the shopping mall was connected to Caesars, it was technically owned and developed by Simon and Gordon, who were the landlords for Spago. Spago itself was built as a two-part restaurant, a café for lighter, less expensive fare facing the shopping mall and an interior restaurant separated by a bar for more serious Spago food.

Spago was the first upscale restaurant run by a celebrity chef in Las Vegas, and Wolfgang had no assurances it would be a success. "We opened in December 1992, which we didn't know is the slowest month of the year," recalled Kaplan, who became the Spago Las Vegas general manager. "There was a rodeo going on. We did 100 dinners the first night, but the cowboys were thinking that there was going to be a buffet. They took up their plates to the open kitchen to collect food. The next three weeks it was the same thing." By Christmas, they were serving 300 covers a night, but that was still not enough to cover the rent.

Then, a few days after Christmas, a consumer electronics convention hit town, and "We went from 300 dinners a night to 2,000!" Kaplan said. "Business went haywire. The conventions came, and we never looked back." Spago reigned almost without competition for a half a decade, as few other chefs came to Las Vegas until Steve Wynn opened the Bellagio Hotel and Casino in 1998. In reply, Wolfgang also opened a Chinois outpost in the Forum, Trattoria del Lupo in the Mandalay Bay Resort, and Postrio Las Vegas in the Venetian's Grand Canal Shops, all in 1998.

WOLFGANG continued to expand Fine Dining under the leadership of Tom Kaplan with more Spagos. In 1994, Wolfgang opened Spago Mexico City, but the deal fizzled.

In 1996, he opened Spago Chicago, with his brother Klaus as general manager. Designed by Adam Tihany, the restaurant proved overlarge. Spago's California Cuisine was less than popular because the city's taste was "strictly meat and potatoes, or pasta," said Klaus. "What amazed me more was that young people expected the same." With the lease finishing in early 2004, Spago Chicago is likely to close.

In 1997 Wolfgang opened Spago Palo Alto on the site of one of Jeremiah Tower's Stars restaurants. Initially, Jeremiah Tower had underbid Wolfgang, but his restaurant failed within a year, leaving the investors to come back to Wolf. With customers at Postrio in nearby San Francisco, Wolfgang believed he saw a good opportunity. Tom Kaplan initially oversaw the new restaurant. Adam Tihany designed again.

Also in 1997, Wolfgang opened Spago Beverly Hills. Barbara returned as designer. Rather then simply remake the humble original, she created an elegant restaurant around an open-air courtyard filled with exotic trees. Guests could still watch the chefs cook in an exhibition kitchen, but it was set in the back of the restaurant. The move there marked the coming closure of the original Spago, which Wolfgang decided not to renovate when the Beverly Hills location became available. Beverly Hills was "much more California" and closer to the talent agencies, which drove movie stars to Spago.

After successful openings in Palo Alto, Chicago, and Beverly Hills, a Spago was announced for Kuwait City, Kuwait, in 1998. During negotiations, the agreement switched to a Wolfgang Puck Café. Wolfgang sent out chef Virgo Romano with the further mission to open up a catering company in the region as well as cafés. Wolfgang said, "They had wanted a Spago, and they treated it like a Spago." Eventually, the owners "policed" the entry and demanded coat and tie, "so rigidly that the young crowd fell away. They lost the business clients, too, and closed."

The most recent Spago opened on Maui at the Four Seasons Hotel in December 2001. Wolfgang sent over trusted veteran front-of-the-house manager Jannis Swerman from corporate headquarters, where by then she directed corporate communications, to oversee the opening during the Christmas holiday. Wolf owns the restaurant outright, and it has proven so successful that Wolfgang Puck Fine Dining is discussing a second property with the Four Seasons.

TOP chefs in France have produced or endorsed food products for over a century. Escoffier made sauces. In 1976, Michel Guérard started a barrage of chef-corporate deals by becoming consultant to Nestlé's Findus line of frozen gourmet food. Within a few years, Paul Bocuse had Disney (Chefs of France at Disney World), Alain Senderens had Carrefour, Joël Robuchon had Fleury-Michon, and the late Bernard Loiseau had Unilever and Royco.

Earlier in the 1970s, Julia Child had endorsed Cuisinart in America. Chuck Williams, founder of Williams-Sonoma, said that whenever she talked about a product on her show, the product sold out in his stores the next day. Before her, James Beard had advertised for Mouton Cadet and less known products.

In 1961, advertising giant George Lois tried to license James Beard's name, but Beard refused. Eventually, Beard agreed to endorse a few minor products. "It was a strange period," Lois said, "when a guy like Beard said he would be hurting his reputation. I said, 'Jimmy, what are you talking about? We could create an empire here! I mean, people worship you!' . . . I had all the plans in the world. I wanted to put his name everywhere with terrific products. He wouldn't do it, and he could have had a giant business." Lois went on to make Tommy Hilfiger famous, as well as MTV (he coined "I want my MTV"), ESPN, and Lean Cuisine (he named the product), in addition to his famous covers for *Esquire* magazine.

A doctor whose patients included O. J. Simpson's lawyer Robert Shapiro lured Wolfgang down the same road. In 1983, Dr. Robert Koblin approached him to participate in a frozen food company along with chefs Roy Yamaguchi, Piero Selvaggio, Mark Miller, and Michael Roberts. Koblin had noticed that his cardiac patients could not easily find healthy prepared foods and that most of America's large food producers had chemists rather then chefs devising their recipes. He envisioned Chef's Choice, a company with American Heart Association approval, to sell frozen entrées prepared from chef recipes, with no additives. When the American Heart Association refused to endorse him, Koblin decided to start with Spago pizzas, frozen and without any additives.

At first, Wolfgang turned him down. According to Koblin, Wolfgang feared that if the pizzas failed, that would reflect badly on Spago. Koblin accepted Wolfgang's choice of frozen desserts and chose several recipes from pastry chef Nancy Silverton's repertoire. Spago was famous for its desserts. Koblin raised $3 million from among his patients and Spago customers to form the Wolfgang Puck Food Company (the Food Company, to insiders). Soon it became apparent, however, that the exquisite desserts were too expensive for supermarkets.

Conceptually, however, Wolfgang favored food product expansion. Koblin went through another round of financing and raised some $7 million. By then, Wolfgang had noticed that some of his customers at Spago were buying extra pizzas to take home. When he asked them why, they said they were going to freeze them to eat later. Convinced, he allowed Koblin to launch the pizza line. It took months to get approval from the U.S. Food & Drug Administration, since the pizzas were not tomato-based and thus outside the usual pizza definition. When a third round of financing approached in 1989, the board replaced Koblin with Selwyn Joffe.

Joffe had his work cut out for him because he was not building the company from scratch. "A lot of people questioned the concept of why would you go frozen when you have a gourmet guy?" Joffe himself claims he would have started with restaurant concepts, then shelf-stable products, and lastly frozen products. Instead, he had inherited a frozen food company. According to Joffe, he farmed pizza production out to KT's Kitchens, then relaunched all three varieties of frozen pizzas in Vons, a big Los Angeles supermarket chain.

Joffe created a marketing plan that focused on the Wolfgang Puck brand. He reasoned that the pizza had to be premium, made with the best quality ingredients, to separate it from typical frozen pizzas. He emphasized that Puck's pizzas were handmade.

"What is the difference," he said, "to the supermarket whether it's Wolfgang Puck's or Gino's? They are going to get the dollars from the category no matter what. So we developed Wolfgang Puck and Wolfgang Puck lifestyle positioning. I was not competing with other frozen pizzas. What I was doing is competing with home delivery. The home delivery market was about $25 billion at the time. The frozen pizza category at the time was about $900 million."

Against the claim of Domino's, one of the leading delivery pizzas, that they could deliver in 30 minutes, Joffe claimed his pizzas would cook in 15 minutes. "I positioned it as an incremental revenue source for the supermarket. I could generate more dollars per cubic inch than they could from any other product because we were more than double the price than anyone else." By 1996, Joffe claimed to have captured 18 percent of the frozen pizza market in California.

In 1995 frozen entrées were introduced. When Tom Warner took over marketing for the Food Company in 1997, he added seven new pizzas and thirteen new frozen entrées. Joffe also hired an advertising company to help him refine the Wolfgang Puck positioning, which he had distilled into the phrase, "Where food meets life." They developed an advertising campaign around the phrase "Live, love, eat!," which eventually took over as the corporate slogan.

Joffe said, "The thought was that I wasn't going to focus on taking the product to everybody. I was going to focus on people who knew him and cater to them wherever they went." That meant if Spago customers were throwing a child's birthday party, then the pizzas or frozen entrées were available.

"Most people knew Wolfgang at Spago as chef to the stars. We tried to convince people that the way he caters to the stars, you could cater to your friends at home and enjoy that lifestyle, or to yourself. Feel the way these people feel—that is the lifestyle. . . . It was the lifestyle of the event of going to Spago that I was trying to capture."

After the pizzas were re-released, Joffe focused on meal replacement with "To Go Units." These in-supermarket stands featured freshly made foods that consumers could take home. "Wolfgang Puck To Go" started in 1995 in an upscale, southern California supermarket chain called Gelson's. The name evolved to "Grab and Go." According to Tom Warner, the per unit cost was high because each location had to have a small pizza oven, and sales did not rise quickly enough to offset that cost. Further expansion was put off, though the units still exist.

AT the same time as the frozen pizzas were taking off, Joffe started casual dining restaurants. Postrio had opened in San Francisco in 1989, and Wolfgang was gaining some name recognition in northern California. The Food Company had followed with free samples of Puck pizzas at Macy's on Union Square in San Francisco. According to Wolfgang, "Rudy Borneo was then the [vice] chairman of Macy's West, and he was very good friends with us and still is. He said, 'Why you don't do a little place down there, serve them the little chicken salad?'" Joffe opened up a 14-foot-long counter in the Macy's Cellar and made $600,000 the first year.

After opening a second outlet in a Macy's in Bloomfield, Illinois, Joffe looked around for great real estate that would give him the exposure he had at Macy's, with low or no investment by the Food Company. Lew Wasserman, a Spago regular, was at that time the head of Universal Studios and had been trying to get Wolfgang to put in a restaurant there. Joffe talked Wolfgang into it, resulting in the first Wolfgang Puck Café on the new City Walk of Universal City.

Joffe brought on board real estate expert Irv Siegel, who had once been a restaurateur as well as an attorney, to oversee site selection. The City Walk site was a no-brainer, Siegel said. "Anytime you can have a location in a highly trafficked, controlled environment with exclusive use, it's difficult not to be a winner." The small café exposed the Wolfgang Puck brand to more consumers from outside southern California.

Joffe asked Barbara to design the Wolfgang Puck Café concept. "I thought she should be involved," he said, "because the combination of Wolfgang and Barbara is what really built Spago and that together we could use their personas to build the cafés." Barbara designed the cafés based on the color scheme of the frozen pizza boxes. Chairs, floor tiles, and wall décor all integrated a pizza shape she created.

"I wanted to make them colorful and vibrant," Barbara said. "I wanted an iconography so that people would immediately know that is what it was, sort of like McDonald's golden arches, the idea that when you looked at the storefront kids would say, 'Oh, Mom, that must be a Wolfgang Puck Café!' All the colorful tiles and vibrancy were supposed to be stimulating and create a sense of fun and celebration."

Successful at City Walk, Joffe opened another Wolfgang Puck Café in Las Vegas at the MGM Grand, where he thought he could attract consumers not only from all over the country but also important convention goers. "The biggest real estate conference was held in Las Vegas at the MGM Grand, and I wanted exposure to all the big developers." Joffe claims that a number of developers cut deals that included restaurant build-out for free. In all, Joffe rolled out nine Wolfgang Puck Cafés and three Wolfgang Puck Express units in just three years, so that Wolfgang Puck Food Company surpassed the number of outlets opened by Wolfgang Puck Fine Dining in 10 years. Joffe rated these outlets several notches above other fast-food and casual concepts. "The concept was to have them intimate, special, and chef-driven as opposed to big feeding machines. I wanted to keep the integrity of Wolfgang's name and the integrity of the product."

Frank Guidara took over the Food Company in September 1996 from Joffe. He was a restaurant operator with a long career, including 10 years as president of the restaurant division of Restaurant Associates of New York. He had been responsible for both fine dining and food service concepts. His clients had included Carnegie Hall, the Lincoln Center's Metropolitan Opera House, the United Nations, Goldman Sachs, and Morgan Stanley.

Guidara found the Food Company practically out of money, just as his predecessor had found it. Joffe had expanded the cafés quickly, stretching the Food Company's resources to the limit. An industry analyst confirmed Guidara's assessment, calling it "a ball of string" losing massive amounts of money, with millions more going out than flowing in.

Wolfgang knew the performance had been poor, said Guidara. "He knew they were almost out of money, but, remember, he was working a million hours at Spago, Postrio—he didn't have an organization at that time, and how much can one person do?"

Guidara joined just as the Food Company was launching another new concept. In November 1996, Wolfgang and Barbara opened an Asian café concept in Beverly Hills based on Malaysian, Indian, Chinese, Korean, Japanese, and Thai cuisines. It was to be followed by outlets in Seattle and other locations. "ObaChine isn't just another Wolfgang Puck Café in Chinese guise," the *Los Angeles Times* reported. "It's Puck riffing on all the flavors and spices of Asia. And that sense of fun comes through in the food as ObaChine plays bistro to Chinois' *haute* Asian food." Others closely associated with Wolfgang disagreed. "We had everything incorporated from Indian to Thai to Chinese—you needed a translator for people to read the menu! It was insane," an associate said.

Compared to Barbara's other designs around Los Angeles, ObaChine seemed "understated." She furnished it with *objets d'art* that she found across Asia. She said that some were real antiques and others she antiqued herself "with a rock in my backyard." She estimated the artwork in one ObaChine restaurant at $100,000.

The two-story restaurant seated 200 people. Typical of Barbara's designs, the restaurant overran costs on construction and décor. Food reviews were positive, but expectations and food costs soared after the new Spago Beverly Hills opened a few months later and only one-tenth of a mile away.

ObaChine Seattle opened in January 1998. "We think Seattle really supports a restaurant scene," Guidara told *The Seattle Times*. "We see a lot of apartments and condos being built downtown. It reminds me of Boston, tightly packed, a good place for restaurants. It's also a young market, with about the right amount of money. And people seem to like good food." They would also open a Wolfgang Puck Café there that summer.

The Seattle Times commented, "Though restaurateurs such as Wolfgang Puck and Il Fornaio cringe at being called chains—a term suggesting the mass production of food in the style of McDonald's or Pizza Hut—to locals with one or two in-town restaurants, that is what they are." Locals often tend to favor local establishments, while tourists, as they become better food educated, tend to seek out local fare as well.

ObaChine opened in Phoenix in January 1998 to little fanfare.

The next month, a furor arose in Seattle over a print hanging behind the reception desk. *The Seattle Times* described the artwork as "a turn-of-the-century depiction of a Chinese man in a servant's jacket holding a cup of tea. He is wearing a long braid, or queue, and the slant of his eyes is exaggerated. Originally, the image was used as an advertisement for a colonial French tea company, but Lazaroff has since had it altered to include the restaurant's name." ObaChine Beverly Hills had the same poster, which was mentioned only in passing in the first *Los Angeles Times* review as, "a bright, Chinoiserie poster advertising ObaChine," but Seattle's huge Asian community felt differently. Pickets and boycotts assaulted the restaurant over the "yellow sambo," despite calmer reasoning from *The Seattle Times* that "bullying innocent businesses into insult avoidance won't change the past—and will only make future efforts to prevent bona fide discrimination more difficult."

Barbara, the designer, felt her artistic freedom threatened and rejected the charge of racism, given the ethnic diversity of her 5,000 employees. Paris-based art dealer Annie Rousseau came to Barbara's rescue. Not only, as she pointed out in an editorial, were her great-great-uncle Henri Rousseau's paintings similar in that they depicted exotic foreigners (in Rousseau's case, Africans), but she herself had sold the ObaChine work to Barbara—and another copy to the famed social China Club in Hong Kong.

The media lost interest, and the poster remained in place. The boycotts, however, continued. Then the scandal spread to ObaChine Phoenix. In February 1999, word leaked out that ObaChine would close. By May 30, 1999, *The Seattle Times* reported that "it's all oba for ObaChine" as all three outlets closed that weekend.

Publicly, Guidara cited strategic reorganization within the Food Company as the reason for the closures, not the poster controversy or anything else. Critics in Seattle and Phoenix disagreed. "Coming to Seattle (from California, no less) to serve pan-Asian cuisine is, at best, bringing coals to Newcastle."

Instead, the Food Company would focus efforts on the Cafés, Grand Cafés, and Expresses, as well as food products because "the Asian-oriented ObaChine concept wasn't as adaptable," Guidara told the *Los Angeles Times*. Admittedly it was not as profitable, either.

Later, Guidara said of ObaChine that when he had joined the company, "I was led to believe that the concepts were worked on, that two chefs were working on it from Spago, Asian chefs developing the menu. Nothing had been done. There was no management, no menus, nothing. Unfortunately, we had commitments on real estate to open them."

Irv Siegel cited two further problems. First, the myriad cuisines, each one a fusion, created not just confusion but aversion. Second, the two-story setup created problems they had not encountered before: vertical transportation, unusable space, and access for the handicapped.

After the ObaChine fiasco, Guidara figured that if the small cafés were bringing in good returns then he could make more with much larger spaces, which he christened Wolfgang Puck Grand Cafés. The first went into Disney World's Downtown Disney section in Orlando, Florida, in 1997. Wolfgang signed a worldwide agreement with Disney. This "one of a kind" restaurant was really four restaurants in one: an Express, B's Sushi & Raw Bar (named after Barbara), a Café, and the Dining Room upstairs for finer dining. The Food Company built four more Grand Cafés from 1998 to 2000 in Denver, Colorado; Orange County, California; Sunrise, Florida; and Evanston, Illinois.

In February 2001, Wolfgang Puck Food Company's last new concept opened, a first-ever seafood restaurant with 250 seats (and another 100 seats for a bar and lounge) overlooking the Paradise Pier section of Disney's California Adventure in Anaheim. Avalon Cove (pictured on p. 32) by Wolfgang Puck was a "a 350-seat restaurant and lounge designed in an elaborate undersea world motif." The restaurant closed at the beginning of October 2001, with both Disney and Wolfgang claiming a mutual decision to close, while observers cited the economic plunge after 9/11. The restaurant was limited to the theme park's customers, who not only grew scantier after September 11 but whose children were less interested in Casual Dining than their baby boomer parents.

In all, the Food Company had opened an average of nearly three restaurants each year for the past decade. Guidara realized that they needed better training and greater consistency. He brought in new managers, some from Fine Dining. He made Jennifer Jasinski, who had cooked at Eureka, Granita, and several Spagos, executive corporate chef for Casual Dining.

As the menus became more ambitious, the restaurants strayed from Casual Dining into Fine Dining, confusing customers with vast offerings under one roof. The Grand Café at Disney World was a prime example.

Jasinski and other chefs assembled a corporate cookbook to get all the cafés to cook the same food. She found her Fine Dining background a hindrance. "Puck taught me, whatever you make, do it well, use the best ingredients, make it right, take pride in your work. It didn't matter if you were at a four-star restaurant or a café: the wiener schnitzel still had to be

Courtesy of Jeff Keller

EXTERIOR OF AVALON COVE

good." Top management was no different, as Joffe's brand lifestyle focused on a Spago experience, while Guidara, like the chefs, was also a product of Fine Dining. Earlier, Joffe had feared that if Casual Dining food was not up to expectation, then customers would not buy food products like pizza.

Of course "mini-Spagos" needed well-trained chefs, not just line cooks. Managers fought to keep menus simple and profitable. The original Wolfgang Puck Café at the Universal City Walk had 140 seats. The café often did 1,100 covers in a kitchen that had a 14-foot line. Once the cafés got more sophisticated, however, the price for the build-out went up, along with the décor. The lines went up to 25 feet and included back kitchens and production facilities. "It wasn't a cookie-cutter place anymore," one former manager said.

Others agreed that larger sizes and higher food costs translated into lower profits. "Wolf is successful because he listens to the people," a longtime associate said. "Whatever they want, they get. That is a wonderful thing if you run a fine dining restaurant—but not if you run a café." People came into the cafés asking for Puck's pizza with salmon and caviar—

for $12 instead of the $30 charged at Spago. Landlords were no better; they all wanted cafés turned into "mini-Spagos."

Barbara said, "The expectation level is extremely high with his name on it. They keep expecting a Spago. They want Spago for one-fourth the cost."

Irv Siegel, the company real estate guru, pointed out that the cafés fared better the farther away they were from Wolfgang's Fine Dining restaurants. Tom Kaplan went further, saying that the Grand Cafés have been less risky than Fine Dining outlets like Spago when entering new territories, such as Denver; conversely, however, the farther Fine Dining spreads, the more it might undermine Cafés. And there could be hidden costs, like the noncompete clause signed with Disney, which stopped a deal with the Ritz Carlton for a Fine Dining restaurant in Orlando.

ALTHOUGH the initial expansion of Casual Dining under Joffe and their continued growth under Guidara had taken precedence over food products, new items were introduced. New people entered, too. They started with David Sculley.

Sculley had worked for the H. J. Heinz Company for 22 years and left as senior vice president for global frozen food operations. After Heinz, in 1995 he formed Sculley Brothers, LLC, an investment company, with his brothers Arthur, a former president of J. P. Morgan, and John, formerly CEO of Pepsi and Apple Computer. David Sculley had studied the soup market and found that there was room for a premium canned soup. He made an investment and got a seat on the board of directors of the Food Company. He formed a manufacturing company called Country Gourmet Foods, LLC, a licensee of the Wolfgang Puck Food Company, based in Pittsburgh, Pennsylvania. By 1998 the company had test-marketed the soups, which scored high with consumers. Distribution began on the West Coast in 1999.

"David Sculley had provided an example of marketing Wolfgang Puck as a brand name, mass-market, with a truly competitive, very strong product," said Rob Kautz, then CFO of the Food Company. "It's having tremendous success in a very competitive market against Campbell's. This is a market that is extremely tough. Progresso took 10 years to go from zero to 10 percent market share, and Wolfgang was at 6 percent the first season in Denver."

Tom Warner saw the new soup line as a great boost to the frozen pizzas he was managing. "If you take a commodity and do it better than anyone else, you can charge a premium, like I did on pizza, but not so much that you drive people away. Then you are going to get a fair share of the business."

One industry observer summarized by saying that he thought the Food Company had too much "basic stuff" wrong, like overpricing and physical size and weight of pizzas. "It's a classical example of a man [Wolfgang] who is brilliant in his area of expertise, but he doesn't have the toolbox, as it turns out, to manage things outside, which includes hiring partners."

This is not to mention the egos involved, the observer continued. "The Wolfgang Puck Cafés was a project that was to showcase Barbara's design abilities. . . . When the Wolfgang Puck Grand Café opened in Orlando, there was Barbara, personally picking out the tiles to glue on the bar. Everyone knew Wolfgang Puck was not behind the wall. It was not a fully developed concept. The financial performance speaks for itself."

Wolfgang and Barbara's experience in the Casual Dining sector came up too regularly in the red, according to former managers. Barbara's flamboyant expenditures often overburdened their creations, and Wolf's softheartedness when it came to customer demand made it unlikely that there would ever be margins high enough to recover the opening losses. However, this same combination almost always succeeded in Fine Dining, where Barbara's flamboyance grabbed attention and maintained snob appeal, and Wolf's generosity could always be added to a guest's bill.

Frank Guidara resigned at the end of 1999, when he was offered a job to head up the Au Bon Pain chain. He turned over the company to his CFO, Robert Kautz. Kautz had joined the Food Company in 1995, after heading up the Koo Koo Roo chain of restaurants. Kautz's strength was as a deal maker in the Casual Dining sector. His first effort was to turn the Food Company into an Internet vendor, selling products from a sophisticated website. Kautz spent heavily on website development but quickly dropped the initiative once the dot.com bubble burst in 2000.

Kautz inherited a confusing conglomerate under the Wolfgang Puck Food Company aegis. The company ranged from food products to casual food and quick service food. Kautz decided that reorganization was critical.

In May 2000, Kautz established Wolfgang Puck Worldwide to hold all of Wolfgang's and Barbara's companies outside of Wolfgang Puck Fine Dining and Wolfgang Puck Catering & Events. Their considerable charitable activities would also remain separate. The model was Martha Stewart, who just had gone public in 1999 with her Martha Stewart Living Omnimedia, but the collapse of stock markets globally that began in 2000 frustrated that plan. Still, the reorganization allowed Kautz to create a consistent brand message and product lines.

In 2002, Kautz hired Barbara Westfield as senior vice president of consumer marketing. Westfield had been head of product development and marketing at Salton and Bullock's. Her mission was both to lead an assessment of the brand and to expand it into lifestyle products just as Martha Stewart had. "It doesn't matter if you are in London, Hong Kong or LA, Starbuck is Starbucks. As the brand grows, it has to be a seamless experience. What the brand represents is value for your dollar in all categories," said Westfield.

According to Wolfgang, "My field extends from the kitchen to the dining room, to the outside dining—whatever is entertaining. I am not going to do living room furniture, but I could certainly do a dining room set, with plates, glasses, all that stuff. That would make sense because it is related to the kitchen. The same thing, entertaining outside, you need different chairs, a table, an umbrella. I can see myself in Target with the 'Wolfgang Puck Collection.' "

Kautz leveraged existing product lines to raise funds. First, following Frank Guidara's plan, he licensed the frozen pizza line to ConAgra Foods for an amount of money widely reported to be $20 million. The new frozen pizzas were relaunched in March 2002, with great hoopla including a press party on top of Hollywood & Highland and banners of Puck's face draped on surrounding buildings.

Kitchenware was already an active area for Wolfgang. In January 1995, he signed with Sydney Silverman to form Wolfgang Puck Products Company, which would produce pots, pans, utensils, and small appliances for the kitchen. Rather than market them in houseware departments and specialty stores, Wolfgang went straight for television. He sold his cookware sets first on QVC and then moved to the Home Shopping Network (HSN) based in Florida near Wolfgang Puck Products Company headquarters. Chefs have endorsed or designed kitchenware over the years, but Puck's success set a new standard. His example has been followed most competitively by Emeril Lagasse working with All-Clad to market Emerilware.

Many chefs got into the act: Daniel Boulud has enameled cast-iron pots, Jamie Oliver (the Naked Chef) a line with Tefal, and Nigella Lawson a Living Kitchen collection designed with Sebastian Conran. Still, Wolfgang is king. During his one-weekend stints he has sold over $10 million of pots and pans in 2000, $15 million in 2001.

Kautz also incorporated Wolfgang Puck's extensive media presence into the new company. Media had started with Wolfgang's first cookbook back in 1981. In all he has written five books for Random House. His latest, *Live, Love, Eat! The Best of Wolfgang Puck,* is a compilation led by Norm Kolpas, a veteran cookbook writer and consultant and more recently senior vice president of media content at Wolfgang Puck Worldwide.

Wolf started making appearances on local Los Angeles TV stations in 1981, spurred by Barbara. Besides regular appearances on ABC's *Good Morning America,* Wolfgang had cut a video in 1987 called *Spago: Cooking with Wolfgang Puck,* in which he cooked with movie star guests. Over the years, he appeared in films, including appearing as himself in *The Muse* (1999). He appeared on TV shows, such as *The Simpsons* (2002), *Frasier* (2002), *Tales from the Crypt* (1992), *Blossom* (1991), and *Who's the Boss* (1987).

Spurred by the success of Martha Stewart and Emeril Lagasse, Kautz and Kolpas decided Wolfgang had to have more TV media presence. For years, the Food Network had asked Wolfgang to do a show, but he would never leave the West Coast long enough for the shoots. Kautz offered a simple solution: shoot the show in Hollywood. In the summer of 2000, the Food Network accepted its first West Coast–based show.

The Food Network contacted veterans Weller Grossman Productions, who had coincidentally worked with Wolfgang on another TV show concept a year earlier. The show premiered on the Food Network in January 2001. *Wolfgang Puck* won a Daytime Emmy for Outstanding Service Show in 2002.

In Kautz's estimation, TV presence meant that the Wolfgang Puck brand was going to "automatically" rise by virtue of the televised omnipresence of the lovable Puck himself. "This is a chef you can trust to steer you the right way, and he really is genuinely that way." Having shot over 80 episodes in three seasons plus specials, however, the program changed format and relaunched in October 2003 as *Wolfgang Puck's Cooking Classes.*

THE original Casual Dining outlet at Macy's was relaunched as a Wolfgang Puck Express in 1993. By 2002, the newly formed Wolfgang Puck Worldwide had 19 Express units. Then, in May 2002, it announced that it would begin national franchising to expand its fast Casual Express concept to 300 units by year-end 2005.

Within a month, Wolfgang Puck Worldwide announced that it had signed five of nineteen regional franchise territories. The strategy was to form territories worth about $15 billion each in sales. The development schedule is fifteen units over the next five years: one the first year, two the second, and so on. This plan does not include airports, universities, or convention centers, where Wolfgang has proven successful already.

All preprocessed ingredients, such as pizza dough and sauces, are prepared in a factory in Phoenix, Arizona, and then trucked across the country. Wolfgang Puck Express charges a 10 percent administration fee; otherwise, they give their recipes at no other charge (albeit exclusively) to the manufacturer, who supplies them to franchisees.

Franchising requires very little capital. Of course, returns are far lower—roughly, a 5 percent royalty on sales for Wolfgang Puck Express as franchiser. Risk transfers to the franchisee in return for 15–20 percent profits, however, while the franchiser is free to supervise and support a number of franchisees simultaneously. Franchising is one of the best models for fast corporate growth.

Making franchise happen is Don Karas, chairman of Wolfgang Puck Express since it reformed as a franchise in March 2003. Karas is a longtime member of the board of directors at the Wolfgang Puck Food Company and now Wolfgang Puck Worldwide.

When the franchise offer came his way, Lee Magnes had already run the most successful Wendy's franchise in the country. He was in semiretirement but decided he could not resist Puck. "It's a unique concept, and New York is just a spectacular market, especially for Wolfgang Puck's great food. Having the whole market was really an exciting opportunity. It's like doing that with McDonald's 50 years ago or Wendy's 30 years ago." In his first Express in Hoboken, Magnes hired three CIA graduates because the food is complicated to prepare. He compensated their salaries with lower service costs. The restaurants were all self-service. He plans to open 42 restaurants in seven years, starting slow and eventually opening in Manhattan.

Courtesy of Larry Falke Photography

EXTERIOR OF WOLFGANG PUCK EXPRESS IN COOL SPRINGS, TENNESSEE

Tom Moats opened his first franchised Wolfgang Puck Express, the twenty-sixth in the group, in May 2003 in Franklin, Tennessee. The opening was noteworthy for two reasons. It was the first of the newly designed restaurants, and its location was in an unlikely spot to an industry outsider. Moats's participation and strategy made waves inside the industry. This was the man who had developed his own concept, Logan's Road House, a full-service casual dining restaurant that he grew in eight years to 60 outlets and then sold in 1999 to Cracker Barrel. When Tom Moats speaks, franchisees listen.

Moats gave three reasons why Wolfgang Puck Express had attracted him. Wolfgang was passionate about food, which meant that new recipes for the Expresses would be coming out of the Fine Dining restaurants. The Express menu had a little from each of Puck's Fine Dining restaurants, Southwestern, Asian, or Italian, and therefore it would appeal to more people than the typical single-cuisine restaurant menu. Lastly, he liked the new design, whose quality elements, such as real cherrywood finishes on tabletops, granite countertops, and stone tile floors, make for a truly upscale feeling.

Neither Karas at Wolfgang Puck Express nor franchisees such as Moats have many illusions about the challenges facing this concept's expansion. Together, they will attempt to penetrate demographic regions traditional to the casual dining sector but new to Wolfgang's typical haunts in airports and tourist resorts like Disney.

Nationwide franchising was on schedule in early 2004, according to Karas, and international franchising had begun as alluring offers came their way, such as an Iranian's for the Middle East concession and Magi-Corp Entertainment's deal for Canada. Another franchisee bought rights for 70 units in Japan alone. Moats believes the national expansion rate is reasonable, though he believes it will take seven, not five, years for the Expresses to reach the 300-unit number. Moats hopes to hit 30 himself rather then 15.

WOLFGANG started catering out of the back of his first restaurant Spago in Hollywood. Originally, he catered off-site private parties of up to a few dozen people, with revenue reaching about 5 percent of total restaurant sales, no more then a few hundred thousand dollars. Spago was already a watering hole of the celebrity set in Hollywood, but it became even more exclusive because of the parties. "It was really a service to his customers," noted catering's president, Carl Schuster.

The Oscar party originated when Puck was approached to do an after-party by Irving "Swifty" Lazar, the most famous agent in Hollywood, and so Lazar moved his parties to Spago in 1984. After Swifty's death in December 1993, Puck waited a year and then accepted an invitation in 1995 from the Academy of Motion Picture Arts and Sciences to cater food for the dying Governor's Ball that Swifty's party had so long eclipsed. Restaurant Associates (RA), the large East Coast catering and restaurant company, was trying to gain a foothold on the West Coast at the time and was called in to cover the front of the house. The man in charge of RA operations at the ball was Carl Schuster.

The Governor's Ball seats over 1,600 guests and requires staffing of 450 waiters and 150 cooks. "You don't ever get this many people in one room of this magnitude," Schuster explained. "In that sense, it is the most important party. Plus there is a lot more press and exposure than any other parties, too. If you don't look good, it can hurt you really bad."

After the successful 1995 party, Schuster pitched Puck for a job in catering. Schuster said, "I wanted to build a national catering company utilizing his name and his reputation for food with what I did. I thought we could easily create it."

Wolfgang had Schuster write and present a business plan. They spent one Saturday afternoon reviewing revenues and markets over the next five years. Wolfgang liked the plan and shook hands with Schuster. "I'll never forget driving home that day and thinking, 'I can't believe that happened,'" Schuster said.

Wolfgang made Schuster vice president of operations for catering. Their aim was not to be in all 50 states but to have a presence in major markets like Los Angeles, San Francisco, Dallas, Phoenix, Seattle, Chicago, and New York. By 1998, Schuster had become president, with Wolfgang and Barbara vice presidents of the Wolfgang Puck Catering & Events group, which has been the long-time caterer to the Academy of Motion Picture Arts and Sciences, most famously for the Governor's Ball during the Academy Awards.

In 1998 Wolfgang made Schuster a partner with equity in the new catering division and gave him equity in the Fine Dining division along with existing partners, such as Tom Kaplan, Bella Lantsman, David Robbins, Lee Hefter, and Joe Essa. In return, Puck gave Fine Dining partners shares in the new catering company to reinforce cooperation. The logic was simple: many catering jobs involve kitchens and staff from Puck's Fine Dining restaurants. Growth depends on keeping the team of top managers.

Schuster brought the organizational know-how to cater large events that Wolfgang had been missing. "We have an 18-step process in catering, from the inquiry call to the thank-you letter. We are very specific on how the paperwork flows and what is on the event order. . . . We have it down to a science. We have standards, and when you have these standards it's easy to grow bigger."

The core of the business is not the big media events, according to Schuster. "Entertainment would be our biggest volume, but we really need the day-to-day, 10 or 15 parties a week we do at people's homes. No matter if there is a studio strike or whatever, that business continues to grow. We have loyal customers."

Schuster recognized great potential for catering in Chicago, piggybacking on Spago Chicago. His first coup was a contract with the Graduate School of the University of Chicago. During the day, the company catered to the corporate conference center, a $3.5 million business, with a state-of-the-art kitchen from which Schuster could launch further business and help pay the bills and overhead. He added the Museum of Contemporary Art, which built a café for the company, and food service for a Goldman Sachs corporate dining room. Schuster hired a manager, a chef, and sales people. Between 2000 and 2003, he increased revenue from $6.5 million to $28 million. Chicago Spago's executive chef François Kwaku-Dongo serves as executive chef for catering as well.

By then, October 2002, Wolfgang Puck Catering & Events had its own catering kitchen at the Hollywood & Highland entertainment complex, which also houses the Kodak Theater used for the Academy Awards. The complex is a huge shopping center with a Renaissance Hotel run by Marriott, retail stores, a ballroom used for the Academy Awards, and another Puck bistro, Vert, run by Wolfgang's younger brother, Klaus, among many other restaurants.

The developers of Hollywood & Highland built out the catering kitchen for Wolfgang under a lease agreement. According to Schuster, Wolfgang put about $1 million of his own money into the kitchen to modify it further. The 7,500-square-foot catering kitchen supports southern California from Santa Barbara to San Diego. The company has refrigerator trucks to carry the food and then often works with a local hotel or restaurant from space near the site. The Renaissance Hotel provides a lot of opportunities for catering and the Kodak Theater a lot of award shows, but Schuster would like to see more concerts and Broadway plays to round out the calendar, to bring more people into the facility.

After growing the Chicago business, Schuster added catering at the Las Vegas Caesars Palace Coliseum, built for Celine Dion. From his Chicago base he expanded to the new St. Louis Contemporary Art Museum's café Tempt, with on-site catering for parties, and also the St. Louis Science Center. "Puck was just much too good of an offer," said Jean Cavender, the Contemporary Art Museum's director of operations. "They have a great name and will make this a destination." Schuster also got a deal for food service at the St. Louis Art Museum, so with three St. Louis venues he plans to expand to off-site catering. "That represents $5 million in new business," said Schuster. In 2005, catering will start operating in the Walker Arts Center in Minneapolis with a museum restaurant suitable as a base for off-site catering.

Schuster is going after the same kind of business that his old employer, Restaurant Associates, pursues. In 1999 RA bought the Patina Group from Chef Joachim Splichal precisely because it had built up a catering business of museum cafés and restaurants and food service at performing arts center venues on the West Coast. Splichal and Puck are, in a sense, long-standing rivals, as well as longtime friends.

Splichal's flagship is the Patina restaurant, but he has a string of more modestly priced bistros under the Pinot name, Pinot Bistro, Pinot Hollywood, and so on, supervised by his right-hand man, Octavio Becerra. Since 1991, Splichal's catering has built up a business of film openings, Emmy Award dinners, and venue food service that rivals what Wolfgang Puck has done. What Splichal lacks is Wolfgang's natural showiness and outgoing personality. None of Splichal's restaurants bear his name, and he does not appear on the pages of *People* or *Forbes* with any regularity. Despite his lack of comparable celebrity, Splichal made a deal with Restaurant Associates while Wolfgang aborted several attempts to go public. Splichal's RA deal at the end of 1999 sold the Patina Group for $40 million; he and his wife own 75 percent. Splichal and his team would remain at the helm of the Patina Group for five years, which became RA's West Coast arm. Splichal's East Coast restaurants were then managed by RA's East Coast operations.

Unlike Wolfgang Puck's other companies, catering has grown without much of a hiccup because of Schuster's expertise, free rein, and ability to piggyback on existing Fine Dining restaurants.

Puck and Schuster did not stop with event catering. In 2000, they cut a deal with Levy Restaurants to provide concierge service for Los Angeles' Dodger Stadium. Puck food would be available to the 350-seat Stadium Club restaurant and Dugout Club. Levy Restaurants provided chef Robert Moore to reproduce Puck foods in addition to Levy offerings. He showcased his ballpark catering in an episode of *Wolfgang Puck* on the Food Network entitled "America's Favorite Pastime."

In March 2002, Wolfgang Puck announced a major upgrade in his decade-old relationship with Crystal Cruises, Chinois at Jade, in which food from Chinois on Main would be available at the Jade Garden restaurant aboard the Crystal Symphony. For years, Wolfgang had cooked aboard Crystal Cruises ships, as have many other celebrity chefs. He had also shared a recipe for grilled Mongolian lamb chops in *The Crystal Cruises Cookbook,* published in 1999. For the remainder of 2002, however, Jade Garden would be transformed in décor as well as food into Chinois at Sea, led by Bella Lantsman, Chinois on Main's general manager, and Luis Diaz, executive chef. Thereafter, Crystal Symphony featured a Chinois at Jade menu, with five signature dishes from Chinois on Main, executed by chef John Poh, who trained under Diaz at the Santa Monica restaurant.

The year before, Crystal had launched a shipboard partnership between restaurateur Piero Selvaggio, owner of Valentino's and other restaurants in Los Angeles and Las Vegas (and godfather to Puck's sons). The result was Prego, which features five signature dishes from Valentino's. Both Puck and Selvaggio sent top chefs on voyages in 2002, including Spago's pastry chef Sherry Yard and Valentino's executive chef Angelo Auriana.

In January 2003, Puck said on National Public Radio that airline eating is "a great way to be on a diet," because they are not famous for serving great food. Three months later, Wolfgang Puck Worldwide and LSG Sky Chefs of Arlington, Texas, announced an exclusive agreement to sell Wolfgang Puck gourmet meals on domestic flights without meal service, part of the LSG Sky Chefs In-flight Café program. LSG Sky Chefs, which caters 260 airlines, chose Puck to help "return some excitement" to in-flight dining. The licensing agreement comprises breakfast, lunch, and dinner, including Chinois chicken salad. The meals will be on a few airlines starting in early 2004. The challenge is to get Puck's food, especially his bread, to taste the same in the air, where pressure and temperature changes make food taste different. Later in the year, Puck (and RA's Au Bon Pain) tested coach-cabin airline meals like sandwiches and salads in Delta Airlines' Crown Room Clubs at the Atlanta, Chicago, and Tampa airports.

Schuster's company is not involved in airline catering because it lies outside the premium arena for which he aims. He was not happy with the airline deal because he believes Wolfgang Puck Catering & Events should stay in the premium market. "People get confused if you start doing casual. 'Hey, what is casual?' I think Wolfgang Puck Worldwide has wrestled with that themselves. People come into a casual dining restaurant, and there is a tablecloth on the table. The server makes a quarter of the money they make in fine dining, but once you sit down and a waiter comes to the table, the expectation when it's Wolfgang is much higher. The same with catering. Anything we do, even if it's a sandwich, people expect more than from 'XYZ' caterer."

Wolfgang Puck Catering & Events is an extension of Wolfgang Puck Fine Dining. Carl Schuster fears that Wolfgang Puck Worldwide's entry into catering intrudes and threatens to undermine the core brand. The catering conflict reflects tension between Fine Dining and Casual Dining that has dogged the Wolfgang Puck brand since it moved into lower price points. The future forebodes continued tension. On the one hand, Wolfgang Puck Worldwide represents the majority of the company in terms of revenues and assets; on the other hand, Wolfgang Puck Fine Dining and Wolfgang Puck Catering represent the core brand itself, which is fine dining food. These two contending forces, with different sets of partners and investors, need to reach a mutual understanding through Wolfgang and Barbara because they are the common factor as owners and as the personal brand in the name of Wolfgang Puck.

VERT: A Brasserie by Wolfgang Puck opened at Hollywood and Highland in March 2002 around the time of the Oscars. It was Fine Dining's first attempt since Eureka to come up with a lower price point formula. Wolfgang and Lee Hefter, a Fine Dining partner and executive chef at Spago Beverly Hills, developed the menu. Vert (French for "green") was supposed to be the first of several "colored" series brasseries. The restaurant opened amidst heavy post-9/11 security surrounding the Academy of Motion Picture Arts and Sciences' annual Oscar ceremony and its Kodak Theater showcase, housed in the same Hollywood and Highland complex. Business was slack for months.

Klaus Puck, Wolf's younger brother, is general manager at Vert, after several years at Spago Chicago. He visited Los Angeles the year after Spago Hollywood opened and worked there for many years in the summers. Later, he attended Cornell University's prestigious school of hotel management. Over the years, he has quietly worked not only at a number of Wolf's restaurants but also in restaurants owned by restaurateur Drew Nieporent and fellow Super Chef Charlie Palmer. These days, he also appears with Wolfgang during his Home Shopping Network weekends. Klaus is becoming more involved in his brother's business, but Wolfgang has made it clear that he has to prove himself at every step.

Wolfgang Puck Bar & Grill is yet another attempt by the Fine Dining group to find a moderately priced concept that works. Harking back to the original plan for Spago Hollywood for a beach bungalow, Tom Kaplan, the lead general partner, turned to designer Tony Chi to update that concept's look.

The first Wolfgang Puck Bar & Grill in America is expected to open as early as May 2004 at the MGM Grand in Las Vegas. It will replace the Wolfgang Puck Café there, now a decade old. To take advantage of a new Cirque de Soleil theater opening just across from it, Kaplan will open up this new restaurant, with a moderately higher price point gauged to bring in higher profits and to keep foot traffic coming in as well. Wolfgang's name remains for continuity with customers. Unlike most others, the restaurant will not have its ownership taken over by the hotel.

Various executives in the group speculate that Wolfgang Puck Bar & Grill and Wolfgang Puck Express are the likely mutations of the Cafés and Grand Cafés, as they are phased out by either raising or lowering the price point with the more successful, newer brands. Klaus Puck has expressed interest in opening more restaurants; look for Vert to quietly disappear, only to relaunch as a Wolfgang Puck Bar & Grill, and Klaus to open each new venue.

Despite past failures in the sectors below Fine Dining, however, Wolfgang has nevertheless set up the makings of further consumer confusion. He has allowed his Japanese partner to establish Wolfgang Puck Bar & Grill outlets in Tokyo with an entirely different menu that is clearly lower priced, Casual Dining rather than the Fine Dining outlets envisioned for America.

Confusion is also possible in the franchised Expresses. The reformulated Expresses are on the upper boundaries of Fast Casual both in price and in service. One franchisee contemplated turning his restaurants into casual units by adding a full bar, table service, and a few extra dishes. He even considered launching casual catering out of his Express units in the future, though the franchise license does not include catering. Already franchisees have added runner service to units, which is one step away from waiters.

Other mistakes loom. Almost concurrent with the first round of franchisee announcements in June 2002, Wolfgang Puck Worldwide announced acquisition of the Cucina! Cucina! restaurant chain. The Bellevue, Washington-based group had fifteen Cucina! Cucina! cafés and seven fast-food Cucina! Presto! Italian restaurants. Kautz bought the ailing group because, "We found we can buy 22 restaurants in Cucina! Cucina! for the same capital commitment from our investors that it would take to open two Cafés." The competition is formidable: Brinker International, whose brands include Chili's and Macaroni Grill, Outback Steakhouse, and California Pizza Kitchen. In 2003, company insiders admitted that Cucina! Cucina! would be sold: "They knew they couldn't run what they had. Why do you allow $10 million to be spent on more restaurants that you know you can't run?" a former executive said.

The true mark of a Super Chef, however, is to risk mistakes, learn from them, and move forward. Certainly, the Puck-powered machine is still growing at a tremendous rate.

WHAT credit does Barbara deserve in Wolfgang's success? Mark Peel said, "Certainly without Barbara he wouldn't be who he is today." Said Wolfgang, "Her contribution was her style," even after she had filed for divorce in December 2002. She did great flowers and things like that. So, it was certainly a big part of the look of the place. If it had been up to me, the first place would have looked like a cheap Italian restaurant," he added. The press had speculated about a breakup since the pair had fought vocally and publicly for years.

Her style continues to permeate all concepts, whether she has directly designed them herself or not. Look at the new Wolfgang Puck Express design. It is Barbara's style that still gives the new Express its distinctive, upscale look that has attracted major franchisees like Tom Moats: the real cherry wood finishes on tabletops, the granite countertops, and the stone tile floors.

Barbara has often likened their situation to Jimmy Stewart's in *It's a Wonderful Life:* who knows what Wolf might have done without her? "To a lot of people," she said, "I seem like a girl who gets up and walks around the dining room and says 'Hi!' Other people who saw me on the job site and never saw me dressed up, completely filthy all the time, sleeping on concrete floors, you know they probably thought I was crazy and had no idea that it was also *my* restaurant." To this day, Barbara still reviews all contracts, despite legions of attorneys at their beck and call. She has also likened Wolf and herself to Gracie Allen and George Burns, except that Wolf mistook her to mean that she wore the pants, when what she meant was that he was the funny man and she the straight.

Like any of the great talent managers of Hollywood, fundamentally it has been Barbara all along who has understood Wolfgang best and who has helped to make him the phenomenon he is today. Whereas the humble village boy might have hesitated and cautiously undersold himself, Barbara constantly oversold him, confident that Wolf would always live up to her billing. And he did.

Barbara remains Wolfgang's partner in almost every undertaking, as company literature is careful to cite, so ultimately her credit is safely tucked away in the bank, further guarded by California's generous divorce laws. Besides, as she said, there was too much going on in her life—building restaurants, hosting restaurants, managing the restaurant businesses, and raising children, and having a relationship with her spouse. In one year alone, she built six Wolfgang Puck Cafés. "It used to be [in Puck's accent] 'If there is a problem, give it to Barbara. She will take care of it!' I am very happy not to be in that position any more." Now that they are separated, "I have a much saner life."

WHAT makes up Wolfgang Puck? One might think that he is first and foremost a great chef—and he is. In fact, when Puck muses about his legacy, it is as a great innovative chef. But Wolfgang's simple secret is that he works all the time. He even claims to get as little as four hours of sleep a night.

Klaus Puck said, "From day one, I had to work in the kitchen during the day and on the floor at night. It was nonstop, but you get motivated by him, because that is what he does. He works very hard—he sets an example for everybody."

Mark Peel explained, "He is always afraid of the future. He is not overconfident, and he's that way today. When Spago opened in Las Vegas quietly for lunch the first week and no one walked in for 25 minutes, Wolfgang was a mess. He is like that even after Spago, Chinois, Granita, and the rest."

"You can have a few stars and starlets, but they leave to make a movie and don't come in for six months," Wolfgang Puck said in 1998. "You have to be here to serve everybody as if they were big stars."

Reflecting on his life and career over a lunch of butternut squash agnollotti with truffles at Spago Beverly Hills in early 2003, Wolfgang commented:

> I am not nostalgic. For me, the past is not important. I mean, I learn from it and I hope I don't make the same mistakes, but . . . I don't want to talk that much about the past.
>
> I don't care about the awards [either]. I got an Emmy [for *Wolfgang Puck*], but if they would not have given me that, fine. They gave me a James Beard Award: I left it at Larry Forgione's restaurant in New York. It's not like

the Austrian government gave me an award, the same one that Billy Wilder got when he was 80 years old—if you were to ask me, 'Can you show that to me?' I would have no idea where it is, because it's nothing.

At the end of the day there is what is today and what is tomorrow. Now, we can enjoy all these things, with the children, and look back and think, that's great, look back at so many friends, that's good, that's life, and I have a good feeling. But I am not going to sit in my office and think about all that. I never do.

It's interesting, because I have talked to people about that. I talked to Kirk Kerkorian not too long ago about that, and it was the funniest thing, because he said basically the same thing. I said, "I can't believe this! Now I know why you are 85 years old and still keep on doing things." I hope I'm the same when I'm that old, too—not to think about the past, not to stop—because once you stop . . . there is no future.

And so the ever-working Wolfgang appears everywhere. Sid Feltenstein of Long John Silver's said, "When my daughter got married, we rented a place in Malibu, and she hired Wolfgang Puck's catering company. It was a relatively small wedding, but he showed up and cooked. It was amazing! I mean, I didn't expect *him:* it only lasted two or three hours!"

Wolfgang has re-created this story hundreds of times over the past two decades. Take any day of his life, and he is working long, hard hours. Here is a snapshot: in September 2002, a tourist asked for directions from a small man who was trudging along in kitchen whites on the backstairs of the Hollywood and Highland complex. The face that turned around to answer was Wolfgang Puck's. With a quiet smile, Wolf said a simple hello and gave the directions. Then he trudged on, heading to his car from a chef photo shoot on top of the Renaissance Hotel so he could drive over to the Universal Studios lot to oversee preparations for the annual American Wine & Food Festival.

Wolfgang is neither the pre-eminent nor the most brilliant chef, though most agree he is among the very best. Like Henry Ford did for cars, however, Wolfgang Puck has done for food: he has made fine dining accessible to the masses in America. The secret ingredient has been obvious all along—he has been serving up himself, again and again and again.

2

CHARLIE PALMER

Courtesy of the Charlie Palmer Group

"Slow and steady wins the race"
—Aesop, "The Hare and the Tortoise,"
Aesop's Fables (Sixth Century B.C.)

On November 17, 2002, just a few hours after his annual speech at COMDEX, Bill Gates and a swarm of Microsoft employees poured into Aureole Las Vegas to launch the new, Tablet PC-based eWinebook. Purple and blue beams lit Aureole's two-story entrance inside the Mandalay Bay Hotel, while the restaurant's walls displayed giant images of Tablet PCs made by major hardware vendors. Scores of Microsoft technocrats packed the restaurant to gorge on mounds of caviar and shrimp and slurp rivers of champagne—and wine. *Wine Spectator*'s publisher Marvin Shanken led a toast to Super Chef Charlie Palmer on the stairs before Aureole's famous Wine Tower. Billionaire Bill Gates could be spotted from time to time floating furtively across the restaurant floor from a private reception room.

Gates spent most of his time in Aureole's kitchen. He talked with Charlie and posed for a few photographs of billionaire and Super Chef. For the historically conscious, there was a strange flashback to the days of Carême or Escoffier and their patrons—except that those chefs would have never been portrayed with their employers.

The Aureole employee responsible for the eWinebook, Andrew Bradbury, was busy showing guests how easy it was to use this electronic notebook and search through Aureole's vast wine collection and pair vintages with dishes on the menu. Later in the evening, Bradbury found himself led back to shake the hand of Bill Gates, after PR advisors had instructed him about how to behave during the one or two minutes of audience. Instead of two minutes, however, Gates interrogated him for thirty about what Bradbury planned to do with the "software applications" (a technical, legal term) that drove the eWinebook utilizing Microsoft's Tablet PC and related software products. The tired, pallid appearance of Gates started to make sense: tied to his empire, he never rested.

Bradbury had come as wine director to Aureole Las Vegas from Seattle, where he had started work at 14 in the front of the house and then focused on wine. By 1994, at the age of 26, he had become a sommelier at the Salish Lodge and Spa and was consulting to two other restaurants before moving to Aureole Las Vegas in late 1998. Once his feet were firmly planted on the ground at Aureole, he approached Charlie with an idea.

Back in Seattle, Bradbury had long ago noticed how customers would jot down wine notes on napkins or punch them into PDAs (personal digital assistants) and dreamed of creating an electronic wine list. Aureole Las Vegas was a perfect place to work out his idea. Charlie had an immense wine stock there, so big that Adam Tihany had created a giant wine tower to showcase it. It would take an encyclopedic tome to list and describe the 3,500 choices and 50,000 bottles, valued well over $10 million—or a computer.

The idea was to allow wine bibbers not only to choose easily, with plenty of detail at their fingertips, but also to track their findings by creating personal accounts of likes and dislikes. Now, with Charlie's support and the help of Cursivecode from hometown Seattle, Bradbury began development of a proprietary application to drive the electronic wine book. The operating system first used was the open-source (free) Linux: an eBook was the intended hardware. Running Linux, the eWinebook started its test run at Aureole Las Vegas in May 2001 and went into use at Aureole New York in April 2002.

Linux proved to be technically limited when it came to functions, of which perhaps the biggest drawbacks were that it did not work in real time and could not work with many common Microsoft products. Needed was newer, wireless technology that would keep the eWinebooks constantly up-to-date with stock. The user interface should be "touch-based" with pencil or stylus.

Thanks to his sommelier days in Seattle, Bradbury knew a number of top Microsoft executives. In fact, he had been tracking a particular development in notebook-related technology—Microsoft Tablet PC software, much anticipated in the computer industry. The Microsoft executive in charge of developing Tablet PC was a longtime customer, as were others in Microsoft who ran vertical industry solutions, such as the retail and hospitality division—people desperately searching for press-friendly initial customers. For Microsoft, Charlie Palmer's Aureole Las Vegas with its Wine Tower was an attractive showcase for the new Tablet PC's capabilities. With new Tablet PC software from Microsoft, the team targeted its launch in time for COMDEX, the international computer show in Las Vegas synonymous with dot.com success.

The eWinebook had proven a hit with diners in Charlie's restaurants. Older diners particularly enjoyed the eWinebook, at last like their juniors able to manipulate the latest technology as much as the plethora of information available to them. During 2002, Charlie's restaurants saw wine sales increase by 15 percent or $750,000, thanks to the eWinebook. The eWinebook received press attention from technology's hippest *Wired* magazine to the venerable *New York Times*. With the help of Microsoft and hardware partner Hewlett-Packard, press expanded into television, including CNN.

Charlie Palmer chalked up another carefully considered investment.

LINUX and Microsoft-driven eWinebooks seem a quantum leap for Charlie, the fifth son of a machine-parts store owner. For that matter, being a chef at all seems quite a stretch for a boy who grew up in Smyrna, New York, population around 350. The initial drive was very simple: this strapping boy needed to eat. A neighbor, Sharon Crain, encouraged him to take home economics, where Charlie could eat all he could cook. Later, Crain pushed Palmer to apply to the Culinary Institute of America (CIA) in 1978 and drove him down for his interview.

His stamina Charlie credits to his high school wrestling coach, who instilled in him the drive and discipline that have propelled him to the top of his profession. "My high school wrestling coach, Pete Hausrath . . . made you believe in yourself at a stage in life when you are easily influenced. He made you believe that you can do incredible things—and would drive you to the point of physical breakdown. After you have had an experience like that, after four years of wrestling for this guy, everything else is a piece of cake. I could get up at 6 a.m., run 6 miles around a track, and lose 30 pounds in 18 days—this guy could make you do things you never thought you could do. It's an incredible power."

Charlie finished coursework at the CIA. He was working on a fellowship at the school's restaurant when he and a group of students played a joke on the *maître d'* of the restaurant, icing his car shut with aspic. Someone tipped him off to lay low for a while, so he headed down to Manhattan in 1980.

Charlie's CIA mentor, Belgian chef Leon Dhaenens, had recognized his gifts and had already lined him up a job at the newly opened La Côte Basque, one of New York's leading French restaurants owned by the illustrious chef Jean-Jacques Rachou. Just working there was a major coup for Charlie and other CIA students, said former La Côte Basque colleague and one-time Chef & Cuisiniers Club (CCC) partner, Rick Moonen, now chef of rm and Branzini restaurants in Manhattan. "Jean-Jacques Rachou was the first French chef to have unconditional confidence in 'American-American' chefs. It was taboo before him."

From the start, Charlie showed his drive to excel. To learn cooking, one must practice, which means work, so he spent off-hours at other French restaurants. While working full-time at the 160-seat Le Côte Basque, he made pastries on the side at the 80-seat La Petite Marmite and moonlighted at the 150-seat Le Chantilly whenever French cooks went on vacation.

"I was an insane, high-energy guy; I had stupid energy in the morning," said Moonen. "Charlie was quite steady, a smart worker. He had no wasted moves. I would stop by early in the morning and help him make dough; he wanted to soak up everything he could learn."

After four years of nonstop working and learning in New York, Charlie took a job in 1983 at the Waccabuc Country Club outside Manhattan in Westchester County. There, he could practice and experiment without worrying about critics. He soon became virtual master of the restaurant as his sumptuous and inventive foods had the heretofore quiet country club restaurant rolling in dough—green dough. "Regulars started complaining that they couldn't get a seat, it was so popular," said Charlie.

After a year and a half, he got a call from Michael "Buzzy" O'Keeffe, owner of the River Café. In 1984, the 110-seat restaurant's current star chef, Larry Forgione, was just leaving to open his first restaurant, An American Place. "The staff thought he [Palmer] was a country boy: they thought we needed a star," said O'Keeffe, who intentionally did not hire a star. In the unknown chef he found a hardworking, passionate cook who brought with him a staff of equally inspired young cooks. "If they already think they are a star, they are a pain," quipped O'Keeffe. "Besides," he added, "star chefs are more expensive."

The River Café, then holding two of four possible stars from the *New York Times,* became Charlie's launchpad. From its vantage point at the bottom of the world-famous Brooklyn Bridge, jutting out on a barge, the River Café quite literally commanded one of the finest public views of Manhattan. The restaurant's commitment to American cuisine provided the perfect setting for Charlie's robust food. In tow, Charlie brought young chefs like David Burke (next chef of the River Café and then his own Park Avenue Café), Rick Moonen, and Rick Laakonen (who followed Burke as chef of the River Café and opened Ilo).

The River Café's cuisine used local American ingredients as much as possible and French technique with creative turns whenever possible, such as cooking with a smoker. Gerry Hayden, Aureole's first executive chef after Charlie and now chef-owner of his own New York restaurant, Amuse, also worked for Charlie at the River Café. "The reason it was so creative was that we were constantly compared to the view. It kind of drove us nuts—we wanted people to come for the *food*!"

Under Palmer, the food remained theatrical but increased in flavor and never wandered into the weird or startling. One of Charlie's signatures, the use of intensely flavored stocks, came to the fore at this time. Rick Moonen said, "Charlie is straightforward, clean, rich. You never walk out of his restaurant hungry. He is not one to do teenie-weenie, little things, nothing silly. Everything has a reason and a purpose. There is a sensible understanding of food."

Charlie's great respect for ingredients started at the French restaurants in New York, where he noticed that they were using frozen Dover sole. "I wondered, why are we doing this, when we can get the best fish in the world right in New York City? You just had to ask yourself this question." Later at Waccabuc he asked the groundskeepers to put in an herb garden next to the kitchen, and even he was stunned at how aromatic locally grown herbs turned out to be.

Charlie came to the River Café to follow the pioneering work of Larry Forgione in locally sourced ingredients. "Larry had buffalo from Michigan, free-range chicken before they were even called that, and he was flying in oysters from Oregon," Charlie said. "It didn't make sense financially, but the idea as a whole was great."

Charlie ran the kitchen and dining room with little interference, according to O'Keeffe and Palmer. Joe DeLissio, wine director at the River Café since 1978, said, "If Buzzy likes what you are doing, he'll give you free rein and a place to experiment." DeLissio remembered Charlie as a shy country boy who was driven but cautious at the same time. "It was hard to get him out of the kitchen. He had the inner confidence, but it's like going from off-Broadway to 42nd Street." He got the reluctant Charlie his first press interviews, practically dragging him out of the kitchen.

After two years, Charlie won the River Café its third star from *The New York Times.* In a long article in 1987, *The New York Times* cited Palmer as "in the forefront of those who are trying to redefine American cuisine by working out eclectic and sophisticated variations on traditional techniques." It noted that "he has risen with heady speed to near-celebrity level . . . drawn to food it [the public] can describe as 'inventive.'" After four exciting but grinding years at the River Café, like Larry Forgione before him, Charlie decided to open up his own restaurant. He had a very narrow, very lofty vision of what he wanted—no less than an American answer to Lutèce.

FOR over 30 years, Lutèce and its chef André Soltner dominated the restaurant scene in New York. Lutèce's star was just starting to dim as Aureole's was rising in 1988. "This is the first year since the [Zagat] survey began that Lutèce was not No. 1," noted *The New York Times* that year. The name "Lutèce" was synonymous with "best of," and such references to the restaurant flourished in the newspaper's pages for years. In 1988, *The New York Times* asked the fateful question, "Is Lutèce over the hill?" and speculated that "André Soltner, the chef and owner, was losing his spark." (In 1994 Soltner sold Lutèce to ARK Restaurants, which brought in Chef Eberhard Muller from Le Bernadin the following year.)

With such sights, Charlie decided his new restaurant, to be called Aureole, had to be in the quadrant between Fifth Avenue and Lexington and 55th and 70th Streets, in a townhouse, like Lutèce. "I wanted to be the owner of the real estate, and I wanted it to be a long-term prospect, something I knew would grow in value. Sure, it was about wealth," said Charlie. "I was single, 27, a young guy with no expenses, making a lot of money well beyond my needs, driving nice cars, dating a lot of women . . . I already knew how to live poor: I had lived poor most of my life. Hell, if I could get even an idiot to invest a few million in me, I would have taken it!"

Three groups of investors courted him, but the only one that met his criteria was the duo of restaurateur Steve Tzolis and designer Nicola Kotsoni. Part of Charlie's reasoning for the Tzolis-Kotsoni team was monetary: he received an unheard-of 35 percent stake in the restaurant. Charlie and his partners purchased a townhouse on East 61st Street and renovated it for $3.5 million, with an apartment on the top floor for Charlie. His partners put together initial funding and a $3 million mortgage.

In January 1988, Charlie resigned from the River Café to prepare for this first venture. He became general contractor for the new restaurant, which was finished in October. While the 90-seat restaurant was being built, Charlie invested in another restaurant with Tzolis and Kotsoni, Periyali, and devised the first menu. He had assembled a team from the River Café who were waiting for Aureole to open, so he sent them to work at Periyali. That way, Charlie made sure his Aureole staff was being paid. This kind of practical, general consideration for everyone involved won him much loyalty from staff and became a hallmark of his operational style.

Later, Charlie decided to terminate his relationship with Tzolis and Kotsoni. He believed that they had different plans for the future than he did. He sold his shares of Periyali and bought theirs in Aureole, so that by 1995 Charlie owned 90 percent.

Opening a restaurant in Manhattan in the late 1980s required in-house preparations, general contracting, and perhaps most of all skill in cutting through City Hall's building regulations and red tape. Toward the end of construction, Charlie found himself delivering a suitcase from Tzolis to motivate a rent-controlled tenant who was otherwise unwilling to vacate the building. Charlie had no idea what was going on. "I remember one day I delivered a suitcase full of cash," said Charlie, "though I never looked inside." Tzolis claimed the suitcase contained $200,000 cash.

Aureole opened in November 1988 and received two stars from the *New York Times* two months later. Within half a year, Aureole had received three stars; *Times* critic Bryan Miller cited "the top-notch service and the

Courtesy of the Charlie Palmer Group

EXTERIOR OF AUREOLE NEW YORK

consistently captivating food" as the reasons. "Waiters at Aureole have a professional bearing without being stiff. Like good basketball centers, they know when to float in and when to stay on the perimeter."

At Aureole, Charlie began to get away from theatrical presentation, now that he did not have a view with which to compete. "At the River Café, if we did veal, we might have the bone standing high, playing up to the skyline," said Gerry Hayden, who was also Aureole's first pastry chef. "At Aureole, we didn't have to do that. Charlie concentrated more on flavor."

Flavor for Charlie is central. "My cuisine is about concentration of flavor. We always try to figure out how you can boost the flavor level," he said. To do that, he carefully chooses cooking methods, like roasting beets rather than boiling them or using a variety of hearty stocks. He sources great ingredients. "The old analogy used to be that a great chef could take something mediocre and make it great. Why do that?" said Charlie. "Why not buy the best ingredients? If you start with the very best, it's going to taste better."

In terms of presentation, Charlie started concentrating on what he calls "plate sensibility." He emphasized using appropriate plates and bowls and utensils. He also cut down on the number of ingredients in a dish so as not to mask the main ingredient. "Presentation is not playing with food, not turning it into art," said Hayden.

"When we looked at a dish, Charlie enforced a simple notion: how is a person supposed to eat it?" Hayden said. "He made us think. If a dish falls in a woman's lap, it's embarrassing: you *don't* want that to happen. It's not something a cook thinks about, but a chef does."

Last but not least, there was discipline. "Discipline is the hardest part, not only for yourself, for your chef, but also for your cooks," said Hayden. "It's fine and dandy to do it right once, but you have to do it right every single time. You have to go to the extreme of getting fish in every single morning. You have to discipline yourself to continue to search for great products every single day."

The mood of Aureole's kitchen resulted in part from its architectural layout. The prep rooms and pastry area were in the basement, while the main cooking was done on the second floor. Dining was on the main floor, between them. That meant a great deal of climbing, and thus a premium on efficiency, so that a cook did not have to climb up and down the stairs too often lugging crates and pots. Joe Romano, who started at Aureole straight out of the CIA and then headed up Charlie's restaurants in Las Vegas, said, "Aureole New York is and will always be the most intense restaurant I have ever worked in. The facility, those 36 steps to the basement where all the *mise-en-place* were, all the walk-ins, to where you actually did the prep work and cooking upstairs—well, space was a *big* issue."

It also made for a great deal of competition between cooks to get out of the basement and literally up to the main kitchen. "There were always people who wanted your job upstairs. They were downstairs, waiting for a chance. It was very competitive," said Michael Mina, who started working at Aureole while still studying at CIA. Mina went on to become executive chef and partner in the Aqua restaurant group based in San Francisco and now owns his own Mina Group of restaurants in San Francisco and Las Vegas.

Many of the young chefs whom Charlie brought into Aureole came fresh from the CIA with the same grounding in French technique that he himself had. This CIA crowd and others became the nucleus of his expanding empire, well schooled in Palmer's Progressive American Cuisine, able to execute whatever he envisioned. Palmer protégé Romano is a perfect example of this.

"My style is the same as Charlie's style, and vice versa," said Romano. "I have been with him for over a decade, because I agree with his philosophy of food and business, which is the same as mine. He groomed me from infant stage to what I am today, but even so, a person who has different philosophies and different thoughts and ideas of food—those guys stay for a year and a half, then go and do something else."

Aureole soon became a top destination for both New Yorkers and tourists and remains so to this day.

AFTER Aureole, Charlie's next project was the Chefs & Cuisiniers Club, or CCC, located in the Flatiron District of Manhattan. The restaurant was open to the public but was meant to be a place for chefs to hang out at night after their own restaurants had closed. In 1990, he joined two other chefs, Rick Moonen and Frank Crispo (of Andiamo), and brought a *sous chef* from Aureole, Peter Assue, to work full-time at the new venture. (Assue is now corporate chef and wife Tracy Kamerdyk Assue pastry chef at the City Limits Diner group, owned by the same Livanos family who own Rick Moonen's last restaurant, Oceana.)

"It was a ton of fun," said Moonen. "We all chipped in and painted. I built the tabletops and the wine rack and put new tile in the bathroom. I even brought in a Cuisinart and mixed music cassettes." Charlie wanted a hamburger joint with sawdust on the floor, but CCC turned into a serious restaurant. "That poor guy Assue had three chefs spoiling his pots," Charlie said.

Profits were ploughed into parties that the chefs threw for their friends and colleagues. "It was a playhouse for me and my friends, not a business venture to make money," Charlie said. "Sports people and business people had bars: we needed one, too!"

In 1990 Charlie met his future wife, Lisa, a former ballet dancer, who at that time was general manager of the restaurant in which Jean-Georges Vongerichten first worked, Lafayette in the Drake Hotel. She, too, came from upstate New York, from a large family of seven children. She had seen Charlie and his chefs at the Lafayette many times. They began to date. Because Aureole was already an established restaurant, she did not get involved in running it. Her role was largely to establish front-of-the-house systems, including reservations, staff training, and setting the tone for service and hospitality. "I am the one who shows up with the vacuum cleaner," Lisa said. "It's the last thing people think about, vacuuming before they put down the rug." Charlie and Lisa married in 1993 and now have four boys.

Charlie started getting serious and none too quickly when it came to CCC. The three chef amigos Palmer, Moonen, and Crispo may have been having fun for a few years there, but the public was less and less pleased. The *New York Times* had already written a scathing article about CCC in late 1990, stating, "They forgot to train the staff," which are in dire need of "attitude adjustment . . . Mr. Palmer and company need to spend more time at the Triple C . . . on the floor and in the kitchen and not at the chefs' table." In the end, they got off with a warning: "With few exceptions, being a chef and owner of a multi-star restaurant and being a multi-restaurant mogul are mutually exclusive."

Here was a direct challenge to CCC heavyweight contender Palmer. Bachelor fun days were over. Now a married man, Charlie undertook to run his budding empire masterfully from then on. By 1994, the CCC partnership was falling apart, and Palmer and Moonen wanted out. "We weren't losing money, but we certainly weren't making any money there either, not with the parties we threw," said Charlie. Crispo was launching a new restaurant and needed cash, and eventually Charlie wound up with a deal on his hands and bought everyone out.

Charlie brought in a new partner, Cuban-born designer and bartender Fernando Saralegui. The designer took the spartan looks of the New York diner and transformed it into an homage to the bare electric light, hence the restaurant's new name Alva, after Thomas Alva Edison. Palmer developed Inventive American Bistro Cuisine, with prices targeting the local neighborhood. Together, they reopened the restaurant as Alva in October 1994. He later bought Saralegui out of the 65-seat, 40-barstool restaurant. Alva proved a steady profit maker for many years.

Next, Palmer launched into another project with 120 seats in the restaurant and 30 in the bar. The Lenox Room opened in April 1995 with Tony Fortuna, former *maître d'* of Monkey Bar and Lespinasse, and American hotelier Edward Bianchini, owner of Hôtel Les Muscadins in France.

Lisa Palmer made the introductions; she had worked for Fortuna at the Tavern on the Green and the Palm Court at the Plaza Hotel. At first, Palmer envisioned a casual restaurant but wound up creating another "destination" in a style similar to Aureole: American food concentrating on flavor, whether straightforward and robust or delicate and intense.

Having set the menu and brought in chefs from Aureole, Palmer sold his shares in the Lenox Room. The reason was simple: Charlie keeps decision makers in his company to a minimum. His fellow decision makers were controller Richard Femenella, in-house lawyer Tim Bartley, Aureole New York manager Richard La Pouza, and whatever executive chef was involved in a given project. "I want to be in tight control of what we do," he said. "We are efficient. We get on a conference call, we discuss an issue, and we change it. That is it."

Meanwhile, Aureole's success had created a rising demand for catering and private parties, but Charlie would not close down Aureole for private events. For one thing, Aureole, though seating only 90 (and another 30 outside during the summer), typically had three seatings, or "turns" in restaurant parlance, per night. Three turns per night is unusually high in fine dining restaurants like Aureole. High turn is how most successful restaurants make big money, but some restaurants are designed for only one turn, such as Alain Ducasse at the Essex House. Detailed service or labor-intensive menus (such as Ducasse's) are factors limiting the ability to turn seats.

Well-managed restaurants set percentages for the costs of food, wine, and other beverages, though these vary widely between restaurants because of cuisine and menu. Restaurants have fixed costs, such as labor and benefits, rent, utilities, and other expenditures associated with operating any business. Rent is often about 10 percent of gross sales, and few restaurateurs own their own buildings like Charlie does at Aureole. They also have unique costs like promotions, such as food given away for a variety of reasons, often running at 2–5 percent of average food costs. Profits again vary widely but typically run 5–15 percent for a restaurant and higher for catering or special events.

These were the background considerations Charlie had in mind when confronting the rising demand for catering. Further, he had to balance this demand with the loss of revenue and customer dismay caused by closing the high-turn Aureole to regular guests. "I didn't want our customers to come to Aureole and find it closed for a party. If that happened too often, they might not come back." So he waited patiently while things started to fall into place.

First, Lisa introduced Charlie to Spero Plavoukos, whose successful private catering events had included a Swatch party at the 1996 Summer Olympics and the opening of Disney's film *Pocahontas*. Plavoukos began catering parties in private homes from the Aureole kitchen as Aureole Events & Catering with Lisa's help. Given demand, though, this could only be a stopgap measure.

Then, Charles Cohen of Cohen Brothers Realty approached Charlie to look at a space in his Design & Decorations (D&D) Building near Aureole on Third Avenue at 58th Street, which he had just renovated. "He kept bugging me to come see the space," Charlie said. "It was on the 14th floor, with a terrace, a conference room with a wall of lights from the 59th Street Bridge. As soon as I saw it, I said, 'That's it!' We made a deal in three days, and we opened in four weeks." Plavoukos accompanied Charlie to see the bare space. "I was a little worried," he said, "wondering, 'Who is going to throw parties in an office building?' but Charlie saw the potential."

About this time, one of Charlie's chefs at Aureole was ready for promotion. Typical of Palmer's protégés, Dan Shannon had begun at Aureole right after graduating from the CIA. He had moved up quickly and was expecting to be made *sous chef* at Aureole or at another Palmer restaurant or to find another job. Rather than lose a trained chef to competition, Charlie offered him the position of *chef de cuisine* at the new catering company.

Catering suited Shannon perfectly—no more 12-hour days. "I knew what Charlie wanted," he said. "In the beginning he gave me the recipes, but later I could do the menu, which he would approve. The desserts came directly from Aureole." Charlie spoke to Shannon and Plavoukos usually once a day to review menus and any problems. The result was the Astra dining and catering facility, serving dinner for 140, buffet for 250, and cocktails for 300 at one time, one of Charlie's most profitable operations.

The only hitch was that Cohen insisted that the new facility serve lunch to the building's tenants and their clients; by night, the place was Palmer's to do as he pleased. For such a deal, Cohen offered a licensing agreement in which he receives a percentage of net revenue after costs rather than a lease or management contract. Daytime returns carried little weight for Charlie; evening was his time.

"Astra is great," Palmer said. "It's been busy since it opened because of the high demand for events. We do very little advertising, just some marketing. In fact, in the beginning it was pure referrals from Aureole. We make bigger money in catering than restauranting, 18–20 percent rather than 10 percent markup." Astra's gross revenue was, for instance, $2 million in 2002.

One secret to Astra's success is catering at its own site. "We have our own controlled catering space, with our own incredible kitchen," Charlie said. "You know those catering events where they go into the field and cook out of hot boxes? Quite honestly, I can't do that. When people say, 'Why is the food better at Astra?' it's because it's cooked to order, not heated up, put in a truck, shipped over 60 miles, and then cooked up over a Sterno®! It's hard to make something really good like that. Sometimes it's not too bad, but usually it's just horrible."

Astra brought in celebrity parties and put Charlie in the news again. Executives who dined at Aureole now had a venue to hold major corporate parties. New York's entertainment and finance circles crowded Astra, with regulars including DreamWorks, Goldman Sachs, J. P. Morgan, Merrill Lynch, Estée Lauder for product launch parties, and even the WWF.

CHARLIE took pains to understand the entire business cycle of his restaurants. Like many chefs, he developed special relationships with growers in the New York region who supplied him with produce like exotic greens or heirloom tomatoes. Unlike most chefs, his next step was actually to invest in selected suppliers.

Charlie realized that he was spending a fortune on flowers; Aureole was costing him up to $150,000 a year. In 1993 when he came across freelance floral arrangers Jennifer Kelly and Don Stone, he invested 50 percent in their New York storefront shop, Stonekelly. They supplied him at a discount and also supplied other hotels, restaurants, businesses, and special events in the New York area.

Later in 1993, as a judge at a butter contest in Manhattan sponsored by the New York State Dairy Producers, Charlie tasted an exceptional cheese made by Jonathan White. He joined a small group of investors in White and put $20,000 into an initial capital of $150,000. In April 1994, they started Egg Farm Dairy in Peekskill, New York, which made and distributed cultured butter, clabbered cream, and cheeses to nearby Manhattan.

Initially the business went well, as there was a big demand for cheeses. Among restaurant clients were Le Cirque, the Water Club, and Union Square Café, while retail included Fairway, Dean & DeLuca, and Murray's Cheese Shop. First year projections ranged up to half a million dollars.

To date, Charlie has no idea what in fact Egg Farm Dairy actually earned: "No one knew what was going on there." White kept raising funds in chunks as large as $300,000 from investors. Eventually, White raised over $2 million before the whole investment soured. He started producing different cheeses practically every week—mozzarella, truffle-flavored cheese, whatever he felt like, according to Charlie.

"My view of it was, let's make four cheeses," said Charlie. "Let's make them really well, and then we can add a fifth cheese." According to him, White saw himself as more of an artist than a businessman. "There was a point when someone needed to raise a lot more money, and I would have had to run the creamery," Charlie said. "I didn't have the time for that, but that's what it would have taken." White brought in an attorney who quit his practice to figure out the problem with the company. "He figured out the problem all right—the problem was Jonathan," said Charlie, who closed down Egg Farm Dairy with his partners in mid-2001 and sold off the remaining assets.

"Stonekelly are ambitious; they listen when they need help," Charlie said. "With Jonathan, his answer to the business was 'I am going to go raise some more money.' I would say, 'You can't run a business and never make any money.' I don't think that classifies as a business."

For Charlie, White betrayed him. "I dislike the fact that he used this company to travel to Italy to go to a cheese conference or to go to Holland because he said he was going to sell cheese there. It's OK if the company is successful, but he was broke!" He took the failure to heart, because for him it reflected on his choice of business partner.

White countered that indeed a cheese business does need continual investment in its first few years of existence for new churns, vats, and storage for growing production. "He [Charlie] didn't understand that it's more complicated than running a restaurant," White said. "If you run out of something, the only solution is to make more of it *six months before*." White also said that all the various cheeses sold well. "When I left Egg Farm Dairy, it was profitable. I left not of my own choosing, and nine months later they went bankrupt." White said that he was advised by friends not to bother fighting and to put the whole thing behind him.

With his signature labeled as Progressive American Cuisine, Charlie decided to put American bottled water on Aureole's tables instead of French. In 1998 he set up a 50-50 joint venture with Grayson Mountain Water of Columbia, South Carolina, to produce Astra Ridge springwater in blue bottles for all his restaurants. Astra Ridge did very well, growing from $750,000 in sales its first year to a projected $2 million the following year. Grayson also managed to attract a number of baseball investors, including the Cardinals record breaker Mark McGwire, other Cardinals team members, and New York Yankees manager Joe Torre.

Grayson was overwhelmed by its own success and started to falter late in the second year of production. It failed to put up its half of the money for the bottles and missed important order deadlines. In due time, the company went bankrupt. Charlie was left with 12,000 cases of water, which he used, and a possible licensing deal with Grayson Mountain Water's buyer.

Charlie came out with a line of pan sauces and chocolate sauces produced at a factory in New Jersey under the supervision of chef-author Judith Choate. Although originally intended for sale in specialty stores, they have been used primarily as promotions for special customers and at Astra Catering events. Unlike Wolfgang Puck, Charlie has resisted selling on QVC or Home Shopping Network. "I don't think I am the QVC type of person. Once you start doing that sort of thing there is no going back: it cheapens you."

To three restaurants, a florist, bottled water, cheeses, and food products, Charlie added cookbooks. He coauthored his first, *Great American Food,* with Judith Choate. The book sold poorly and was relegated to a spot alongside the pan sauces at his restaurants. A second cookbook, *Charlie Palmer's Casual Cooking,* also coauthored with Judith Choate, was published in part to counter claims that the first book was unusable by most home cooks. The second cookbook sold better, but Charlie was dissatisfied. In October 2003, he published a third cookbook, *Art of Aureole,* again with Choate. *Publishers Weekly* described the third as "Charlie Palmer's extremely haute and formal cooking."

BY 1997, Charlie felt ready to open restaurants outside New York. His first venture afield was with business partner Oliver Grace, Jr., of the

Grace family of New York. The Graces had built their fortune in the mid-1800s on the trade of Peruvian bat guano, upon which they founded such venerable New York institutions as the Grace National Bank (later Marine Midland Bank). Oliver's great-great-uncle William R. Grace, the dynasty's founder, had also been the mayor of New York who accepted the Statue of Liberty from the people of France in 1885. Oliver's second cousin was J. Peter Grace, who headed up W. R. Grace from 1945 to 1992. Himself part of the family-owned Sterling Grace capital management group, Oliver Grace ran hedge funds and was perhaps best known to the public for fronting for a Japanese family to buy the Empire State Building in 1991.

A former employee introduced him to Grace, and Charlie started discussions to sell him an equity stake in Aureole alone. Grace, though, wanted right of first refusal for all of Charlie's ventures. "It made sense—to him it doesn't matter if I am spending time on a project in Las Vegas or New York since he has a piece of everything. You can't ask for a better partner. If I need advice he is there, and he has pull from banking and financial institutions, which I didn't have at the time." Grace set up Aureole Investments, and then a string of limited liability companies for each investment, to insulate the partners. Charlie, in turn, invested with Grace in some of his own projects.

Grace asked Charlie to open a restaurant in Palm Beach, Florida, where Grace already owned a building and had been spending large parts of every year. Charlie and Grace formed a partnership that invested in the property. As a result, Charlie launched the 120-seat Aquaterra in March 1997, sending down longtime disciples Joe and Megan Romano from Aureole as cochefs.

For the first time Charlie hired a market research firm, which assured him that the new restaurant would be a great success. It was not. "Palm Beach, as wealthy as it is, is busy only three months a year," recalled Joe Romano. With two chefs, a *sous chef,* and a general manager plus other costs, profits were meager. "It brought $20,000–100,000 to the bottom line for all the aggravation, and by the time you split that between the partners, for a guy as hot as Charlie and opening restaurants like Charlie was, business-wise it didn't make sense," said Romano. Luckily, The Breakers, a private hotel in Palm Beach, offered to lease the place from Grace and Palmer in 1998, just as they were contemplating closing it down. Charlie, who had never warmed up to Palm Beach, was glad to get out without losing money. "I learned one thing: don't ever do business if you don't feel good about it."

Surprisingly, the misadventure cemented the partnership with Grace. Though Charlie speaks in vague terms, Grace's name has hovered near every deal that he has pursued. Originally in need of cash after he paid off partner Steve Tzolis, Charlie had been eager to diversify away from a single restaurant. "If something had happened to Aureole, that was everything," said Charlie.

Before Palm Beach, Charlie himself had begun considering Las Vegas, uncharted fine dining territory Wolfgang Puck had pioneered with a second Spago in 1992. In addition, Palmer loved Las Vegas. "The deciding factor," he said, "was that there is no place in this country that you can be in the forefront of a great dining area. New York has great restaurants. It's had them for a long time—so has Chicago, San Francisco, L.A. . . . Here was the chance to go do a seriously phenomenal restaurant in a place where you are literally a trailblazer."

Finding the right deal took time. Charlie began negotiations with the Venetian Hotel but walked away from the deal. Then, Bill Richardson, Vice Chairman of the board of the Mandalay Bay Group, went after Charlie, flying him out to Las Vegas to look at the plans of their unfinished hotel. Charlie liked what he saw and made a deal with the group for a second Aureole, which opened in March 1999.

Charlie negotiated a management fee for the restaurant but also formed a partnership with the Mandalay Bay that paid him based on an annual budget reviewed between them. The multiple contracts Palmer signed in his deal with the Mandalay Bay for Aureole were outstanding, in his opinion. The management contract gave him a straight percentage of gross sales. "So if we do one cover tonight, the company makes money," said Joe Romano, "and if we don't, we're not out a penny." The Mandalay Bay built out the restaurant and retained ownership and employed all of Aureole's non-management staff.

The contracts were quite complex, however, and one problem plaguing Charlie and other chef-restaurateurs in Las Vegas was the high cost of unionized labor. "Our payroll at Aureole Las Vegas is double that of New York," Romano said. "The difference is front-of-the-house staff. In Vegas, a waiting captain makes $10.50 an hour, plus $1.75 per fringe benefit, plus tips, while in New York he makes minimum wage plus tips." In addition,

Courtesy of Andrew Bradbury/Aureole

INTERIOR OF AUREOLE LAS VEGAS WITH WINE TOWER DURING EWINEBOOK LAUNCH

Palmer has not been free to move staff from one restaurant to another in slow periods, a big obstacle compared to New York.

Deal making may have taken time, but construction took less than four months, including the famous $1.2 million Wine Tower, designed by Adam Tihany, made of stainless steel and glass and stocked with impressive wines largely from the collection of a Mandalay Bay partner. The gimmick included waitresses ("wine angels") and even the master sommelier who swung up the tower in aerial harnesses to pluck a desired bottle from its numbered space. According to Tihany, he was inspired by a scene with Tom Cruise in the 1996 film *Mission: Impossible.*

The 340-seat Aureole Las Vegas, four times the size of its New York original, shared many elements: tan woods, rich materials, and modern touches, as well as a waiting staff that is more informal than in a typical French restaurant. The Romanos were duly moved from Palm Beach to Las Vegas to head up the new venture, with Joe Romano as executive chef and Megan Romano as executive pastry chef.

The opening was insane. The Mandalay Bay had not anticipated just how many people would attend its grand opening, and no other restaurant was opening to support the onslaught, neither China Blue nor Wolfgang Puck's Lupo nor Milliken and Feniger's Border Grill. "No one was doing food except us," said Joe Romano. "When the word got out that we were doing food and it was free, there were thousands of people at the door." Aureole had to hire security guards, because there were several points of access for guests, including a door from a fountain court with swans, not to mention the kitchen door.

Opening night, Charlie called Joe out of the kitchen. "Charlie said, 'You gotta see this!' I walk out to the swan court, and there are six people walking through the pond to get into the restaurant! They were soaked and waist-high in water!"

No sooner did Charlie start negotiating with the Mandalay Bay than the Four Seasons began chasing him. Randy Morton, then general manager of the Four Seasons in Las Vegas and later at the Bellagio, had known Charlie for several years. Morton knew that Charlie could bring the Four Seasons what it had otherwise been unable to bring itself—restaurant customers. Located at the southern end of the Las Vegas Strip, the Four Seasons was barely attached to and almost completely hidden by the larger Mandalay Bay, so that it missed both car and foot traffic.

Location can make a difference to the success or failure of any restaurant, but for high-end restaurants so can a host of other factors, such as the reputation of the chef, the ability to raise money, the choice of cuisine, and a chef's history of success. A Super Chef's name alone is enough to make any restaurant a destination in itself, according to Charles Baum, a New York-based restaurant consultant. "It's easy to say 'Location, location, location,' but we all know that destination restaurants do work," Baum said. If the name is not enough, the food itself can be (and some would argue, always should be) the draw. For instance, long before he became a TV star, Emeril Lagasse opened his first restaurant in a warehouse in a low-income New Orleans neighborhood. "These restaurants gentrify neighborhoods that once upon a time no one would go to. So, it depends, it depends, it depends," concluded Baum.

In the Four Seasons' case, it was sufficient that Charlie Palmer, a destination name, open there for the hotel to draw guests to its remote location. Morton began to talk about opening a steakhouse, something Charlie had wanted to try his hand at. "Quite frankly, I was afraid to do it in New York, because there are a lot of what people consider great steakhouses, so this was an incredible opportunity."

Part of the reason they settled on a steakhouse had to do with what was going on in other restaurants and hotels. Chef Jean-Georges Vongerichten had turned an unlikely space of chocolate brown velvet and baby blue marble into the highly successful Prime, his French take on an American steakhouse. Vongerichten had been in talks with Las Vegas legend Steve Wynn to open an outpost of his Vong restaurant chain, and they had come up with the sophisticated steakhouse instead. The restaurant had already been designed by Michael de Santis without a particular chef or restaurant in mind to fill the space, as is often the case in Las Vegas, where restaurants had been typically run in-house without an outside chef, much less a Super Chef. Charlie Palmer Steak was the Four Seasons' response to Vongerichten's Prime at the Bellagio and Emeril Lagasse's Delmonico Steakhouse at the Venetian, both of which opened a year earlier in 1998.

"The Four Seasons was smart," said Elizabeth Blau, hotel and restaurant consultant and former senior vice president for restaurant development at MGM Mirage. "Their restaurant wasn't making the grade. They looked at the mix next door in the Mandalay Bay and saw they didn't have a steakhouse. So it was a no-brainer. They couldn't open a corporate chain like Ruth's Chris—that wouldn't make sense," not with the exclusive nature of the Four Seasons brand. The Four Seasons and Charlie Palmer, however, both had management contracts with the Mandalay Bay, so it was easy to proceed with Charlie.

Once the deal got going, Charlie found himself transformed from the hunted to the hunter, chasing Isadore ("Issy") Sharp, founder and CEO of the Four Seasons. Until Charlie, the Four Seasons had never contracted restaurants outside, at any location. "Quite honestly," Charlie confided, "it became a thing where I had to convince Issy that this was a good idea. The Four Seasons philosophy is about taking care of people on a high level, like mine, but he was afraid to give up control of something that was going to take care of his Four Seasons guests. In the end, he felt comfortable, and I got a straight lease." Unlike Aureole Las Vegas where Charlie owns nothing, everything is his inside Charlie Palmer Steak, though he did take over an existing restaurant.

Charlie appreciated Sharp's decision immensely. "I always try to think of our associations," he said, "and you cannot be associated with any hotel better than the Four Seasons as top-of-the-line service. So, in that sense, it was exciting to have an opportunity like this. . . . There are many examples where restaurants have damaged hotels. At the Four Seasons, I feel responsible for the hotel's guests."

The 180-seat Charlie Palmer Steak with a lounge seating an additional 20 opened in November 1999 just as successfully as Aureole a few months earlier. With Joe and Megan Romano to oversee both restaurants, deals on supplies to cut down costs, and Palmer's philosophy not to waste anything, the restaurants brought in more than 20 percent to his bottom line. Annual gross revenues at Aureole have run in excess of $10 million and $5 million at Charlie Palmer Steak.

CHARLIE found himself back in New York for his next restaurant. A group with rights in the newly renovated space in Grand Central Station, just across from Michael Jordan Steak, approached him. Chef Matthew Kenney had pulled out of the deal at the last minute, leaving the partners, East Balcony Associates, in need of a name chef. Charlie, who had more chefs in his kitchens ready to be promoted, jumped at the deal, along with Oliver Grace and former Lenox Room partner Tony Fortuna. He opened Métrazur in January 2000 with a menu that combined his Progressive American Cuisine with Mediterranean influences. The restaurant seated 110, with an additional 90 seats in a lounge bar.

The effect of opening three restaurants in two cities within one year brought tough criticism from the *New York Times* food reviewer William Grimes: he downgraded Aureole by one star to two. "Diners fill Aureole's tables day after day and night after night," Grimes wrote, "partly because it serves very good food but mostly because, like Everest—the quintessential celebrity mountain—it is there, and famously there. In the last 10 years, however, the surrounding peaks look a lot higher. . . . The restaurant has changed little, in fact, but the world around it has changed a lot."

Charlie was, in fact, no longer at the helm of Aureole to make sure quality in the preparations was constantly upheld. He was already in discussion with Gerry Hayden, who had risen at Aureole to *sous chef* before leaving for a string of highly successful restaurants, including those of colleagues Michael Mina at Aqua in San Francisco and Don Pintabona at Tribeca Grill. Charlie approached Hayden originally to run Métrazur but eventually decided that he needed an executive chef at Aureole, as he could no longer handle that position himself. "Charlie was branching out, but he needed to realize that New York is the base," said Hayden. "It's OK to expand, but you need to have someone back here cooking."

In November 1999, Charlie appointed Hayden *chef de cuisine* of Aureole, and in September 2001 anointed him executive chef, while Charlie stepped back to the role of owner. By then, he was no longer head chef in any of his restaurants, although he remained closely involved with each new restaurant.

Two months later he opened Dry Creek Kitchen in the new Hotel Healdsburg. The project had been brewing for years. Charlie had come to the area over a decade earlier for the vines and since 1995 had been blending a *cuvée* for his flagship Aureole restaurants at the Iron Horse Vineyard in nearby Sebastopol. He kept coming back, discovering the richness of the area. “From my standpoint, there are hardly any places that have all the things we have here: great wines, incredible produce, and Pacific Coast fisheries.” As a result, he decided to limit the restaurant to the nearly limitless agricultural bounty of Sonoma County and particularly Healdsburg. For Sonoma, read “America,” and you have Charlie’s philosophy of cuisine: the best local ingredients and cooking to enhance the flavor of food.

Typical of Charlie, he had also taken advantage of an excellent business opportunity. Thomas Keller’s French Laundry and Hiro Sone’s Terra in next-door Napa Valley had already done the hard work of bringing serious diners up from food-savvy San Francisco to California wine country; both chefs are James Beard award winners. Following good game on proven grounds, Charlie staked out Sonoma County for his own with the coolness of a seasoned hunter. Wine, food, flowers, Charlie was serving it all up in his restaurant, under his national banner of Progressive American Cuisine. Who could compete with that?

Dry Creek Kitchen lay in a corner of Hotel Healdsburg, which stretched along the town green. Of the $22 million investment in the hotel (“rather high for a 55-room hotel, even if it is boutique,” said partner Paolo Petrone), only $6 million came from the partners, of whom Charlie was one; the rest came as loans. Charlie’s contribution was a combination of cash and in-kind investment of restaurant and catering. Charlie was last in the group, introduced by the hotel’s designer.

The boutique hotel was completed in November 2001. The main façade had an overhanging roofline, French windows, and views of the town’s youngish yet already towering redwoods. Its courtyards contained an herb garden, grape arbor, and fruit trees along a sizable swimming pool, with onlooking meeting rooms and a luxurious health spa. The

Courtesy of the Charlie Palmer Group

EXTERIOR OF DRY CREEK KITCHEN AT THE HEALDSBURG HOTEL

hotel's long east façade housed a café-bookstore filled with the latest magazines. A flower shop drifted out of its own space, gracing the restaurant's entrance. Despite the economic downturn that had begun before its opening, the hotel flourished. Charlie's restaurant manager, who had previous experience managing hotels, took over management of the hotel shortly after it opened. In August 2003, *Travel & Leisure* magazine listed Hotel Healdsburg among the top 100 hotels in North America.

In addition to 70 seats in the restaurant proper, Dry Creek Kitchen offered catering in special spaces at the hotel, including an event green for 150–200 guests, a grange hall for 75, and a quiet wine library for 14. The interior featured a set of vaulted ceilings resembling a wine *cave,* clean lines, and lots of glass to look out onto the town green. Its colors were soft and autumnal: olive greens, warm browns and reds, and huge displays of russet and yellow mums (courtesy of the next-door flower shop). While the lighting featured modern chrome-and-glass faux candles (also found at other Palmer restaurants), the chairs were covered with classic etchings of giant ripe pears in light yellowy brown tones that turned the whole modern look on its head. Along a wall, a teak armoire displayed Charlie's cookbooks.

Charlie's next venture, Astra West, relocated Spero Plavoukos and Dan Shannon to another Charles Cohen property, the Pacific Design Center in

Los Angeles, in August 2001. The Astra West facilities, which opened at the end of that year, accommodated over 800 guests for a sit-down dinner and offered a 1970s-style lounge. Many of Astra's New York clients were also in Hollywood, and Astra West was planned to become a celebrity hangout. The facility's gala opening included stars like Janel Moloney of *The West Wing,* Rosanna Arquette, and Tori Spelling.

The deal with Cohen differed from Astra in New York. In Los Angeles, Charlie was actually a partner with Cohen in the facility and spent just shy of $1 million on the interior and kitchens. By this time, he had decided to go with Martin Vahtra, previously with Adam Tihany's firm, as his main restaurant designer. For Tihany, Vahtra had designed Aureole Las Vegas and had then left to found Project Labs based in New York, with Charlie Palmer as a client. Vahtra also picked up work from Palmer protégée Gerry Hayden when he left Aureole in New York to open his own restaurant, Amuse, in 2003.

After many bad experiences as a charitable celebrity, Charlie found a charity that he believed was truly effective: City Meals on Wheels. His conscientious efforts to fight waste fitted very well with this charity, so it was small wonder that he favored a group that donated nearly 100 percent of all money raised. "I do some guest cooking," said Charlie, "though I've been cutting back, because you can get caught up in the 'event thing.' I'm on the board of City Meals on Wheels, and I try to concentrate on that. Otherwise, you could do an event every night. City Meals, it's incredible what they do. Literally, 99¢ out of every $1.00 goes to charity; it's incredibly well run. That makes me feel like I'm really doing something, too."

For one of the charity events that the organization hosted, corporations paid $2,500 for dinner and wine for six at restaurants around New York. Typically, chefs donated one or two tables, but Charlie often gave more. "It's a lottery, so if I have a last-minute person calling who wants to pay for a table and they are all gone," said Maryanne Bloomfield of City Meals on Wheels, "I call Charlie, and he usually gives another. We can always count on him."

AFTER the collapse of the two World Trade Center towers on September 11, 2001, like many colleagues Charlie felt the need to do something. He recalled, "After 9/11, it quickly became apparent to some people—Gray Kunz, Daniel Boulud, and me among them—that we could not get food downtown." All week, they had been sending down food by whatever means possible: taxis, police cars, delivery trucks, whoever would volunteer transportation. Near Ground Zero, Don Pintabona, one-time Palmer protégé and chef of Tribeca Grill, was completely shut down, with food rotting, and had gotten in touch with Spirit Cruises. He and Gray Kunz lined up the *Spirit of New York* for food deliveries.

"Don got them to loan us their boats," Charlie said, "and got clearance to take the boats down to the marina area right behind the World Trade Center. Then, we had a shuttle bring food and volunteers to the boat. By Friday [September 14], we were serving some 6,000 meals a day. Then, the Red Cross took over and told us that we could not serve food with bones or anything with red sauce, because it reminds the workers of blood—all kinds of nonsense. I mean, these were New York City firefighters! They were so appreciative, too—you cannot imagine how happy they were just to have something hot to eat, just to sit down, clean up—the boats had showers. We donated all the food. Would you believe, after we got on the phones, within three hours we had too much food to handle?"

According to Don Pintabona, New York's finest chefs fell right into line wherever they were needed. Daniel Boulud and Andrew Carmellini worked the ship's kitchen. Gray Kunz handled supplies and serving stations. Charlie and Lisa Palmer served with wait staff; Pintabona was boss. Grateful recipients sent a note of thanks scrawled on a paper plate.

Daniel Boulud went so far as to issue a day-by-day account by press release and by Internet. He called their group "Chefs with Spirit" and listed Drew Nieporent, Owner, Myriad Restaurant Group; Don Pintabona, Chef, Tribeca Grill; Gray Kunz, Chef (formerly of Lespinasse); Charlie Palmer, Chef-Owner, Aureole; Nick Valenti and Stefano Cordova, Restaurant Associates; and himself.

Like so many New Yorkers who rushed out to help in the aftermath of 9/11, Charlie suffered some sobering losses of his own. His Manhattan restaurants failed to qualify for Federal Emergency Management Agency (FEMA) relief despite their losses because of their location well above downtown. Virot, a midtown restaurant in the Dylan Hotel, closed in November 2001 along with many other newly opened restaurants; Charlie was one of the investors in this French restaurant opened by Jean-Georges Vongerichten veteran Didier Virot.

Alva fared well, as did so many local neighborhood restaurants. Aureole and Astra suffered somewhat as high-end, celebration-oriented sites.

Métrazur was hit hardest: there was little or no traffic in Grand Central Station, vacated by the disaster and briefly an object of fear as another terrorist target. For the first two months after September 11, Charlie kept Métrazur open simply out of loyalty to his staff. "With all the layoffs in the City, I did not have the heart to send my waiters out into a market where they had little or no chance of finding other work." Over the next few months, Métrazur hung on and slowly returned to something near normal business, like the rest of Manhattan.

In December 2001, Charlie announced a deal with Seabourn Cruise Lines, part of Cunard. Charlie would supply three, 208-guest ships with not only his signature Progressive American Cuisine but also Mediterranean, Southeast Asian, and Latin American cuisines. Charlie's take on the move was that, like the Four Seasons, Seabourn Cruise Lines guarantee a level of excellence in quality that he strove to maintain at his own restaurants. In addition to creating over 200 menu items, Charlie trained Seabourn cooks onshore at his own restaurants and then onboard.

Charlie went a step further: in February 2003 he announced with Seabourn the creation of a "chefs circle," a guest chef format in which many respected and familiar chef friends cooked, taught cooking, and took passengers on food-shopping trips ashore during special European cruises: Rick Moonen of rm, David Burke of Park Avenue Café, Michel Richard of Citronelle, Andrew Carmellini (*chef de cuisine*) of Café Boulud, Jean Alberti of Kokkari Estiatorio, and David Pasternack of Esca (a Mario Batali–Joe Bastianich restaurant). Charlie did not market as aggressively as Wolfgang Puck did with Crystal Cruises. Wolfgang branded a section of the Jade Garden restaurant as Chinois at Jade and has sent at least three chefs (Lee Hefter, Luis Diaz, and Sherry Yard) to sea in his stead; Charlie is giving space to his friends. Ultimately, however, it remains to be seen whether Wolfgang will cinch up brand recognition and loyalty or tire out his brand, or whether Charlie's lower key approach lasts longer.

Charlie kept expanding. With catering on both coasts, he began looking for another venue in Las Vegas for larger events than his two Las Vegas restaurants could handle. Many of his catering customers were staging events on both coasts and were interested in working with him in Las Vegas as well. The Soffer family approached him to take over catering at the Stirling Club, a $40 million semiprivate club nestled between the four towers of the $650 million Turnberry Place condominium complex. Turnberry's condo prices range from $500,000 to $5.25 million. In April 2003,

Charlie accepted charge of food and beverage for the club, including club catering functions, in return for the right to use the venue for his own catering needs. The Stirling Club serves up to 1,000 guests: across the street is the Las Vegas Convention Center.

Charlie decided to change the concept again at the Alva location. With new no-smoking regulations threatening to ruin Alva's famed smoking bar, Charlie realized that it would soon be out of business. His new concept was Kitchen 22. He thought of it as the ultimate neighborhood restaurant, one that combined great décor and service, good food and wine, and reasonable prices. The old CCC and Alva site closed for extensive renovations, including a new bar, kitchen floor, and electrical paneling. The new Kitchen 22 offered a three-course prix fixe menu for $25 and a wine list with bottles for $25 and $35.

The margins were tight, but the volume was higher than previous guises as CCC and Alva. Kitchen 22's success persuaded Charlie to open a second outlet on Manhattan's Upper East Side, Kitchen 82. He started planning for a third. His designer for Kitchen 22 and Kitchen 82 was again Martin Vahtra. "It's a concept for cities like Cincinnati, so big restaurant groups are interested in buying. I might sell it to them," said Charlie.

OVER time, part of Palmer's profitability has come from keeping food costs within a given percentage at each restaurant, something he started while still at the River Café. "Your food costs have to be 30 percent or lower, and every chef has an incentive program that benefits him if his costs are in line." Charlie said, "Every chef knows that if their costs go above a certain point, they're not going to be around for long."

Charlie himself monitors food and labor costs at each restaurant daily through flash reports. Each restaurant is set at a different food cost percentage point with an incentive plan for the top chef. To make sure that a chef does not cut numbers by using inferior products, he also reviews all products. However, much of that risk has been eliminated by the fact that most of his top chefs have worked under Charlie anywhere from six to a dozen years or more.

"I set the metrics, because each place is different," Charlie said. "For instance, Alva was a place I wanted to keep for the neighborhood, so we actually knocked prices down. Alva's food costs were set above 30 percent, whereas Aureole Las Vegas is set below 30 percent. Richard, our controller, and I call those numbers. Food costs in catering are below restaurant food costs."

Joe Romano commented further, "Charlie's cuisine helps make him lucrative as a businessman. And part of his success is that he simply uses everything. A lot of chefs in these high-end restaurants get baby carrots but will only use two-and-one-half-inch carrots—anything longer or shorter, and they throw it away. We utilize everything."

Another part of Palmer's profitability has come from his ability to keep chefs who have worked for him and whom he can trust—the talent. Traditionally, cooks in France used to start as unpaid apprentices in important kitchens. Most chefs in America, including Charlie, follow this tradition of hiring very young cooks. Chefs then teach them in their particular style. Most of the chefs in Charlie's employ who have advanced to executive chef level have come to his restaurants through externships from the CIA or after completing their education there; few have come from other, outside restaurants. Loyalty to Charlie is thus instilled from the beginning of their careers.

The modern chef's career path was organized and regimented by Auguste Escoffier. In his *Le Livre des Menus* (1912), Escoffier outlined the following hierarchy for a "kitchen brigade": *chef du cuisine* (chief of the kitchen), *sous chef* (deputy), and *chefs de parties* (chiefs of stations). The major *parties* or stations are *saucier* (sauce chef), *poissonier* (fish chef), *rotisseur* (roaster), *grillardin* (griller), *garde manger* (pantry chef), *entremetier* (vegetable chef), *patissier* (pastry chef), and *tourant* (relief chef). There are further chefs, *commis* (assistants), and *apprenti* (apprentices). Each station forms a line for the various stages of food preparation and is assigned a "company" of assistants and "line cooks." Escoffier first conceived of his system during the Franco-Prussian War of 1870 to create efficient cooking while serving in the French army, and it remains the basis of most large fine dining kitchens today.

In traditional *haute cuisine,* the variety of food is so vast and its preparation so complex that a cook must spend years paying his or her dues by learning each and every step in a station's line. Someone like Escoffier had to devise a kitchen brigade to regiment not just operational efficiency but the progress of a cook's proficiency. The accumulation of hands-on cooking skills continues all the way to the top; in fact, perhaps the deadliest criticism to level against any chef is to accuse him or her of no longer cooking.

When Escoffier instituted his kitchen brigade hierarchy some hundred years ago, most cooks were happy just receiving the decent salaries and sanitary conditions he offered. "He spent a lot of time teaching his employees," CIA president Tim Ryan said, "trying to upgrade their skills, talking about the notion of working together and being a team, how to behave professionally by not swearing, by not going out and drinking and carousing, by living a healthy life. In those days, kitchens were pretty unhealthy. There were charcoal stoves, and they were breathing in the dust and so forth, and they were prone to some abuses. He even developed a barley drink, which was supposed to be healthy and restorative." Thanks to Escoffier, an *haute cuisine* chef became a more respectable profession, and fine dining became comparable to architecture, law, and other service industries, requiring long training and high skill levels (although there are no comparable chef partnerships at the present time).

There is a natural attrition rate, particularly at the lower levels, as not everyone is cut out for the demands of an *haute cuisine* restaurant. This attrition, however, is part of the success of the hierarchical kitchen brigade, which wages its own constant, internal war to weed out the unqualified or apathetic, keep the qualified, and advance the exceptional to chef levels. The result is trained talent—and that is when the tables can turn against a Super Chef. Once a chef has become trained talent, the trick for chefs and restaurateurs is to retain that talent. Once a dedicated cook has advanced through the ranks of the kitchen brigade, once the investment starts to see a return in a highly skilled *chef du partie* or *sous chef,* a Super Chef like Charlie Palmer has to work at creating team loyalty to keep that chef with him.

A primary factor in loyalty is the drive for self-preservation because of the fundamental risk of striking out on one's own, into the unknown. "It is stressful to do your own business," said Daniel Boulud. "Most chefs are better off working for someone else. There is more money, more security, and less headache." Slaving in a kitchen for years as a *sous chef* under the master chef can be vastly more appealing than losing one's shirt within a few months of opening a first restaurant.

Further, striking out on one's own assumes that a *sous chef* or *chef du partie* could muster the investment necessary to open a restaurant in the first place. Charlie's disciples, many who have worked for him for years (some going back to days at the River Café), are all too aware of the advantages Charlie had when he opened Aureole. He was not only one of the hottest young chefs of the 1980s but also one of the first American chefs to challenge the French. With so many other chefs who have followed his path, it would not be so easy for Charlie to be starting out again today, 15 years later—nor is it easy for his disciples.

There are factors more positive in loyalty considerations than self-preservation. One is job satisfaction, particularly with the restaurants of a Super Chef like Charlie. A chef may have spent five to eight years under Charlie and risen to become a *sous chef* and stayed there another three, but being a *sous chef* at a Charlie Palmer restaurant is often far better than being executive chef or chef-owner at many other restaurants. In addition, there is the prospect of working among equally qualified people. Also, chefs and cooks within a group like Charlie's share the same experience and cook according to the Palmer School, which eases many aspects of daily operations, starting with the never-ending repetition of food preparation *à la* Palmer.

In the specific case of Charlie, all his people praise him for taking care of his own, as well as his being admirably kind amidst his striving for perfection. He does not scream out orders; he plays classical music in his kitchens. In fact, Charlie's people ascribe to him a long list of admirable qualities, including being down-to-earth and having lots of common sense. Charlie has not forgotten who he is or where he came from, and he seems far less at home in Manhattan than in Healdsburg, which is much more like his own hometown of Smyrna.

With respect to loyalty and retention of talent, the CIA's Ryan agrees on these points: Charlie is so innovative in cuisine that talent is interested in staying, so innovative in business that talent has new opportunities within his organization, and so "very personable" and interested in his people (for all his being a tough taskmaster) that "they return his interest with loyalty."

With all these considerations in mind, however, a *sous chef* without room for further advancement under his or her *chef du cuisine* will inevitably consider using the accumulated knowledge and experience not only in cooking but also operating a restaurant out in the unknown. It is at this point that Charlie's restaurant expansion fits into the rest of his business dynamics. His first restaurants after Aureole—CCC (later Alva, later Kitchen 22), the Lenox Room, and Astra—were not only less fancy and less expensive but were also safe outlets for staff to grow. A rising chef whose path was blocked by a *sous chef* at Aureole could take over at Astra and gain tremendous experience as *sous chef* or *chef du cuisine*, as Dan Shannon did. By the time he or she was ready to expand outside of New York with investments comparable in size to Aureole New York, chefs like Joe and Megan Romano were ready to run them, chefs with whom Charlie had worked for nearly two decades collectively.

Thus the empire-building Super Chefs have an advantage over chefs who stay in one kitchen: as they expand, they offer more opportunities to their increasingly trained staff. By contrast, a chef like Daniel Boulud, who until recently had not expanded outside New York, cannot afford to keep chefs who are ready for promotion beyond the *chef du cuisine* level. "Unless a particular chef is going to be my successor, it's inevitable that they will want to take the risk and jeopardize the security I offer them, in which case they are free to leave," Boulud said.

Meanwhile, Charlie has offered his chefs competitive salaries and incentive bonuses to keep food and labor costs under control. Such compensation has been common practice among top-tier restaurants; only the top chef used to be offered a share in ownership of a restaurant by restaurateurs. Chefs like David Burke of Park Avenue Café only offer chefs incentive plans with standard salaries and compensation. For key players in Charlie's company, however, generous pay and compensation are not always enough to keep them. After a couple of years at the top as an executive chef, they are even more qualified and experienced to strike out on their own.

His top staff found a solution to their desire to keep working for him and their need to build their own equity. "I slowly put it into Charlie's ears over the years that we should be allowed to invest in his ventures. Because . . . what else is going to keep you?" Joe Romano said. He suggested that Charlie allow key people in his organization to create an investment company of their own. "We dubbed it 61st Street Investments in reference to Aureole's address," said Romano. It has pooled employees' money to invest on an equal footing with Charlie and his partners in new projects, like Dry Creek Kitchen in Healdsburg and Astra West in Los Angeles.

Romano explained, "Profit sharing has been around since Day One, but this is actually an investment company. Charlie is not in our company. It's myself, Richard Femenella [the controller], Aziz Zhari [head *maître d'* at Aureole], and my wife Megan—we are the ones who developed the company and set the ground rules. We have full say about who is in or not in the company." In practice Palmer still has a big say. "If Charlie says, 'Look, I got this guy Gerry [Hayden] in New York . . . ' then we're gonna listen."

The investment company launched in September 2001, with $25,000 from each of the partners and smaller amounts from other employees. Though Charlie was initially reluctant about the idea, since their shares would come from his, he has embraced it wholeheartedly as a way to keep talent. "It's good for us, because otherwise no matter how far you rise in the company you are still an employee, you are still getting a paycheck, and that is all you are getting." Romano confided, "I had actually considered leaving Charlie because I wanted more than a paycheck, so that's the whole idea: it keeps people in the company."

Charlie has a dream: his chefs help him build it, so it becomes their dream, too, commented business guru and coach Bruce Hodes. "The situation in most companies is, I, the employee, am going to make you, the boss, get rich—but I go as soon as I get a better deal." Subordinate chefs often trade on their master chef's name for something better, he explained. "So, you have to change what 'I' do to what 'we' do. It's the same situation with any entrepreneur: he gave birth to something, then he has turn it into something for the group. After all, people of talent have a choice. They may hunger for wealth, but they also want to make a difference." Charlie has obviously convinced his people that his dream is theirs, too.

Charlie has not been the only Super Chef to change compensation for chefs. Take Wolfgang Puck's counterpart to Joe Romano, David Robbins. Hired by Wolfgang to head up Spago Las Vegas when it opened in 1992, Robbins is now not only in charge of Puck's six venues in Las Vegas but also partner in them, as well as Spago Maui.

If his chefs have become savvier in business under his tutelage, Charlie has not slowed down himself. His venture in Healdsburg is a hotel-restaurant partnership with three businessmen: while his chefs have been carving into his empire, Charlie has been extending it.

Geographically Charlie is quite concentrated. Outside of his New York base, his only other area of operations is a western triangle formed by Las Vegas, Los Angeles, and San Francisco (Healdsburg), all within two hours of each other by plane. By restricting his growth to where restaurant development is hot, Charlie also makes his traveling relatively easy, an important consideration for someone who moves around regularly to each restaurant. He refuses to book any event far in advance so he can remain focused on his daily operations. He also refuses to go international ("too far"), nor will he ever consider commercializing into chains—with the possible exception of the Charlie Palmer Steak and Kitchen concepts. At present, he has reached or is reaching an ideally manageable size and does not expect to grow much more, other than to accept offers he cannot refuse (and even those have to be better than best).

As for celebrity, Charlie seems to regard it as dangerous, a threat that could easily undermine and cheapen his credibility as a chef. Back at the River Café, although O'Keeffe had his chefs do their own publicity and chase after restaurant reviews, he warned Charlie not to let fame go to his head. These days, Charlie generally limits his TV appearances and rarely cooks promotionally.

"TV has become very dangerous to a top-tier chef. Once you are looked at in that light, you aren't going to be taken seriously as a chef anymore," said Charlie, who has even turned down several offers for a TV series. "You see that happening with Emeril. I mean, I like the guy. I think he is a talented cook, but if you talk to people in the industry they think his food stinks and his restaurants stink. If you spend all your time doing television, your restaurant suffers."

Publicizing chef names contradicts advice from some top business gurus. Dr. Ichak Adizes, a former restaurant owner himself, warns, "It is essential that they not build up a name." Yet nowadays as Charlie pursues print reviews, he hopes to have his top chefs prominently mentioned. "If it takes me to be a part of it, that is great," Charlie said, but if it includes one of his chefs, it is better. Charlie's chefs are getting press. On his own website, Charlie lists his chefs. Executive chefs are Dante Boccuzzi at Aureole New York, Philippe Rispoli at Aureole Las Vegas, Mark Purdy at Dry Creek Kitchen, Bryan Voltaggio at Charlie Palmer Steak in Washington, and Stephen Blandino at Charlie Palmer Steak in Las Vegas. *Chefs du cuisine* are Michael Lockhard at Métrazur, Christopher Ennis at Astra West, Chris Bradley at Astra, Scott Romano of Kitchen 22 and Kitchen 82. (The Stirling Club is not listed.)

SOME have said that the 1999 Grimes article in *The New York Times* marked a serious embarrassment if not decline for Charlie. Others said that he turned his back on his home base as he opened in Las Vegas in 1999 and was penalized for a drop in food quality in New York. That is an easy mistake to make with a cursory reading, but the Grimes article never faulted Charlie's food outright. Quality, one of Charlie's chief concerns, went unquestioned. Also, Charlie was most certainly not the only chef to be docked a star. When Daniel Boulud reopened the new Restaurant Daniel after a $10 million transformation, Grimes demoted the restaurant from four to three stars. Of Roy Yamaguchi's New York opening, he said, "If clowns had a cuisine, this would be it."

The tough criticism from Grimes sparked a reply from several prominent chefs and restaurateurs in the *New York Observer* soon afterward. "I think it's unfortunate that someone like Bill Grimes," Charlie said, "is allowed to use *The New York Times* as a vehicle for his own personal agenda." He claimed that Grimes' review was "a critique of our success with Zagat" rather than of Aureole. Further, he said, "my clientele at Aureole is a very educated group, and they dine in the best restaurants in the world. Probably 75 percent know more about food and wine than Bill Grimes will ever know."

In 1988, *The New York Times* ran a similar article by Bryan Miller critiquing Lutèce, and the Miller and Grimes articles make for interesting comparison and contrast. Miller complained that Lutèce was "hardly a gastronomic trailblazer" and concluded that "you dine at Lutèce not to ride the latest wave in French cuisine, but rather to stroll leisurely through familiar terrain, sniffing the flowers along the way. And how sweet they can be." Here, Lutèce and Aureole seem to be relatively on par, choosing quality over innovation.

Yet regarding Lutèce's innovation, Miller said, "The classic French menu is merely a formality, for Mr. Soltner and his staff conjure up a host of daily specials that should be carefully considered," while Grimes makes no such mention about Aureole's menu. Moreover, unlike the new Super Chefs, Soltner was famous for living upstairs above his restaurant (as Charlie did at first above Aureole), and Miller attributes much of Lutèce's appeal to "Mr. Soltner himself, the affable, self-effacing host who wouldn't leave his cherished restaurant unless under subpoena." In contrast, Charlie has executive chefs cooking for him in every one of his restaurants. Lastly, Miller left Lutèce's four stars intact, while Grimes dropped Aureole from three to two stars.

As if in reaction to the Grimes article, Charlie brought Gerry Hayden back to Aureole. Hayden rewrote the menu and brought in West Coast and international influences of lighter cuisine and smaller portions. Then, when Hayden left to open his own restaurant, Amuse, Charlie brought in Dante Boccuzzi, who had worked not only for him but also for Nobu Matsuhisa. Will a new executive chef be enough for Aureole to recover its third star? Possibly, but Aureole may have to wait a long time for its turn at a new review, because *The New York Times* has a responsibility to review literally thousands of restaurants in New York.

The two articles indicate two further findings. First, they are a reminder that Aureole has never achieved Charlie's goal of surpassing Lutèce, at least in terms of achieving four stars from *The New York Times.* Second, together the articles imply that perhaps Grimes was simply trying to warn all restaurants of his high standards—by knocking off a star from a restaurant that can take the knock. After all, there will always be new competition, new mountain peaks, that will make jaded diners question how good a meal is in an established or older restaurant. As Grimes himself said, the stars are really just for "consumer convenience" and that "the review itself should clear up any confusion"—and he did compare Aureole to Mount Everest.

Other print coverage has been kinder if not copious. Charlie was listed as one of the "Chefs du Buck" on the *Forbes* Celebrity 100 list of March 2000. In May 2001, *Time* magazine wrote a very favorable article called "Palmer's People" about the loyalty he has won in the front and the back of the house. His Wine Tower and eWinebook at Aureole received mention on Warner Bros. *ExtraTV* on Christmas Day 2002 in a piece on Las Vegas. And since 2000, Charlie has been showered with awards from the magazines of M. Shanken Communications: 2000–2002, the *Wine Spectator* annual grand award for Aureole Las Vegas; 2000–2002, the annual award of excellence for Charlie Palmer Steak; 2001, the *Wine Spectator* annual best of award for Aureole New York; and May 2003, the monthly *Food Arts* Silver Spoon Award for Charlie Palmer.

Charlie has made national television about every other month or two for some time, particularly on NBC's *Today Show,* to compete in a gingerbread house contest, cook mussels, and make Easter chocolates. He has brought four of his closest aides onto the show—sons Courtland, Randall, Eric, and Reed. Charlie has also appeared on numerous Food Network programs: *Cooking Live* with Sara Moulton, *Tasting Napa, Wolfgang Puck, Food Nation* with Bobby Flay, and *Follow That Food* with Gordon Elliott.

HERE is a dilemma facing all Super Chefs: none of them are cooking daily in their increasing numbers of kitchens and yet perhaps the main reason many eat at their restaurants is to eat the food cooked by a Super Chef. Charles Baum, son and partner of the late Joe Baum, speculated, "You have a highly skilled *chef de cuisine* [under a Super Chef] who should get the credit and often does. Still, is that why I am going—where there is a chef I don't know or I don't associate with the place? Does that make me feel good, or does that complicate having a memorable meal—because now I am in 'just a restaurant' and really not in, say, Charlie's restaurant?"

Charlie replied that what is essential is to keep up a quality and style that meet the expectations of anyone eating at a Charlie Palmer restaurant. Romano elaborated candidly. "Can you have a bad meal at any one of Charlie's restaurants on any given night? Yes, you can. When you're feeding mass amounts of people, anything can happen; it *is* possible for you to have a bad experience. But let me tell you something: if an average person goes to one of Charlie's restaurants five times, I *guarantee* you, 4.75 times you're gonna have a great experience, borderline phenomenal experience. That's my personal opinion. I think you can go to other people [other Super Chefs] who are expanding more rapidly, and it could be a crapshoot, two-to-three bad experiences out of five."

Meanwhile, Charlie himself has claimed to be cooking these days *more* than he has in the past half-decade of empire expansion. This claim is hard to qualify or judge. Charlie, now free of direct executive chef responsibilities for any specific restaurant, said that he has been acting as group chef, particularly when it comes to developing new dishes.

In his established restaurants, he has been reviewing menu changes that come from his executive chefs, with whom he is in touch daily. His focus has remained on maintaining quality in his kitchens. Besides watching menus, Charlie said that he often walks into the kitchen of a group restaurant and simply chooses to work with someone for the night (not *so* often, chuckle some of his chefs). On any given night a line cook could find Super Chef Charlie Palmer standing beside him or her for the duration of the shift, helping with style and technique.

"Look, I don't cook the same as I cooked five years or even two years ago. Cooking is a progressive kind of thing." His signature has not been static but dynamic and ongoing, a work in progress; further, he has a "school" to which his chefs not only adhere but add to and influence. "I don't want Aureole to be my signature food," he said. "If Aureole is my signature, what is Métrazur? What is Dry Creek? Is *that* my signature food?"

Tim Zagat said, "When he started Aureole it was a big deal; it was the opening of the year. It had aspirations of being the best restaurant in New York within its first five years. It was supposed to be the next Lutèce. Lutèce was everyone's idea of number one, as it had been for years. Aureole has never made it. Mind you, Aureole has always been an excellent restaurant, but what people wowed about in the beginning is now just more common." To date, *Zagat Survey* finds Aureole to be still among the top 20 most popular New York restaurants, after a decade and a half.

If the jury is out on Charlie's role as a leading, innovative chef, there can be no doubt that he has developed into a formidable restaurateur and businessman. He has been cost conscious in his operations and treasures his most valuable resource—his staff. As a result, his costs have dropped while his productivity has risen over time. Meanwhile, he has taken his time considering business deals and partners and has done business almost exclusively with people whom he has known for some time, whether partners or staff. Consequently, he has made few mistakes when he has stepped forward into a new venture.

"Bottom line, it's all about my guests," Charlie said. "I want people to go to any of my restaurants, eat good food, and have a good time. That's it."

BARELY a month after its opening in May 2003, Charlie Palmer Steak in Washington, D.C., hosted a bash that rivaled Hollywood for celebrities—and silliness. At a party for outgoing Recording Industry Association of America (RIAA) chairperson Hilary Rosen, celebrity politicians did not so much populate the pulpit as perform on it. Guests included former President Bill Clinton and Senator Hillary Clinton (D-NY), former Vice President Al Gore and Tipper Gore, Senator Tom Daschle (D-SD), Minority Leader Senator Orrin Hatch (R-UT), Republican National Committee deputy chairman Jack Oliver, Washington power lawyer Bob Barnett, NBC News reporter Lisa Myers, Internet gossip Matt Drudge, *Crossfire* co-hosts Tucker Carlson and James Carville, CBS radio host Laura Ingraham, and Aspen Institute president Walter Isaacson, formerly chairman of CNN and managing editor of *Time* magazine.

On video Representatives Billy Tauzin (R–LA) and Mary Bono (R–CA) rapped to the tune of Eminem's "Lose Yourself," chanting, "Piracy bad! Piracy bad!" while the whole group sang to the tune of Edelweiss of their griev-ing now that Hilary was leav-ing. The event was covered gleefully by *The Washington Post* and *Slate*.

The restaurant was bedecked with such personal touches as pink lightbulbs everywhere (Hilary Rosen's favorite color), and happily helping as host was investor Craig Fuller. Currently the president and CEO of the National Association of Chain Drug Stores, Fuller wields the ultimate lobbyist's resume. After serving eight years in the Reagan and Bush White House, he went on to hold top-three spots at Hill & Knowlton USA, Philip Morris, Burson-Marsteller, and Korn/Ferry International. He had never invested in a restaurant before, but when Charlie Palmer's people called him, he not only agreed to help them look for investors but became an investor himself.

The convivial Fuller is an ideal restaurant investor. He believes in his chef and adores his food. From personal experience, he appreciates several aspects of convenience in the restaurant's location. Charlie Palmer Steak sits right on Capitol Hill, where no fine dining restaurant of this caliber has ventured. I-395 actually makes the restaurant more available than the rest of downtown Washington for weekend diners. The rooftop allows catering to another 600 people, and one of the other tenants allows Charlie to rent their balconies overlooking the Capitol Building for private dining functions. "Imagine that you're a chairman with a senator," said Fuller, "and the entire backdrop is the United States Capitol—that has an impact."

Fuller knew of Aureole in New York and Las Vegas, though he had never eaten at Aureole Las Vegas or Charlie Palmer Steak. During a Las Vegas trade show, he dined at both and was then approached by PR maven Jack Cassidy of Cassidy & Associates. It turned out the Carpenters' Union, which also knew Charlie from Las Vegas, were opening a new building just off Capitol Hill and wanted Charlie Palmer to open on the ground floor. "I thought I would introduce them to some people, but this is not for me," he said. Then they told him the location, 101 Constitution Avenue, so Fuller and his wife drove by and decided that the restaurant could not fail. They became interested in investing. After meeting Charlie and his people, they were in.

Charlie has used "American" branding with real style in Washington: Charlie Palmer Steak serves only American wines from all 50 states. His corkage policy allows "bring your own wine"—free as long as it is American made and $25 for foreign bottles. Another wine monolith inhabits the space, this time horizontally.

For Fuller, Charlie Palmer Steak has become "home away from home." The restaurant actually lies halfway between his Alexandria office and his McLean home, so it has been easy for him to swing by. People stop by all the time; business associates are even tenants in the building. Senator Fred Thompson—now movie star Fred Thompson of *Law & Order*—has come by. Long-time acquaintance Tracy Mullin, president of the National Retail Federation, quickly became a regular.

There will always be room for venerable Hill haunts. The Monocle, just behind the office buildings of the U.S. Senate, will remain a perennial hangout of senators and staffers; La Colline, at nearby 400 North Capitol, co-habits a building full of numerous news agencies. Partisanship spills over into restaurants: after a 1996 union dispute in which La Colline employees picketed the union, Democrats never really came back, giving La Colline a reputation as a Republican hangout and the Monocle became more of a Democrat hangout.

Charlie Palmer Steak is a bipartisan restaurant. Private breakfasts are perhaps even more important than lunches and dinners for such positioning. Senator Frist (R-TN) was one of the first breakfasters. With an eye on the street, he could stay to the last minute before an 8:45 meeting across the way in the Capitol. It is a perfect spot for members of Congress or fund-raisers. Early on, Charlie Palmer Steak held fund-raisers simultaneously for Republicans in one private room and Democrats in another.

Wolfgang Puck may have locked on to Hollywood early on, but Charlie Palmer has found and captured Hollywood East for himself, and *his* Capitol Hill stars make national news every night of the week.

3

TODD ENGLISH

Courtesy of Carl Tremblay

"He who reigns within himself and rules his passions, desires, and fears is more than a king"
—John Milton, *Paradise Regained* (1671)

ON a blustery morning in the early hours of a clear day in June 2003, a chauffeured sedan was shuttling Todd English to West Hampton, Long Island. Among his entourage rode a publicist and an assistant general manager from Olives New York. Equipment included a couch-sized cooler dangling dangerously at the back of the sedan's roof. The driver stopped occasionally to readjust it before they reached the MTV Beach House to shoot a barbecue *à la* Super Chef. As part of its red-hot Hamptons summer, *MTV Hits* was rolling in a new lineup of segments, special guests, and stunts for the latest in music, style, and events.

Todd, 40-odd years old, sat in front with an electronic device in either ear. He juggled both devices with ease as he stared ahead through the windshield to ward off car sickness. He scrolled through email, called his CFO about a deal, and planned a menu for a benefit. Mobile phones for the publicist, manager, and driver kept chirruping as well.

Upon arrival, he found an MTV crew waiting beyond a rough, weather-beaten staircase laced with heavy TV cable. The set was meager, just a pool with fifty-some teenagers standing around in bikinis, shorts, and the occasional T-shirt, shivering in the unseasonably cool June air. A gray Atlantic Ocean lolled behind as backdrop.

No one was dancing. There was no hip-hopping and certainly no one doing the grind. Every now and then, the kids would explode with cheers and clapping for videos they could not see, cued by the video jockey. No one looked like they were having much fun. They paid no attention to Todd, and he tried not to think about them. "Man, I feel *old!*" he muttered each time he scanned the crowd.

Todd unpacked his gear. MTV had provided a makeshift table around a grill that a teen might use for a weekend party—as adequate for one of America's premier chefs as handing him a butter knife to carve a turkey. No one helped him unpack garnishes, salsa, orange segments, salt, pepper, or roasted vegetables. Todd's assistant general manager vanished with the driver to get corn and fresh clams. His publicist hid from the wind inside the beach house.

Todd pulled out two huge fish, a red snapper and a black bass. Then he piled marinated flank steak onto a plate for the shoot. He fought with the wind to keep foil from blowing away. He left burgers and hot dogs grilled and stuffed into buns for the crew and headed off for makeup. He returned shortly, bedecked in a jungle-print shirt and beach shorts and

TODD ENGLISH AND ASSISTANT AT THE MTV BEACH HOUSE

Courtesy of the Author

looking suddenly very bronzed. The producers plucked an even more bronzed teenage girl in a purple string bikini and silver navel ring from the crowd to assist Todd. Hilarie Burton, *MTV Hits* VJ, finally materialized and introduced herself to Todd. The producer and crew discussed his shoot.

By the time Todd finally started preparing his fish on camera, the one-hour shoot had been cut down to 15 minutes, spent mostly on retakes. Todd had to scuttle the steak, the roasted vegetables, the cucumber sauce, the salsa, the orange segments, the chili rub, the fresh corn, and the red snapper. It was showtime—and time for a Super Chef to improvise under the relentless, high-speed patter of an MTV VJ:

Burton: Al-*right!* That was Christina Aguilera with Fighter, and we are hanging out here with Chef *Todd English!* He is doing some *serious* barbecue for us! This isn't Uncle Paulie's barbecue—no hot dogs and hamburgers! This is the *real deal!*

English: This is actually—What I love doing is—We're doing this hobo pack. It's a very simple thing, very simple to do. We got this whole *bass* in here with, like, everything in here. We're going to throw some ingredients on, some tomatoes and clams, put it altogether, and—on the grill!

Burton: You're going to set it right *on* [the grill]?

English: You're going to see how easy this is. It's very fun.

The camera caught him deftly surrounding bass with chopped tomatoes, leeks, olive oil, spices, and boiled red potatoes, then enveloping the fish *en papillote,* except that Todd used foil instead of parchment paper. Once the fish was on the grill, the cameras shut off.

Twenty minutes later, Todd opened the packet. At first, pungent steam wafted toward the cold, hungry teenagers. By the fourth or fifth take, however, there was no more steam left to waft, though the cameras continued to roll.

Burton: Hey! What's up? Welcome back to *MTV Hits.* I'm Hilarie Burton, and our final request that comes to us from our website is for Bonecrusher. Before we get into that, I've been smelling this food *all* show long. Todd English has something *amazing* for us on the grill here. Show me what we got!

English: Look at this. Remember we had this thing wrapped in foil? Let's open this thing up. There you go!

Burton: It's *beautiful!*

English: Ha-ha! Look at that! The clams popped open. All the vegetables cooked around. Really simple.

Burton: Oh my God, I can't *wait* to dig into this! Now, I hear that you're working with a lot of rock stars these days, right?

English: Absolutely. You know, it's amazing: most of my good customers are rock stars. They love to eat. They love to dine. And most importantly, they love to cook! So I go and cook with these guys.

Burton: That's *awe*-some! Like the guys from Aerosmith and Bono—?

English: —Bono, and drinking Cabo Wabo [tequila] with my friend Sammy Hagar—

Burton: Whoah-whoah-*whoah!* Well, if it's good enough for them, it's good enough for us here at *MTV Hits!* Thank you *so* much for coming by and treating all of us. (You guys, *come* dig in! We're having a *hell* of a meal right here!) You *guys,* don't forget to go to our MTV.com website and check out what we've been up to all summer. Have a great day! It's Bonecrusher with Never Scared. See you later!

"Most of my customers are rock stars" was *not* the line Todd had been practicing just moments before. Besides, rock stars had been more a preserve of Todd's recent *Iron Chef USA* rival Kerry Simon, whose close friends include, for instance, band members of INXS. Then again, who knew about Todd's hanging out with Sammy Hagar or Bono? He explained a few moments later off-camera, "I am planning a special on VH1 where I would cook with rock stars. *Cool!*"

Chow time for the kids had arrived at last. The fish stuck to the foil paper as Todd plated it. He spooned chunks of the bass into mouths of female extras. "I could get *arrested* for this!" Todd muttered in disbelief. Despite his concern, he continued to beam for the cameras.

He carefully cooked some of the flank steak and layered it over the salsa and cucumber sauce. On top of that, true to style, he layered corn relish. Everyone dug fingers into the dish, as much to stave off cold as hunger. The meat tasted juicy and garlicky on its own and fit well with the cucumber sauce; the other sauces seemed unnecessary. Once the shoot was over, Todd packed the coffin-like cooler with heaps of unwanted food and headed back for Manhattan with his entourage. Despite VJ Hilarie Burton's promise that "There will be good eating later on," most of the teenagers never got to sample Todd's food; however, they were placated easily with a massive delivery of pizzas.

Todd tried to convince himself that being the first major chef on MTV had been worth his time. The ride had taken five hours round-trip, plus an hour and a half on-site for 15 minutes of shooting, the result of which was less than 2 minutes of airtime, including nonspeaking shots. There was also the cost of engaging his public relations firm, the chaffeured sedan, food, and extra supplies. MTV teenagers would probably *not* be coming to his Olives restaurants soon, though some might make a pizza stop at one of his Figs outlets or dig into fish at his KingFish Hall restaurant in Boston.

His latest phase of expansion needed TV presence, he felt. Few people knew of him in, say, Seattle, where he had just opened the Fish Club at a Marriott hotel. Still, if *MTV Hits* landed him a spot on VH1, with its older crowd, then it was worth it.

Back at Olives on Union Square, the cooler went to executive chef Victor La Placa, who was thankful for the off-site catering aid. Next on schedule that evening was a fund-raising dinner for AIDS organization amfAR, attended by actors Chloë Sevigny, Liev Schreiber, and Rosie Perez and New York Giants players Dhani Jones, Jesse Palmer, and Armani Toomer. Also attending would be *MTV Hits* hostess Hilarie Burton and fellow chef Rocco DiSpirito, whose show *Restaurant* was just about to premier on NBC Sunday nights. For Todd, the grind would go on that night and into the days and nights ahead.

WILLIAM Todd English was born in Amarillo, Texas, in 1960 to a father from Oklahoma and a mother from New York City. Todd's sister Wendy was born two years later. When Todd was only three, they moved first to Nebraska, where his mother started catering for friends, then to Atlanta, where Todd spent most of grammar school, and then to Branford, east of New Haven, Connecticut, where Todd attended high school. His mother left his father when Todd was a child in Nebraska, and his father never played a role in his life.

His mother remarried an older man, who had little influence on Todd. His mother dubbed this now deceased husband the "evil stepfather," while Wendy remembered him as a recluse like "Howard Hughes, very eccentric and intelligent," who became increasingly removed from the family over the years. He drank. From him, Todd and Wendy have three stepsiblings, but they are not close.

As a child, Todd was passionate about food. Like most Italians, his first-generation, Italian-American mother followed the culinary traditions of Oppido Marmertina in the toe of the boot of Calabria, Italy, home of her mother's family, the Vergaras. Their food was hearty peasant fare, strongly flavored. He was exposed to his mother's family a lot, particularly after his maternal grandmother came to live with them.

Todd's great-grandmother Giulietta used to make her own fresh pasta and dry it on her bedsheets. "My grandmother was a typical Italian, always wearing an apron and stirring something with sauce and fish," said Wendy of Bettina Vergara Arcuni. Todd also experienced fine dining in New York restaurants in the seventies like the '21' Club, thanks to his great-uncle Armando, who had invested in a restaurant in New York and was "a father figure to all of us," according to Wendy.

Todd worked with his mother in her catering business and helped prepare family meals. "My mother is your basic home cook, with Martha Stewart flair and beautiful presentation. She was always doing outrageous birthday cakes and wedding cakes," Wendy said. "Todd, on the other hand, was more into the food and the cooking."

In tenth grade his mother got him a job as a dishwasher at a neighborhood Mexican restaurant called Su Casa. He was promoted to line cook, and she joined him on the line, while Wendy bused tables and helped out in the kitchen. "I was making chips in this tiny little kitchen, the three of us in there. I was in eighth grade; Todd was in tenth. It was great," said Wendy.

Beyond cooking, Todd's passion was sports. He won a baseball scholarship to Guilford College in Greensboro, North Carolina. According to Todd, he decided to take six months' leave to figure out what he wanted to do. Joining friends in Atlanta, he got a job working in a French restaurant in one of the city's small independent hotels. The chef, Donald Browning, recognized his talent in the kitchen and urged him to apply to the Culinary Institute of America.

Todd had to measure his love for cooking against baseball. "I was pretty lost. I was trying to figure out what to do, debating whether to go back to school. The coaches from Georgia Southern and Georgia Tech were calling. I had some baseball options, but I wanted to try cooking." His mother added her encouragement and paid his tuition for cooking school.

Todd started the 21-month program at the CIA in 1978. Following Charlie Palmer, he did an externship at La Côte Basque under chef Jean-Jacques Rachou and graduated in the top quarter of his class in 1982. According to Todd, the CIA was just discovering "American food" when he was a student. His mentor was Charles Nichols. "I got really gung-ho about American cooking." There was no American Bounty restaurant at the CIA yet (it opened in 1982), but teachers and students were starting to explore.

> I was pretty stoked by it. I thought it was interesting being American and trying to understand the roots of where all this stuff came from. . . At La Côte Basque, I was working *poissonier* [fish station], and the chef would do red kiwi on sole—*groovy!*

At the CIA, Todd met his future wife, Olivia Disch, a fellow student from New Jersey who graduated a year later, in 1983, also in the top quarter of her class. Todd's mother described Olivia as flamboyant, energetic, and very competitive; Wendy described her as eccentric, the life of the party, and unusually pretty. Olivia had studied to be a pastry chef, but she and Todd got into conflict in the kitchen, so she went to the front of the house to avoid being "underneath" him.

Todd spent the summer of 1982, after his graduation from the CIA, as a private chef at the home of a CBS TV executive on Martha's Vineyard, then returned to work again briefly at La Côte Basque. During his second tour at La Côte Basque, he worked with such line chefs as Rick Moonen, Waldy Malouf, Henry Meer, and David Bouley.

Charlie Palmer had just left La Côte Basque for Waccabuc Country Club, inside the New York state line, a few miles from Danbury, Connecticut. By the end of 1983, Todd had taken that job when Charlie moved on to the River Café. Like Charlie, Todd wanted to do his own thing, and Waccabuc allowed for just that. Olivia was cochef with Todd, in charge of pastry, and took over the restaurant after he left before the second season was out.

THROUGH friends of Olivia's family, Todd met restaurateur Michela Larson in Boston. Michela's family came from the northern Italian towns of Bordighera (Viareggio), Florence, and Bologna. She ran a small restaurant called Salon Rouge in Boston and had been putting together funding over several years for a new one in the eastern, industrial part of Cambridge.

Michela interviewed Todd and liked his brashness. Unsure about his cooking, however, she invited him over to cook a five-course dinner for her and 13 friends, many of whom were food writers or foodies. She gave him no directions other than to keep continuity between courses and to let each speak to something "Italian":

> At the end of the evening, people said, "Thank God you did this: now you know not to hire him!" I said, "What are you talking about?" "Well, there were so many things on the plate. Nothing spoke to the elements. It was just too over-the-top." I said, "Oh no, he is *exactly* the person I need. Every piece of fish was cooked perfectly, every piece of chicken, every vegetable. The only thing he needs is some editing. He does know how to cook, and he is going to come into his own."

In many ways, Michela consummated Todd's culinary education, at least in Italian food. Before the restaurant opened, she packed him off for a few months to northern Italy to learn Tuscan cuisine. "That is where he learned how to make squash tortelloni, glorious delicate food." Todd's marketing literature over the years has often cited these *stages* at Restaurant Dal Pescatore in Canneto Sull'Og'lio and Paraccuchi in Locanda dell' Angelo. Upon his return, they opened Michela's (1985–1994)—only neither of them had ever opened a restaurant before. Todd said:

> Two days before, I said, "Michela, where is the menu? What exactly are we doing?" I had seen an outline and had a general idea. She said, "I don't know." "You don't have the menu?" I said. "I thought *you* were the chef," she said. She was freaking out, freaking out about opening. So, being the driver that I am, I went home, banged out a menu, and ordered the food, and we opened. At that point we had a take-out shop. I worked there from 7:30 a.m. until 1:00 in the morning for the first nine months, until the restaurant really started to take off, and I got married.

Michela described Todd's menu story as "slightly apocryphal," particularly in that they had both been discussing the menu's elements for some time. "I can imagine that Todd would have thought that I would have written the menu—he had only worked before in establishments where there was a powerful male (frequently French) chef at the helm. I had assumed I had hired a chef who would write the menu."

Michela believes Todd's signature developed at her restaurant, though she grants that his food has become richer since. "He is a very original thinker—and I believe his food can be deeply interesting—but it's very *big.*" She felt he was not a great manager at the time but had potential to become a great leader. Certainly, he was not shy about coming out of the kitchen.

Wolfgang Puck's Spago and some other restaurants were already hot in Los Angeles, San Francisco, and New York, so writers wanted to find the next hot restaurants in the next hot cities. "He was very young, very raw, very unformed," Michela said, and she helped refine the "wild" and "cocksure" Todd and round him out. Her restaurant was a great platform for Todd's launch: "I made sure that happened," she said.

Barbara Lynch, chef and owner of Boston's No. 9 Park, first worked with Todd during his last few months at Michela's. In the 2002 documentary short film *Amuse Bouche: A Chef's Tale,* she said:

> Todd was a tough guy. I was petrified to work for him. He was *so hard.* I just thought he was this high-energy, highly brilliant guy running around the kitchen. . . . He was so militant, that old school, hard-ass chef. "Get organized!" "Don't you know what salt and pepper is?" You know—"Get your shit together!" "Get this food out!"—really screaming, really loud, really ugh—what *not* to do in a kitchen.

In September 1988, Todd left Michela's to open his own restaurant. Todd had been dreaming about his own restaurant since his school days at the CIA. "I remember finding an old rendering I had drawn in school of a kitchen I wanted to do. It is very close to the Olives kitchen." Olivia and Todd raised a paltry $125,000, partially from a bank loan. The only place they could afford was a rough suburb, Charlestown, where they rented a modest storefront. Todd catered parties out of their small worker's cottage, which had a four-burner stove. Luckily the winter was cold so he could use his Volvo as a refrigerator.

They opened the original Olives in April 1989. The restaurant was small, with only 50 seats. One chef dubbed it "very Todd": a wood-burning grill, a rotisserie, an oven, all crammed into a little place, with a tiny, cramped walk-in with baskets of dough everywhere. "Olives arrived like a comet" and was packed shortly after it opened, according to the *Boston Globe.*

Jord Poster, cofounder of Priceline.com and later one of Todd's advisors, visited the restaurant in its first week when it was virtually empty. He ate the butternut squash tortelloni, later an Olives classic. "I was terrified the place was going to close. I started telling everyone I knew, and within the year I couldn't get a table. I had to endear myself to Olivia to get in!"

Olivia ran the front of the house. She explained to *Restaurant & Institutions* in 1997 that from the beginning of their relationship she saw Todd as the main food talent. "So when we married and opened Olives, I knew he would be the food guy. And it was a relief, too, because it gave me a chance to explore the wine, the service, and the overall business of running the restaurant."

By December 1991, Todd had announced plans to move Olives down the street to a larger space that would include a full bar. Up by 75 to 125 seats, Olives took off all over again. "The scene was different for Boston," *Boston Globe* journalist Alison Arnett said, affected more by atmosphere than food. "The actual food had changed here starting with Jasper White and Lydia Shire in the mid-80s. But Olives was newer, younger, hipper, more fun and it had more edge to it. Olivia was at the door, looking gorgeous every night. There were long lines down the street: it was a scene. Boston had a decorous scene at openings: this was more New York style."

By July 1992, *The Boston Globe* had entitled an article "Prepare to Wait at Olives' New Locale." It described a "typical pilgrimage to the culinary mecca called Olives" as one of sheer panic over the lines thanks to "beseeching throngs who would walk on water for a table or wait hours in the cold or the heat to be frozen out at the door." Todd's mother claimed that he had not thought about being the best or a star: it just started happening. "They were shocked to find people standing outside in the rain to get in."

One chef said:

> We would open the doors at 5:30 [p.m.], and 150 people would walk in at the same time. It was the most difficult job I have ever had. . . . People were waiting for their food. There would still be 150 people waiting in line, drinking at the bar. It was exciting but crazy. There was an open kitchen

> and a feeling that you were sort of like the warrior—exhilarating, if you are a cook in a restaurant—and if you don't thrive on that, forget it. One hundred and fifty people—and we aren't making hamburgers, but stuff in ring molds—things falling over—after the fact it was hilarious.

The food was more "conservative" than in later years, recalled Marc Orfaly, chef and owner of Boston's Pigalle, who worked on the line at the original Olives. "We used to have dishes like fried porgie and polenta, bistro chicken, his famous Parmesan pudding with pea sauce. . . . he came up with the olive tart." Overall, it was simpler fare. Todd's mother agreed. "In the beginning it was very honest, straightforward food, no gimmicks or fancy stuff."

Barbara Lynch, who worked for Todd at both Michela's and Olives, felt that there was no dramatic change in his signature between these restaurants. "He did phenomenal things at Michela's. He did a lot of growing up there and found out what he wanted there . . . rustic Mediterranean cuisine, with a lot of wood fire." Another chef of his disagreed about the merits of his multilayered creations: "If you are more sophisticated, you can't eat Todd's food: I can't eat a whole appetizer."

The *Boston Globe* ascribed his success this way:

> Is chef Todd English's food really that good? . . . —yes . . . The ingredients are good in the less complex dishes, but the intricacy of the complicated ones is where Olives shines. . . . English says he believes in "expansive" cooking and in taking chances. "I spill my heart out; I try to give people a lot, to be very generous. I try not to be restrained in any way." People come to Olives, he thinks, because his cooking is "out there sometimes." The excitement he has in trying new combinations and tastes is certainly discernible in all of the dishes. The expansiveness is also a reason for popularity: the dishes are presented on large plates and platters, filled to the edges, and almost every dish has several distinct elements. Even appetizers have this layered effect.

A former chef of Todd's said, "There was something about his food, the 'over-the-top' thing—you felt like you were really indulging. The dishes had all the flavor people wanted."

Just as Olives was reaching a critical mass, Steve Mannino arrived in January 1996. Like several other chefs working for Todd, not only was

Steve an Italian-American, but he had graduated from the CIA. He had worked for Charlie Palmer's successor at the River Café, David Burke, who by then had also moved on to become chef-owner of Park Avenue Café in New York. Within a few months, Burke had shipped Mannino out to Chicago to open a new restaurant of his. Chicago had proven to be a bit farther from his hometown of Amsterdam, New York, than he realized, so Steve decided to leave Burke for Boston. "If you want to go to Boston, go work for Todd English," Burke had told him.

The day Mannino darkened Olives' door, Todd got a photo shoot from *Boston* magazine, so Todd referred to him ever after as "my good luck charm." The work was hard, so hard that Mannino told his wife that he was not sure he could handle it. Soon, however, Mannino had become part of a tight crew that worked five days a week, Tuesday through Saturday, dinner only.

"It didn't matter how long you worked in those five days, because you had two days off," Mannino said. "It is very rare. Everybody hung out together—probably the best food and the best time . . . that I have ever done in my life—just because everyone was there, very close, doing our thing."

Barbara Lynch said, "Best group of guys, the most energy—I had a lot of fun. I still enjoy hanging out with Todd."

Other chefs were not so nostalgic. One chef from the early days of Olives hated the job at first but gained rapport with Todd from working side by side with him. Another said, "We pretty much ran the show. Todd would have dishes he wanted us to do, but in terms of the day-to-day he would be at meetings and photo shoots. He was mostly there at night. He would get on the line and cook, but he wouldn't train."

Since apprenticeship is critical to becoming a chef, no training is a major complaint coming from a rising line cook. Others cooks, however, did not mind learning by imitation rather than instruction. Barbara Lynch said, "I like his energy and drive. I don't think of him as a teacher: he doesn't have the patience to teach one-on-one. You have to come in with your eyes wide open and become an observer of Todd English's and get as much as you can out of it."

By 1996 the main team was Joe Brenner, Steve Mannino, Clay Conley, Victor LaPlaca, Rick Gencarelli, Tony Susi, and David Bazirgan. Over the years, a few have left. Tony Susi opened his own restaurant, Sage. David Bazirgan went to work for Barbara Lynch at No. 9 Park. Clay Conley, who later became executive chef at Olives Las Vegas, left and then came back to man the first few months at Olives Tokyo.

Some very talented women have worked in Todd's kitchen, too, perhaps most notably Suzanne Goin and Barbara Lynch. Of her two years at the first Olives in Charlestown, Barbara said, "Olives was the best education I ever had." After working with Todd, Lynch traveled in Europe and came back to work in a tiny trattoria, Galleria Italiana, for which she was cited by *Food & Wine* magazine as one of the "Ten Best New Chefs in America." In 1999, she opened her own restaurant, No. 9 Park, for which she won the James Beard Best Chef Northeast award in 2003.

Suzanne Goin moved to Boston for love and chose to work with Todd instead of other great names like Jasper White or Jody Adams. "What drew me [to Todd] is the energy. I am hard-core, and I wanted to be somewhere that was hard-core: staying up till 4 a.m. for menu meetings, running five specials when you shouldn't be. It's fun to be in that kind of place. It gets my adrenaline going." Goin admitted the kitchen was very "male dominated," but she was not intimated. Other women were intimidated, she recalled. In fact, when she was applying, another woman chef pulled her aside and told her to keep away because "they're all assholes." Goin, who had learned long ago never to let teasing get to her, "got along with them great."

Nevertheless, Goin—a veteran of numerous reputable restaurants including three in France as well as Alice Waterr's Chez Panisse and Joachim Splichal's Pinot Bistro—said, "It was the most macho kitchen [I've ever worked in], even compared with France, where it's not so much macho as hard." Overall, Goin found Olives "a really good exercise" because it made her think about food differently. "I would suggest, as a special, spring chicken *pot au feu*, then he would put in *raviole* and something else—and then something else again."

Goin then moved to Los Angeles. Eventually, she became executive chef for Wolfgang Puck's protégé Mark Peel at Campanile. Then she opened two highly acclaimed restaurants of her own, Lucques (1998) and A.O.C. or Appellation d'Origine Controlée (2003).

Though their cooking styles were quite different, Goin appreciated Todd's support, describing him not as a father but brother figure. Not only did he encourage her to seek her own way, but he also directed his own customers to her first restaurant, Lucques. "For all the cutthroat reputation of this business, he was really nice."

In April 1993, Todd went public with a new restaurant on Martha's Vineyard. Previously, it had been named Decoys, owned in part by actors Glenn Close and Michael J. Fox and Bruins hockey legend Cam Neely. Todd and Olivia assumed management of the profit-bleeding establishment. They planned to name the new restaurant Uva ("grape" in Italian) and place Paul Borras from Olives as chef. Uva would open during the summer season.

As it turned out, another couple had a restaurant already called Uva on the island, registered in the town of Edgartown as a trade name. Todd and Olivia registered the name with the Commonwealth of Massachusetts and changed the name to Ristorante d'Uva. The other couple, Chris and Diane Campbell, feared they would become "the other Uva." At the time, Todd defended the Englishes' action by stating that the name fit their corporate vision, saying, "We wanted to do the three symbols of the Holy Roman Empire—the fig, the grape leaf and the olive branch. I didn't want to use the name 'Grapes.'" *The Boston Globe* quoted a Harvard scholar, who remarked that he had not "heard of that constellation as Holy Roman" but that "it fits a Mediterranean mentality."

When the renamed Isola ("island" in Italian) opened on Memorial Day weekend a few weeks later, *The Boston Globe* noted more kindly, "It's the kind of place where actress Patricia Neal is quietly having dinner at the next table, and lawyer Alan Dershowitz is walking out with take-out containers." It was also a place that a president might visit—as Bill Clinton did.

The reviewer found it "softer" than Olives but complained, "the same inventiveness in the cuisine that can sometimes veer into too-muchness prevailed—the plates were big and bold and over the top. Even something as minimalist sounding as watercress, endive and green bean salad had a construction befitting Notre Dame with beans piled high and lots of Roquefort cheese—delicious but in no way light," though there were many delicious dishes.

It was clear that the restaurant lost money—"pots of money"—with lots of debt dumped on Neely and partners. The disaster was bad enough that the *Boston Herald* speculated that its demise a year later caused Neely to fire his manager and restaurant partner Mark Perrone, though Perrone denied the restaurant was an issue. "Cam and I fought tooth and nail to rescue the damn thing," Perrone said.

Whatever the cause for Isola's demise before the next summer, which left all parties in debt, Cam Neely would only intimate to the *New York Observer* a few years later, "Todd likes to look after the big three: me, myself, and I.

Back in Boston, Todd had a few months of rent left on the old Olives site. With birth of their first son, Olivia and Todd were thinking about a place they could take their own family for dinner. He was also itching to do something new, outside the menu of Olives.

The original concept was a pasta shop called Bettina, after Todd's maternal grandmother, that would feature such family favorites as macaroni, fired *crostini,* and fish cakes. During renovation, the name changed to Figs and pizza became an important component. Figs opened in 1992.

"Todd decided to try a pizza and pasta restaurant," said Barbara Lynch. "He envisioned Neapolitan pizza, thin and crispy. He was not copying anyone else, not Wolfgang Puck. There were far fewer ingredients and less than ten pastas and ten pizzas. We had takeout. Todd doubled volume without even adding new customers."

"Pizza is an art," she said. "He spent time designing the dough, how long to let it rest, what temperature the oven would be. . . . He was just doing the pizza he loved. He knew Naples. He knows good pasta. That is what he wanted." Barbara was on the line at Olives; when he offered her the chance as chef at Figs just down the street, she leaped at it.

Figs expanded after a few years from Charlestown to Beacon Hill, Wellesley, and Chestnut Hill in Boston. Todd financed the expansion by adding partners drawn from Boston's venture capital firms. A fifth Figs was announced as in the works in October 1997, but Todd's partners opposed further expansion, despite favorable reviews. Todd, a minority partner in his own restaurant concept, had to listen.

Brad Stevens was Todd's corporate executive chef for Figs from 1994 to 2003. He had worked at Michela's during Todd's time and then joined Olives in 1994 to head up the expanding Figs. His biggest challenge was keeping Figs' cooks from turning the small restaurants into Olives copies. "The hardest thing is to keep the chefs down, to keep it simple," since often he would hire cooks from Olives who were used to the more elaborate dishes there. Each Figs varied its menu. The Beacon Hill Figs didn't typically sell very much pizza, and other Figs had virtually no fish on their menus.

MANNINO said that from the day he entered Olives Charlestown, "the deals haven't stopped." Todd wanted to concentrate on media rather than business negotiations and deals. In 1998, he turned to Jim Cafarelli for help.

Cafarelli was a contractor in Boston. His company, Cafco Development, had built the House of Blues in Boston with House of Blues founder Isaac Tigrett. Cafarelli eventually joined the House of Blues as exclusive developer of their clubs and moved to California to develop six of them. According to people who know him, Cafarelli did not like California and after a falling out with Tigrett returned to Boston. Under Cafco, Cafarelli had also built the original Olives in Charlestown for Todd. Together, English and Cafarelli formed Olives Group Corporation, 25 percent owned by Cafarelli, 75 percent owned by Todd.

In 1998, Todd turned away from expansion in Figs toward Olives. In that year he opened a second Olives in the Bellagio Hotel in Las Vegas, a concept called Onda ("wave") at the Mirage Hotel, both under management contract, and Miramar in Westport, Connecticut.

By the time they approached Todd, the Bellagio Hotel & Casino in Las Vegas had already built out most of its restaurants: Jean-Georges Vongerichten's Prime Steakhouse, Sirio Maccioni's Le Cirque 2000, Michael Mina's Aqua, Julian Serrano's Picasso, and others. All were offered a lucrative management contract and were tied to the hotel's centralized purchasing, art department, and maintenance. The idea of introducing so many world-class celebrity chefs to run restaurants was the brainchild of three executives then with the Mirage Resorts: chief Steve Wynn, Kevin Stuessi in food service planning, and Gamal Aziz in food and beverage.

Elizabeth Blau, at the time the Mirage's vice president of restaurant development, led the restaurant hunt. The slot allotted as Olives' home was sandwiched between Hermès, Prada, and Armani boutiques. "It had a title on the plans, 'retail café,' and because of the neighbors, it needed to be a hip, fun, funky restaurant, with approachable, understandable food. We made a list of restaurateurs and chefs around the country who fit the bill," Blau said. "No matter how we looked at it, Todd English kept coming up. He was widely regarded in Boston but not internationally famous, so it was exciting to have a young, up-and-coming chef."

Todd's only contractual obligation for Olives Las Vegas was to hire a management team: the Bellagio took care of the rest. The opening was typical for Todd. "The day we opened the restaurant he changed the entire menu. We had everything in place, what we were going to do, and he changed the entire dinner menu the day before we opened," said Victor LaPlaca, his first executive chef there. LaPlaca remembered the same behavior at Olives Charlestown years before. Todd would arrive at 5 p.m., order new dishes, and expect the restaurant to be open at 5:30.

Vegas is a cash cow for Todd: the licensing fee makes him $1 million a year. According to LaPlaca, "It's busy all the time. With 170 seats, I remember doing 500 for lunch! Just factory business, just crazy out there—we made bonus *there*! There was a line out the door every night."

Shortly after the hugely successful Olives Las Vegas, Todd opened Miramar in Westport, Connecticut, in December 1998. The restaurant went into National Hall, a restored brick edifice built in 1873 on the Long Island Sound that also housed a luxury hotel. Miramar's was essentially a copy of the Olives menu. Todd made Olives veteran Rick Gencarelli chef, assisted by Todd Winer as *chef du cuisine*. When Gencarelli left in 2000 to open Olives New York, Winer became chef. The Westport location drew on local celebrities, headed by Martha Stewart and including Paul Newman, Michael Bolton, and Christopher Walken.

His next restaurant, Greg Norman's Australian Grille, opened in October 1999 and derived from a simple equation. Todd English would do anything to golf. Jim Cafarelli had contacts at the House of Blues in Myrtle Beach, South Carolina. Greg Norman owns the Barefoot Landing golf course in Myrtle Beach. The sum was Todd's barbecue restaurant at Barefoot Landing. It was essentially a high-end Outback Steakhouse with a beach setting. Todd went down a few times to prepare the menu and to open it. Otherwise, Cafarelli staffed it locally. Although Todd had discussed expanding to other golf courses with Greg Norman, as the economy cooled in 2001 the initial restaurant had trouble filling seats.

In November 1999, Todd opened Olives Washington, his largest restaurant to date, with 220 seats and another 30–40 planned. Todd brought Mannino, who most lately had been *chef de cuisine* under Victor LaPlaca in Las Vegas, to run the new restaurant.

According to Mannino, the deal, negotiated by Cafarelli, included high rent. Mannino worked hard to keep food and labor costs down, but the high rent meant that even if the restaurant made over $4 million dollars a year, it was difficult to show much profit. The space itself proved to be very large and awkward. Although the open kitchen was only 15 feet from the front door, allowing Mannino to greet guests and have a strong presence in the dining room, the main bar was tiny, and the downstairs area with a much larger bar proved difficult to use or fill. Nevertheless, the restaurant was extremely popular; lines were out the door when it opened.

Todd himself cooked at the opening but, according to Mannino, rarely returned. Michael Jordan's Washington Wizards held three all-restaurant parties there: Todd did not attend. President Clinton ate there: Todd was not around. Despite his claim to hang out with rock stars, Todd chose not to come to a Pearl Jam party. This was a far cry from the rising chef who had been very excited when President Clinton visited him less than a decade earlier on Martha's Vineyard.

Todd's absence was accompanied by difficulties with management. Olives Washington tore through four general managers in three years. Tony Cochones is the first general manager with previous experience in that position, and Mannino is grateful to have support in the front of the house at last.

Mannino said he sometimes had a difficult time getting Boston headquarters to pay the restaurant's bills in a timely manner. The restaurant's late payments were a particular problem in 2002:

> There were times when we were stuck down here not paying our bills. I had guys calling my house because I have relationships with my vendors. One of my vendors was at my wedding, and this guy calls my house and says, "Steve, pay my bills!" It's *my* name in town!

By 2003, Olives Group was back to paying bills on time, though it was still difficult for Olives Washington to increase the number of purveyors willing to extend credit. Steve Mannino was offered a raise and future partnership to keep him in the group.

Top-of-the-line chain hotels are a force to reckon with in restaurant development in most American cities. By the 1990s, some hotel restaurants competed directly with big-name restaurants, such as Hilton's Spencers for steak against such names as Morton's. Then, Super Chefs ventured into this territory hand-in-hand with hotels in Las Vegas, with Emeril

Lagasse's Delmonico Steakhouse, Jean-Georges Vongerichten's Prime, and Charlie Palmer's Charlie Palmer Steak.

Seeing himself as a restaurant conceptualizer, Todd has partnered time and time again with hotels, leveraging his celebrity for reduced rent or a licensing or management fee. Todd's input is name, concept, and management to supply the demand of a hotel, which has name, location, and a large number of guests to satisfy with more than just rooms.

Other top chefs were getting into the act as well. Larry Forgione opened in the Hilton in Manhattan. Michael Mina opened in the St. Regis in Dana Point, California. Alain Ducasse opened in the Essex House in Manhattan. Todd opened Olives Aspen, his first restaurant with Starwood, in its St. Regis property in Aspen, Colorado, in December 1999. As *Restaurants & Institutions* magazine commented, "It is not surprising that hotels are turning to brand-name chefs or hot concepts to headline their restaurants; they have the power to reel in customers." But the point of opening an Olives in Aspen was to win further rewards, in the form of another deal with Starwood in Manhattan in the future. Todd wanted the biggest bang for the buck, and his venture in Aspen would get him a prize in New York.

The Aspen restaurant is tiny by Olives standards, with only 90 seats and an average of only 70 covers a night. His food did not rate highly there, although business was good in season—Bill St. John of the *Denver Post* said of Olives Aspen that every dish is "designed for excess." He found the simpler dishes the best but, "more often, as if in an attempt to justify the stratospheric prices, Olives schmeers on the goodies, busying plates with three or four accompaniments and two or three sauces, all Pollock-swirled around the plate."

Todd rested for a bit before the next round of restaurants. The Rouse Company developed Faneuil Hall in Boston and turned to Todd to fill an anchor restaurant space. KingFish Hall, which opened July 1, 2000, was Todd's take on a seafood restaurant. Todd and Cafarelli hired the New York architectural firm of David Rockwell to design it. The restaurant was large for the group: 225 seats in two levels with a special raw bar, ceviche, and seafood tapas, all part of a menu to attract tourists. Todd chose David Kinkead as *chef du cuisine,* who had worked at David Burke's Park Avenue Café and Lydia Shire's Biba. Unlike other deals, KingFish Hall was an old-fashioned, straight lease, so Todd and Cafarelli had to come up with some of the money to build out the restaurant, about $2.5 million. Outside of Olives Charlestown, this was the only restaurant Todd owned outright, and overall it has been his highest grossing, most profitable restaurant. In 2001, it earned him $7.5 million.

Todd was still popular in Boston's press and won popular support in a signage controversy. The Boston Redevelopment Authority, owners of Faneuil Hall, forced him to remove his restaurant's sign as noncompliant in the historic locale, though the *Boston Herald* felt that "the slightly retro design fit in ideally with its historic surroundings." The sign issue and cost overruns for the buildout, due in part to the extreme age of Faneuil Hall, meant that Kingfish came in near 10 percent over budget.

Meanwhile, it was time at last to continue expanding Figs. Todd opened a Figs in 2000 at LaGuardia Airport with some success. The next year, however, a trial Figs Express failed. His partner introduced bar food like chicken wings, so the LaGuardia Figs went "off-concept."

John Mariani reviewed Figs for *Esquire:*

> This place, on the ground floor of the airport, flanked by a hot dog stand and the usual Chinese take-out, is a splashy affair with moss green walls, an elongated oval shape, and a staff that exudes the kind of rote, who-gives-a-damn attitude that gives New York a bad name. The wine list is dreadful, and the food I tasted was just as poor. The thin-crusted "pizza bianco" had all the flavor of sawdust, and the toppings (anemic tomatoes, a trifling of onions, and a whole lotta salt) were not what I'd call generous. A plate of orzo pasta (overcooked) with four cheeses was like eating pabulum, only soupier and hotter. Here, too, prices are high for a very insubstantial meal.

In November 2000, Todd made his boldest move yet with the opening of Olives New York in the W Hotel on Union Square. The deal, negotiated with the building's owners, included cooking for not just the restaurant but also the room service needs of the hotel guests and catering events—because there was only one kitchen to serve the whole hotel. Sources close to the deal contend that Cafarelli and others warned Todd not to take the deal offered him, which initially provided for a $10,000 a month apartment in New York. When the deal was finally signed, the apartment had been withdrawn.

The W Hotel sits on the northeast corner of Union Square and was meant to attract hip, young crowds already flocking to neighborhood restaurants like Tom Colicchio's Gramercy Tavern and Craft, Rocco DiSpirito's Union Pacific, B. R. Guest's Blue Water Grill, and Bobby Flay's Mesa Grill.

The W Hotel, owned by Starwood, had already selected David Rockwell as its designer, and Rockwell put Paul Vega in as project manager. The budget for the restaurant alone was about $5.5 million, to meet the challenge of the original structure. The W Hotel had been the Guardian Life Building, but very little was left of the original decoration. Construction of hotel and restaurant was handled by two different companies, each vying for work space. The restaurant kitchen required new plumbing, electricity, air conditioning, and venting, which meant constant costly adjustment of plans as new problems cropped up.

The key elements of the restaurant were a two-story, wood-burning oven and a bar, both of which tied the restaurant to the hotel lobby. Vega focused on the design of Olives Charlestown, which was done on a shoestring budget, like an antique store with lots of things not quite fitting together. Todd wanted something less haphazard. "He wanted a two-story fireplace that was supposed to be a wood-burning, open grill for the food. He was developing the menu around the open hearth, like a home in a way. That was the idea that drove the design and the connection to the lobby." In fact, the wood-burning rotisserie would seldom be used because it violated New York City codes.

Many of the elements are handcrafted, explained Vega, which relates back to how Todd sees his food, "complicated" and "handcrafted."

He brought the executive chef from Olives Las Vegas, Victor LaPlaca, to head up the kitchen in Olives New York, and Todd spent months in New York, finally getting himself an apartment in the city. Interviewed at Christmas 2000 by *Forbes*, he confessed that he would not leave New York after the opening, for worry about the reviews. The reviews were mixed.

In early December 2000, Moira Hodgson of the *New York Observer* awarded Olives New York three stars, saying, "The ingredients had so much flavor, I felt like I was eating on a Mediterranean beach. . . . Once in a while he reaches too far. . . . For New Yorkers who've tired of oversophisticated cooking, Olives offers the sort of gutsy, rustic food that I, for one, love to eat."

Todd made the cut for the *Forbes* Celebrity 100 list for the first time on March 19, 2001, but two days later *The New York Times* restaurant critic

William Grimes wrote one of the harshest reviews in recent memory about a celebrated chef. His scathing, one-star article on the new Olives New York contained a vitriolic rejection of Todd's very philosophy of food. "Any idea that occurs to him is by definition a good idea. He's the Thomas Wolfe of chefs. No sooner is a thought in his head than it's on the plate."

TODD opened a series of new concept restaurants in 2001 that returned him to his Boston base, where he met growing criticism that he was spreading himself too thin.

The first was Rustic Kitchen in September 2001 in Faneuil Hall. Its menu was somewhere between Olives and Figs and featured more braised and roasted dishes. The opening chef, Brad Stevens, who was the corporate chef for Figs, was brought in to supervise the restaurant because he had the most experience with the wood-burning ovens used at Figs. The restaurant focused on casseroles and other comfort foods.

The following month he opened Bonfire Steakhouse in the Park Plaza Hotel, the third Starwood property to bring Todd aboard. Philip Kendall, then Starwood's vice president of food and beverage, who had complete control over chef choice for the hotel chain's restaurants, explained his selection of Todd English. First, Starwood already had Todd in two of its hotels, the St. Regis in Aspen with Olives Aspen and the W on Union Square with Olives New York. Second, the Park Plaza space needed renovation, so there was already money laid aside for it. They cut a management deal, so the staff were still hotel employees. Todd's responsibilities were to manage the restaurant, hire and pay the *chef de cuisine* and a few other positions, and make regular supervisory visits. The hotel was not worried about Todd's already growing reputation about spreading himself too thin because Todd was known to come back to his Boston home base and make regular rounds of all his restaurants there.

According to the press release for its opening, "Bonfire's vast menu offers something for everyone" in an open kitchen whose grill uses long swords for spits so that "the cooking becomes the entertainment." Another feature was the bar's 50 tequilas and mescals and 200 wines. The restaurant seated 125 for dining, 30 at the bar, and another 35 special seats. The Olives Group Wine Director Glenn Tanner assembled a lengthy list of South American wines after several trips to South America. He and

Todd planned to include special tastings of Malbec grape red wines. Todd told *Food Arts* magazine that the Olives Group planned to begin wine making in Argentina in the next several years. Todd was excited about bringing barbecue under one restaurant roof from around the world, starting with his native Texas, but mainly drawing from several trips to South America, especially Argentina.

Todd Winer, who had worked at Olives Charlestown and helped open Miramar, was brought in as executive chef. "Initially, venison chops were just on a plate with sides, or chicken was served roasted with a choice of sauce and side. People wanted more, so we served it with braised bok choy, scallion cream, and orange chili marinade." In short, Bonfire became more like Olives, with a profusion of ingredients in each dish.

The mixed steak cuisines proved quite a challenge, not to mention training new staff and dealing with new hotel systems and logistics. As an extra measure of hardship, Bonfire opened shortly after 9/11 and during the height of global fears of mad cow disease—both the *Boston Globe* and the *New York Times* were running articles during opening month that compared government handling of the then-immediate anthrax threat to mad cow disease.

Said Winer, "I had a tough time hiring people; nobody wanted to leave their jobs for an untested new restaurant. The economy was going to hell, just after 9/11—we were expecting overseas shipments of fabrics, plates—nothing was getting through, but we made it work." Todd stepped in two days before the opening to change the menu.

Boston did not greet Todd's latest restaurant with great fanfare. "Eager to please but rough" was how the *Boston Globe* characterized it in early 2002. A year and some later, they were citing the decline of Bonfire—"once heralded as the Boston lynchpin in the Olives empire"—before the onslaught of two hipper, hotter restaurants, Davio's and Via Matta.

Also in October 2001 Todd opened Tuscany at the Mohegan Sun Casino in Uncasville, Connecticut. Todd was a partner in Tuscany with the casino. He was responsible only for menus, chef, and regular quality inspections by corporate chef Joe Brenner; the casino staffed the kitchen, as the Bellagio did in Las Vegas. Mohegan Sun had already chosen David Rockwell as architect. The restaurant was conceived as a rustic, Tuscan farmhouse that focused on, as usual, a large, open grill.

Todd made John Nordin *chef de cuisine* at Tuscany. The cuisine was less Mediterranean than what Todd called "authentic regional Italian." Items like spaghetti and meatballs, however, made it seem more mainstream, Italian-American—"not exactly a specialty of his restaurant's namesake region," as *The New York Times* archly noted. Clearly, by late 2001, the press was dubious about Todd's expansion, but their doubt focused on the quality of the food.

TODD'S rise had been meteoric. Outside of foodie circles, Todd was off the national radar as late as 1998, but between 1999 and 2002, the press had begun to catch up. There was a short lag time; as late as May 2000, Todd was largely limited to industry publications like *Restaurant Business,* with a circulation of 120,000. The next month, however, he appeared in an advertisement for cheese by the American Dairy Association in *Time* magazine and suddenly catapulted to a circulation of 4 million readers. In September 2000, Todd made mention in *U.S. News & World Report,* with a circulation of over 2 million as well as the cover of *New York* magazine, circulation over 400,000, about the pending opening of Olives New York.

In November 2000 Todd appeared in *Harper's Bazaar* magazine (circulation 700,000). He also received mention in the *New York Times* about himself, Figs La Guardia, and Olives New York, which reached more than 1 million people. At the end of 2000, a nice spread on him appeared in the November/December issue of *Metropolitan Home,* reaching another 600,000 readers. On March 19, 2001, Todd made the list of the *Forbes* "Celebrity 100" issue, reaching 820,000. On May 14, 2001, Todd made the *People* magazine list of the 50 most beautiful people and reached over 3 million readers.

Coverage just grew. On May 21, 2001, *Martha Stewart Living* took a third of an episode to walk through Olives New York and gave Todd reach to an audience exceeding 1.5 million viewers. Todd appeared on Martha Stewart 10 times. On October 21, 2001, Todd was awarded best restaurateur of the year by *Bon Appétit* magazine, which reaches 1.3 million readers.

Back in June 2001, Todd had filmed the first of two pilot episodes of UPN's *Iron Chef USA: Showdown in Las Vegas.* Todd's team included Jim Koch of Boston Beer Company. "I was his *sous chef* . . . I told Todd beforehand, 'I don't do much cooking.'" Koch loved Todd's dishes, particularly because one of them had a Samuel Adams beer in it. The pilot aired on November 16, 2001. Despite its having reached 2.2 million viewers, UPN considered it a failure and did not even run the second pilot episode. Later, *Iron Chef USA* would open unexpected restaurant doors for Todd in Japan. In any case, Lions Gate, the producers, resold the show to the Food Network, which began airing it in the summer of 2003.

At the end of 2001, Todd appeared in *Fortune Small Business* magazine (circulation 1 million) in a special feature entitled "Accidental Entrepreneur." The title and tone of the article started to hint at the troubles that lay around the corner for him. " 'I'm better under pressure. I'm better in a more hectic life. Sometimes it's like I've got 15 TVs on in my head, and I'm looking at all of them.' And he's okay with that? 'I'm okay with that.' "

In March 2002, Todd made *Esquire* magazine's Best Dressed Men in America (circulation 700,000) with Morgan Freeman, Sean Penn, Magic Johnson, Beck, George W. Bush, Brad Pitt, Matt Lauer, and Wes Anderson. The March 2002 issue of *Better Homes & Gardens* brought Todd to another 7.6 million readers with a large spread. In July 2002, Todd lined up with Jimmy Bradley of the Harrison and Red Cat restaurants, Rocco DiSpirito of Union Pacific, and Eric Ripert of Le Bernadin for a *Harper's Bazaar* photo shoot, reaching the magazine's same 700,000 readers no longer as a chef but as a model.

Certainly, Todd was reaching a larger audience.

BY 2002, word had reached the West Coast that Todd English's empire was having serious management problems as a result of overly quick expansion. The hometown folk in Boston had been expecting Todd to overstretch since 1999. "Whether he can expand his restaurant empire without being stretched too thin is something colleagues wonder about privately," *The Boston Globe* reported. Even Jim Cafarelli was cited as cautioning Todd through the papers, "The constant criticism will be that Todd is spread too thin."

Todd did not seem to realize that even the best managed companies in almost any line of business would be hard-pressed to expand as quickly as he had. Between the end of 1997 and the end of 2001, Todd's empire had increased the number of restaurants from five to sixteen, cookbooks from one to three, and mass media from nothing to one new radio show and two new TV series on local PBS stations. In addition, he had been making numerous guest appearances on national TV programs and had starred in the pilot for *Iron Chef USA*. Though his empire grossed him over $70 million that year, he netted only $1.5 million, less than a 2.5 percent profit.

His business foundation was becoming precarious. His media buzz rested on his restaurants; his restaurants were based largely on management contracts in numerous locations without integrated, in-house management systems. Todd seems to have been either unaware of his situation or to have stated incorrectly in June 2000, "I've put systems in place."

Disputes arose between Cafarelli and Todd over cost overruns at Olives New York and KingFish Hall. Olives New York was the breaking point: when Todd became dissatisfied with the lease Cafarelli and then-CFO Mario Mancini were negotiating, he intervened himself, according to one person familiar with the negotiations. *The Boston Globe*'s June 21, 2002 article refers to an affidavit from one of the Chesapeake's officers in which this issue is raised. One insider countered many of the overruns were due to Todd, who kept changing his mind about restaurant facilities. Each late or haphazard restaurant opening meant loss of income. Insiders say the two began to argue about Todd's peripheral businesses, such as small consulting jobs, and whether they would go into the group's finances. What travel costs should Todd be allowed to charge against the Olives Group? Who else could go with him at company expense? If Todd was paid for consulting, was Cafarelli entitled to part?

When the ground started to erupt, it started right on Todd's home turf. His flagship restaurant, Olives Charlestown, had been plagued from the beginning by neighborhood complaints. In March 2002, health inspectors investigated and found improperly stored meat and chemicals, insufficiently sanitized utensils, evidence of rodent droppings, and several maintenance violations. The restaurant was closed twice in two business weeks. Within a month, "stung by negative publicity surrounding back-to-back shutdowns of his famed Olives restaurant in Charlestown," Todd had told *The Boston Globe* that his empire was "maxed out" with no plans to grow anytime soon.

"The Olives closings hurt," said Olives Washington executive chef Steve Mannino. "I would get people sending me articles—'What the hell is going on?!' "

Just after Charlestown, New York inspectors cited Figs LaGuardia for health violations, such as dangerous handling and storage of food.

Family and friends tried to reach out privately to Todd in spectacular enough fashion to receive a write-up in *The Boston Globe* a year later. Reportedly, family and friends staged an "intervention" in late 2001 to talk to him about his overextended empire and out-of-control life. He had to be lured to the home of a friend, where Olivia, his mother, and friends waited to air concerns. "The opportunities were coming at him one after another. It was a very seductive time," the newspaper quoted Olivia. Reportedly Todd flew out to a retreat on the plane of a friend but left almost immediately; according to Todd, however, all he did was fly out to play golf.

His mother ascribed Todd's problems to overtrust. "They have made some bad choices in people," she said, speaking of the business. "Todd just trusts everybody. He doesn't look past the motive."

The Boston Globe was not so charitable: "If English was the 'glamour-hunk chef' on the covers of America's food magazines, as *New York Observer* dubbed him, he was a meddling boss out of his depth as a business executive, according to some of those who worked with him." One chef who has worked with Todd for many years commented, "It had gotten out of hand in a hurry."

It got more out of hand. On June 19, 2002, his partner and an investor filed lawsuits against him.

Chesapeake Investment Services, a secondary lender, whose president was telecom magnate (and one-time friend) Frank T. Gangi, filed first. According to newspapers, Chesapeake believed its $450,000 loan to help build KingFish Hall was insecure and in danger of default; one reported that Todd had already defaulted. Chesapeake demanded that KingFish Hall go into receivership under Cafarelli. Chesapeake's CFO claimed that drastic measures needed to be taken "to restore confidence in the vendors, service providers, and employees," particularly in light of "a pattern of puzzling decision-making and erratic behavior."

Jim Cafarelli filed a few hours later. His lawsuit revealed that he and Todd were the only shareholders of the Olive Group and that Todd served as company treasurer. Cafarelli's lawyers said that he filed reluctantly, after Todd had rejected a proposal he had requested from Cafarelli to divide company assets and then had stopped paying him. In his lawsuit, Cafarelli also objected to some of Todd's trips across the states, the Caribbean, South America, and Europe, exceeding $150,000, which he alleged that Todd had charged to their company for himself, his wife, and a girlfriend, who was listed on the payroll as "Carol." Essentially, the suit was for breach of contract. Cafarelli claimed salary and expenses exceeding $300,000 were owed him.

Some press debated whether Todd was indeed being slandered with allegations of mismanagement and misspending. Other press wondered whether he was simply a top celebrity caught in a messy business dispute amidst a busy schedule.

The Superior Court of Suffolk made its own decision with an initial ruling on Cafarelli's suit in Todd's favor on June 25, 2002. Daily operations would remain in Todd's hands, and KingFish Hall would remain in his possession. Further, Cafarelli's employment contract left him under Todd's control. Regarding Chesapeake's suit, the court determined that the secondary lender could not file without the primary lender.

In mid-August 2003, Todd said that Chesapeake's case was resolved, but the docket of Suffolk Superior Court said the lawsuit remained unsettled. Eventually, Todd and Cafarelli settled out of court. Todd gave Rustic Hall and the soon-to-open Pescado in Coral Gables, Florida, to Cafarelli as well as an undisclosed financial settlement and a mutual agreement to refrain from further public disparagement. Also, Todd took a loan from another financial institution and paid off Chesapeake Investment Services.

Todd characterized the affair as "pretty nasty." The *Boston Herald* reported that Todd found the whole legal thing difficult. "I'm a lover, not a fighter," he said. *Boston* magazine reported tougher words from Todd's lawyer, who said that Gangi of Chesapeake Investment Services and Cafarelli were trying to "usurp Todd's control of the business" and that they "thought they could get away with it."

People involved with his organization blamed Todd for handing over authority to Cafarelli and then not letting him carry out plans without interference and backtracking on decisions. "The partnership with Jim and Todd wasn't a good marriage," one former employee said. "Todd isn't able to be married: he is the ultimate bachelor in business and in his personal life. He isn't good at compromise: what matters to him is what is good for Todd. It was, 'Do what I say!'—that kind of attitude doesn't lend itself to having a partner."

Some chefs had good dealings with Cafarelli; all stayed out of the fray so as not to be affected by the dispute. "I liked Jimmy . . . I listened to what he had to say, and I think he was going towards people who knew how to run operations," recalled one chef.

In the midst of his business affairs, Todd's marriage finally blew apart, also in public.

The Boston Globe had run an article in February 1993 about couples in the restaurant business in which they weighed the pros and cons of working together. "Olives restaurant owner Todd English, who has been working alongside his wife, Olivia, for 10 years, concurs: once they meet with the pressure of the kitchen, the early-morning fight is history; 'sometimes you don't even remember what it was,' he says." Experts advised that couples make time away from work, on a daily, mental plane and with periodic, physical separations. They noted that children can help distract those who are undisciplined in forgetting their business affairs at home.

None of this advice seemed to have reached Todd: according to former staff, a year earlier in 1992 things were already difficult between Olivia and him. In fact, by 1992, Olivia no longer worked at the restaurant. "Everybody knew things weren't great," said one insider. In May 1993, Todd made the following statement, "I put in 22-hour days, and I introduce myself to my kid on Sundays." At the time, his son Oliver was going on four years old.

By December 2001, Todd and Olivia were known publicly to have filed for separation. Cafarelli confirmed that Todd had found himself an apartment in Boston to spend two or three days a week with his children: Oliver, 11, Isabel, 8, and Simon, 5. Cited as properties owned jointly by Todd and Olivia were Olives Charlestown and the Figs restaurants.

By late 2002, Todd was talking a bit about the pending divorce. According to him, Olivia had gotten out of the business for the most part after the first Olives opened. He wondered whether she resented him for his commitment to his businesses and his success.

The "Carol" named in Cafarelli's lawsuit as Todd's girlfriend was never publically identified. However, in the summer of 2002, reports surfaced that Todd was involved with Caryl Chinn, a special events director at *Bon Appétit* magazine. Confronted, Todd described Caryl as a friend rather than "galpal," as most newspapers referred to her. "It's not really a romance," he asserted. "I get up and go to work; I see my kids. She lives in New York. I'm not interested in relationships right now."

Todd received some positive press when he appeared at the Cannes

Film Festival in June 2002. Generally, however, the press was rather merciless, and when Todd protested he was characterized as "miffed." Some of the negativity seemed driven by a media need to dramatize events for ratings. "Lawsuits, power struggles, health-code violations, fickle fans, gossip-page exposés—this is the price of being one of America's most famous chefs," began one *Boston* magazine article that Todd hates, particularly after he gave the writer a whole day with him in Las Vegas: all she saw was "the whirlwind that consumes his life while fueling his ego."

AFTER a year of negative news and Todd-bashing, what did Todd have left?

Cafarelli had received Rustic Kitchen in Boston, Pescado in Coral Gables, and an undisclosed financial settlement.

There had been other losses over the years. The Onda contract had died within its first year at the Mirage Hotel in Las Vegas. Miramar had slipped away by March 2002, when ownership decided not to renew the consulting contract. The destination restaurant proved unprofitable without the volume a large city could provide, according to operations manager Marco Degl'Innocenti. The restaurant site is now a bank. Todd felt he lost the concept when the new owners changed the menu because there were too many other restaurants called Miramar to contest the name. The contract with Greg Norman's Australian Grille was not renewed after Todd dissolved his partnership with Cafarelli. Overall, Todd had suffered the loss of nearly a quarter of his restaurants by 2002.

Olives Associates still owned Olives Charlestown. The Figs Limited Partnership still owned the five Figs restaurants, which he kept, still in a minority ownership position. The Olives Group kept the four other Olives—Las Vegas, Washington, Aspen, and New York—as well as King-Fish Hall, Bonfire, and Tuscany. All told, Todd kept 13 of the 16 restaurants he had owned a year before, which continued to run under the Olive Group Management Company of which Todd is president and COO.

Todd rebuilt, too. He hired restaurant industry veterans Ken Cox as CFO and Sam Slattery as operations director in May 2002. Cox's mission was "controlled, sustainable growth," starting with infrastructure, and Sam was his right arm. Slattery focused on tackling some of the recurring problems that had led to revenue loss in the group. He changed 21 of the

45 restaurant managers in the group and attempted to make corporate headquarters more responsive to the needs of staff as a whole.

He first targeted the Figs restaurants, focusing on service rather than food. "What it took at Figs is we had to realize, it's not all about the food, it's about the experience, hospitality. The old regime didn't get that. There was a real lack of financial accountability and awareness. We needed to get qualified people in play."

Because many of the Figs are geographically close together, and the same customers might visit different Figs, Slattery made sure that recipes accessible through a graphic database were identical in each restaurant. Then he created a standard set of sequences for service and a bonus program that was tied to increased sales. The results were immediate: food costs decreased, and sales rose.

Slattery was able to show quick results to English, who allowed him to continue. "Todd is a classic entrepreneur. He always worked on the food. He steps aside and allows us to deliver what he wants. I am not rethinking things: he knew that stuff needed to take place. He knew hospitality needed to improve, that it's important to be nice and make people feel special. He needed a mechanic to come in and knock it down."

Then Slattery turned to Olives Washington, where he brought in a new general manager and addressed pressing payment and salary issues. He instituted a group-wide purchasing program for many products, like olive oil, to reduce costs while allowing each restaurant to buy their own fish, meat, and vegetables. Renovations are planned to add 65–70 seats to the bar area and 48 outdoor seats, which should increase gross revenues.

To measure the success of the new training and incentive programs, Slattery hired a marketing firm to conduct shopper's surveys in all the Figs locations, as well as KingFish, Bonfire, Olives Charlestown, Olives New York, and Olives Washington. The shoppers, who visit monthly, review service and food in the restaurant according to criteria set by Slattery and his general managers. "It's helpful. It keeps them accountable," said Slattery. It also underscores just how serious Todd and his corporate staff are about turning around the performance of all the restaurants.

Slattery was concerned about the damage done by the Olives closings and the lawsuits on all the restaurants in the Boston area. He hired consultant Holly Young, whom he knew from his own work at John Harvard's Brew House. She assessed the public perception of Todd English and the Olives brand in the Boston area.

"We learned that the closure of Olives and Cafarelli were irrelevant. We could wipe our hands of it." However, he also learned that Olives Charlestown's long-standing no-reservation policy had hurt the restaurant. "What we found was that we had a real reputation of turning people away and not taking reservations. People didn't feel they could make any plans with Olives." Olives introduced reservations and publicized the change on National Public Radio. Yet, Olives Charlestown did lose much of its appeal according to *Boston Globe* reporter Alison Arnett: "If people from out of town come to Boston, why go there? There are more places to go now, the new kids get all the attention. Lydia Shire closed her restaurant last year after 15 years. It was time to do something different. It's not a bad choice to make, because people's interest doesn't last that long." Wolfgang Puck had closed his original Spago; Milliken and Feniger had closed City Restaurant and survived. That wasn't a choice Todd made.

DESPITE 2002's being a difficult year, Todd continued to accept new projects that began to see fruition in 2003. He started with an old friend.

Jim Koch of Boston Beer knew Todd from Michela's back in the late 1980s because Michela Larson was one of Koch's first customers. When Todd opened Olives, Jim entertained clients there regularly.

Over the years, Jim and Todd got to know each other better and better. Their products were paired together in grocery stores. Todd had a short-lived pasta line in the local Star Markets grocery chain called *Todd's* Real Pasta, made by Joseph's Pasta of Boston. Promotion was weak, and Todd had no TV presence. "You need a television presence to do it. It really makes a difference. . . . Mario Batali, Rick Bayless, Lidia Bastianich—they all have TV shows," Todd said. And they all sell retail food products.

Jim felt that Todd and he fit in their respective food and beverage fields. Jim had been part of the microbrewers who had restarted independent brewing in America in the mid-1980s. His great-great-grandfather, Louis Koch, founded a brewery in St. Louis in 1860. Koch has expanded the original family recipe to a large range of flavorful and unusual craft-brewed beers that he thought rivaled the complexity and subtletly of fine wines. He saw Todd's growth into new restaurants and products as similar to his own.

Initially, Koch included Todd in consulting arrangements with his customers. Koch was working with TGI Fridays on getting more dishes either made with beer or paired with fine beer on their menu. He introduced them to Todd English, who he thought could come up with great beer recipes. Another customer, Publix supermarkets, asked Koch to introduce them to Todd English, which led to his appearance in their demonstration kitchen, where he prepared dishes with Boston Beer. Todd also made suggestions to Koch about designing a set of different beer glasses for each of his brews, which Koch adopted.

Todd appeared at the 2002 Aspen *Food & Wine* Classic for Boston Beer, to introduce Boston Beer to the press—the only beer company participating. Koch was also working on high-proof, expensive, cognac-like beers that were noncarbonated and typically sipped in two-ounce servings with names like Triple Bock, Millenium, and Utopias.

For the 2003 Aspen *Food & Wine* Classic Todd prepared a press luncheon at Olives Aspen featuring Koch's beers. Todd steamed Portuguese clams and marinated bay scallops ceviche with Samuel Adams Light. He made a salad with arugula, watercress, poached Asian pears, and a lemon sauce made with Samuel Adams Summer Ale and extra grains of paradise. For the remainder of the servings, "beer sommelier" Koch explained how he had paired each beer. Dessert featured an ice-cream float of mascarpone-cheese ice cream and Samuel Adams Octoberfest beer and ice-cream sandwiches made with Samuel Adams Stout ice cream and chocolate chip cookies. For the finale, Koch held a blind tasting between a $200 Courvoisier and a Samuel Adams Utopias. Utopias won 17 to 5.

The next month, in July 2003, Boston Brewery started advertising Todd English's "summer grilling" recipes, which included their beer Samuel Adams Summer Ale as one of the ingredients for grilled swordfish with avocado butter and corn on the cob with jalapeño butter.

Koch saw more to do with Todd. He noted that some supermarket chains were trying to attract upscale customers with interesting products. One market, he said, promoted recipes to sell a basket of food with Sam Adams. Boston Beer may also back a VH1 special with Todd, if it proceeds.

Meanwhile, in May 2003, Todd opened the Fish Club by Todd English in Seattle with new hotel partner Marriott at the Seattle Marriott Waterfront. Initially the Fish Club was supposed to lead to as many as a dozen restaurants, as new restaurants or reworked existing restaurants within Marriott. In the case of Fish Club, Todd added only Chris Ainsworth, previously at Bonfire, to a preexisting restaurant.

Fish Club was the first opening under the direction of Todd's new operations director Sam Slattery. Slattery got Todd to admit that the group needed discipline, and as a result the opening went smoothly. No extra costs were incurred.

The restaurant was far from free of problems. The Seattle Marriott Waterfront hotel is far from the beaten path, and the restaurant has poor signage. The restaurant itself was not built for Todd and fits the hotel rather than Todd in terms of design. In addition, the hotel's lower level management proved a challenge for Todd. Todd reported that everything was great at the top between Bill Marriott and himself, but managers in between felt unhappy. Slattery was still sold on the idea of multiple restaurants under management contracts with Marriott or Starwood or another strategic partner because of high profits and low risk.

The *Seattle Post-Intelligencer* restaurant review slammed Fish Club after its first three months with a reluctant two of four stars. The "wannabe high-profile restaurant" was expensive for Seattle, and three meals there were summarized as "lousy, OK, not bad." The restaurant was impersonal, "nothing more, nothing less. It's not hip, it's not exciting, it's not culinarily educational. Let's hope it's a hit with its captive audience at the Marriott." The review voiced Todd's own greatest fear, lack of celebrity recognition. "If Puck, Miller, Yamaguchi, and Lagasse brought a taste of 'what Hollywood stars eat,' the Southwest, Hawaii and New Orleans to other locales, what does English bring? In the case of Fish Club, the answer, sadly, may be 'nothing.'"

Toward the end of 2003, Todd opened Todd English's Blue Zoo at Disney's Swan and Dolphin Hotels in Orlando, Florida. The Starwood Hotels & Resorts manages properties at Walt Disney World, the Swan as one of their Westin hotels and the Dolphin as a Sheraton. Disney is the landlord, but the Tishman Hotel Corporation owns them jointly with the Metropolitan Life Group. All parties had to approve plans jointly for the new restaurant. Much of the approval process was under Todd's operations director Sam Slattery and corporate chef Joe Brenner and again went more smoothly than previous restaurants. The menu was drawn largely from KingFish, with added special tables for Mongolian hot pot and *shabu shabu*. The cuisine is labeled "Todd English's elegant and stylish interpretation of coastal cuisine."

Meanwhile, a restaurant negotiated with Cunard in April 2001 onboard the Queen Mary 2 ocean liner launched in January 2004. The ship cost over $800 million, double the cost of any other new ship being built.

Edie Bornstein, vice president for business development at Cunard, was in charge of choosing all the restaurants and other cobranded activities. "The ship has to be the destination. The ship itself has to be the most grand, most fabulous vacation on earth. So through all the deals I did, like with the Royal Academy of Dramatic Arts, which is doing a repertoire theater, everything has to bespeak 'exclusive' to QM2. Everything is exclusive, not to the Cunard brand but to this vessel exclusively. So in the deals I did, the Veuve Clicquot champagne bar is exclusive and the Todd English Restaurant at Sea is exclusive to QM2."

She hired Daniel Boulud as overall culinary advisor but decided against one of his restaurants like db Bistro Moderne or Daniel's because they were "too French." She traveled and ate at America's premier restaurants before finally settling on Todd English's Olives. She believed that his Mediterranean cuisine would appeal to the younger crowd the ship was meant to attract.

Todd assured her that he understood the limitations of cooking at sea. "On a transatlantic crossing for six days you aren't going to get fresh fish three days in," she said. Slattery commented that each recipe had to be documented exactly because the ship had to have all ingredients on hand. Kitchens on cruise ships are entirely electric, which necessitates a change in cooking preparations—especially important for Todd, who has always cooked with wood or gas fire. Todd had to adapt the Olives menu, and his team had to standardize recipes and procedures. Unlike a restaurant on land, Todd English's will not have specials.

In August 2001 Todd went to London to help the ship designers with restaurant plans.

"This restaurant is simply called Todd English's. It's not meant to replicate any of the Olives but to grow the brand and add a different flavor from the genesis of his brand," Bornstein explained. A Cunard chef would train at one of the Olives restaurants, and Todd would be required to come on board a couple of times a year. There will also be land-based joint marketing such as cocktail parties at his restaurants.

TODD began to explore other ways of growing his company beyond adding new restaurants and food products. He toyed with the idea of opening a cooking school that could use the Internet and virtual technology to reach students far outside his home base of Boston. In the first half of 2000, he met with at least one big-name, management consulting firm, though talks went nowhere.

Right around New Year 2002, an old acquaintance of Todd's moved back to Boston, Jord Poster, a business strategist. Poster founded Priceline.com and the American Express VIP subscription service. He had Fortune 500 clients. He began to advise Todd on restructuring and repositioning his company. He also made a passive investment in the company. He called himself a strategic leader, identifying for Todd important relationships that generate capital, sponsorship, and endorsements.

Poster advised against anymore one-off restaurants and to focus on fixing any problems in Todd's existing restaurants, which were under the watchful eyes of Ken Cox and Sam Slattery. He said, "The thing to focus in on is the things that have already been done well, not create any new ones." However, this advice seems to contradict what Todd has often stated is his greatest talent, namely conceptualizing new restaurants. It also contradicts the state of his restaurant empire: by early 2004, 7 of Todd's 18 restaurants were one-off concepts.

Sid Feltenstein, now retired president of Long John Silver's and A&W® All American Food Restaurants, said that of all Todd's concepts. Figs is the one that he could roll out into a quick service or fast casual chain. "What he does with that and how he does that remains to be seen." Todd himself believes it has potential of becoming a national chain. None of the other partners in Figs want to expand further, and Todd is trying to raise money to buy the concept back so he can expand it himself.

Poster argued that Todd should focus on developing his brand outside of restaurants, expanding in food-related and kitchen-related products, both areas Wolfgang Puck and other chefs have already entered, and lifestyle-related products, where few if any chefs have gone.

Poster identified the hospitality and gaming industries as Todd's most "natural, meaningful" partners, who could not only add the most value to his name but also the greatest competitive advantage. Marriott did not seem a good fit, he felt, but Boston Beer was a good match. Most importantly, he steered Todd into television, so he could have a platform to launch his brand nationally.

Todd's first new effort was to be a show called *Open Kitchen,* distributed by WGBH Boston. Todd would coproduce the show with his own in-house production company. Poster sees *Open Kitchen* as a vehicle for selling Todd English lifestyle products: a Todd English travel package, a foodie hotel, clothes, watches, cologne, gadgets. By late 2003, however, insufficient funds had been raised, so the show's status was up in the air, according to WGBH. Todd courted Boston Beer as a sponsor, but Boston Beer was interested in a second show Todd was flacking, with the working title of *Rock 'n' Roll Chef,* in which he would cook with rock stars (hence his 2003 summer barbecue at the MTV Beach House). Todd's latest talent agency Endeavor was involved in selling the show to VH1, MTV, or a similar network.

Todd also planned a cooking DVD that featured a music soundtrack and cooking demonstrations geared around themes like Christmas. These he planned to sell through chain outlets like Barnes & Noble and his own restaurants.

Poster nixed a deal Todd had made with American Woodworks, a division of Timberlake Cabinet Company of Winchester, Virginia, to design kitchens for show houses featured in the homebuilder's convention held in Las Vegas. Though the kitchens were a success in the press, few builders chose the designs or the use of Todd's name to add further value to their homes.

Todd also said that he was designing plates with Wedgwood for his new restaurant on the QM2. Wedgwood aside, Todd is going ahead with a signature line of tableware made by Front of the House (FOH). The dishes, which will be used in many of his restaurants, will be sold at the restaurants, on FOH's website, and at retail stores. FOH is one of the few tableware manufacturers to supply both the hospitality and consumer markets.

Jim Koch, who was a management consultant before he quit to follow in his family's footsteps and become a beer brewer, has acted occasionally as a friendly advisor to English. "Todd and I talked about his brand. It's an issue that has to be managed." Koch said, "One thing that I told him is be really protective of your brand: don't stretch it too far. Everything you do makes your brand stronger or weaker. Part of having a brand strategy is that it enables you to resist temptation."

Poster agrees. "The most important thing which truly is the hardest thing for Todd to embrace is letting go of all the other opportunities that don't fit. That is the essence of all competitive strategy: it's not as much *what* you do as what you *don't* do.

In April 2003, Todd entered into his farthest-reaching venture yet: he opened Olives Tokyo with Soho's Hospitality Group. Numerous celebrities turned up for opening night. Japan's grand champion sumo wrestler Takanohana appeared, as did Japanese models and TV stars. Two famous, overseas-based Japanese chefs came, Tetsuya Wakuda of Australia and Soho's partner Nobu Matsuhisa of the U.S. Reported chief designer Diego Gronda, who came for the opening, "Soho was very excited because the guy who designed and owned the building, Mori, who owns 50 percent of Tokyo, was at our restaurant at 1 p.m. with all the top people from his company. It was a great honor in Japan. It was very big for Soho." Press coverage was huge: newspapers, magazines, and television. Todd made the cover of several magazines.

The road to Tokyo came about in part due to failure: *Iron Chef USA* had not panned out in the States. However, as America's answer to Japan's original *Iron Chef*, it played well in Japan. Having won the first of the two-episode program, Todd had gained a name there.

Meanwhile, Atsuyuki Tsukikawa, the son of Soho's Hospitality Group owner Soho Tsukikawa, had learned about Todd through his case studies involving Union Square's W Hotel at Cornell's hotel management school. Todd's old golfing buddies and chef friends, also chef partners of Soho's, then helped out: Roy Yamaguchi, after encouraging Atsuyuki to dine at Olives New York, made the introductions while Nobu Matsuhisa nodded approval. The deal gave Todd a royalty based on sales, with no investment other than time and training of chefs from the Olives side.

The Rockwell-designed restaurant seated 160 guests. Led by principal Diego Gronda, who had already worked on Asian projects in Bangkok, the layout of the restaurant had been completed before the choice of Olives. The project was part of the huge Roppongi Hills development, which included office towers, residential buildings and hotels, and restaurants, as well as a new, modern art museum.

Soho's built three, connecting restaurants forming a J called the "Roppongi J." First was a bar to attract the young. Second was an Asian restaurant, with sushi prepared by Nobu Matsuhisa, called Xen. Third was Olives. Although all three were joined, Olives had its own entrance and, more importantly, a grand view of Tokyo, which is very rare in restaurants. The concept was the journey through life ending in Nirvana—at Olives. Gronda even designed a small room in the restaurant as a shrine where couples could marry. A glow of low-voltage light fixtures mimicked votive candles, and low-tech lenticulars of candles appeared to flicker. The effect was meant to reflect the usual open hearth or wood-burning oven in most of Todd's restaurants, missing from Olives Tokyo. Here there was no open kitchen. Instead, olive leaf patterns were used in the curtains, and leather, hand-stitched olive leaves fell from ceiling to floor around the private dining room.

For the first six months, Todd asked Clay Conley, formerly executive chef at Olives Las Vegas, to stand in as *chef de cuisine*. Olives Tokyo demanded new twists on the Olives signature, as Mediterranean ingredients were either in short supply or astronomically expensive in Japan. So Todd and Conley worked to incorporate Japanese and other Asian ingredients. Still, many Olives classics appeared on the menu, such as pea ravioli and lamb tagine, tuna tartare, and tuna carpaccio.

The kitchen staff was Japanese, too, except for Conley. Only their chef spoke a bit of English, but Conley got by with a simple list of ingredients for food markets. Todd also sent out a chef from KingFish for the opening, to work with Japanese staff at each station.

OPENING OF OLIVES TOKYO: SOHO TSUKIKAWA, DIEGO GRONDA, TAKANOHANA, AND TODD ENGLISH

Courtesy of Diego Gronda

Courtesy of Rockwell Group, photo by Shin'ichi Sato

INTERIOR OF OLIVES TOKYO

The wait staff in the front of the house needed some tips on American hospitality. "Japanese service is very relaxed. They will never check back at a table. They will never ask if you want something. You have to ask them. It's not as quick as U.S. service: we are trying to get these guys to give service like the States," Conley said. Still, he praised the Japanese general manager. Also, Todd had sent over corporate wine director Glenn Tanner to help out.

Sam Slattery tried to work with the staff but noted that the Japanese do not tip and the pay is fairly low, so it was difficult to motivate the employees. He noted that the front of the house was understaffed compared to an American restaurant.

The opening was the smoothest Conley had ever seen. Work on the restaurant's construction actually finished two days before the opening. The preparation for each staff member was equally good. When Conley made rounds on the second day to check on what kitchen staff needed, he was amazed to find them all set.

Olives Tokyo worked smoothly, too. Sam has done a great job with systems operations, Conley said. Also, the kitchen staff was far more serious than in Las Vegas, which is unionized—there, everybody is just working for their paycheck, he added.

Todd scheduled quarterly management visits to make menu changes and publicity appearances. Atsuyuki will make the most of each visit. "During his stay, we schedule 'Todd week,' sending direct mails to the clients to let them know of his visit. His visit gives a really good spur to the staff," he said.

Conley was happy with the opening, because he was happy for Todd. "He seems like his is getting back to what he likes to do, which is cooking. There were a couple of years where he was trying to do everything, and he wasn't cooking. It stressed him out a little bit."

Todd was pretty stoked by his success in Tokyo. It was almost like La Côte Basque days with lots of fish, but no red kiwi on sole this time. Todd was doing his own thing, and he had his groove back.

Cool.

4

MILLIKEN & FENIGER

Courtesy of Gary Moss

"Poetry [is] a speaking picture, with this end:
to teach and delight"
—Sir Philip Sidney, *The Defense of Poetry* (1595)

WAYNE Brady was not having one of his better days—though lately his days had been quite good. The exuberant comic had received nationwide notice in 1998 with the doubleheader of *The Hollywood Squares* and the American version of *Who's Line Is It Anyway?* By 2001, he had landed *The Wayne Brady Show.*

The shoot on January 16, 2003, started OK but lacked sizzle and pop. Wayne had floundered a bit with a monologue and had not connected too well with interview guest Martin Mull. Halfway through the episode, it was time to get cooking.

"Our next guests have hosted their own show on the Food Network called *Too Hot Tamales,* and they are also the authors of five cookbooks, including *Mexican Cooking for Dummies."* He laughed as he said "Dummies." "Please welcome Mary Sue Milliken and Susan Feniger!"

"We heard that that last book was probably really good for *you,"* Susan said as she walked on stage.

"Yes—because I'm *Mexican!"* shot back Brady.

Mary Sue and Susan had come to teach Wayne how to prepare breakfast for his then very pregnant wife. First, they moved to a blender for fruit juice.

"Our blender is a little 'broke-down' right now," Wayne explained, "so, I'm just going to shake real hard." He seized a blender to demonstrate its capabilities. Brady and blender became one. Teeth on edge, he grated out in a gravelly voice, *"Eeeeh-ou-weeee-uh eeeeh-ou-weeee-uh eeeeh-ou-weee-uh!"*

He took the lid off his imagination-blended drink and cooed, "*Oooo,* that's *good!*"

Next, they tackled turkey sausages and buttermilk pancakes. Susan set Brady to chopping cilantro for the turkey sausage.

"Now, don't chop your finger off!" cautioned Susan.

"They're very sharp knives!" Mary Sue added.

"Keep your fingertips—*back!*" shouted Susan, seizing Wayne's hand and curling his fingertips under a bit in one of the most basic techniques of food preparation. Wayne eagerly grabbed the knife away from her again and leaped back into action.

Suddenly Mexican, Wayne said, "This is how we do things in Mexico—leave me a-*lone!* O-*kay!*" and started chopping as steadily as his untrained hand could manage.

"Stop!" cried Susan and pulled back his hand. Then she broke into a huge smile as she lifted up the cilantro by its ends to reveal long strands of partially chopped, mostly mutilated cilantro stalks. "Good job! Good job!" she said, laughing with the audience, while Wayne, smiling with embarrassment, recovered smoothly by explaining with the cunning of a conjuror, "You see, I just gave the *illusion* of cutting."

Susan cut the cilantro expertly in a tenth of the time, while Mary Sue took the lead for a moment. "Likewise, I'm going to chop up a couple of chilies. Actually, we're gonna put two kinds of chilies in. Smell this," she coaxed.

"It's amazing!" assured Susan.

"Hmmm!" Brady said. "What does it smell like? It's a smoky chili!" He registered surprise, then wile, as he quipped, "It's bad, bad, see, big guy?" in an Edward G. Robinson imitation, complete with smoked chili cigar.

"It used to look like this," Mary Sue continued, unfazed, holding up a green jalapeño, "until it got smoked."

"It got dried *and* smoked," added Susan. "It's used for chipotle—you know, in *Mexico*?"

"Right!" chimed in Brady on cue with a huge smile and arched eyebrows that confessed utter ignorance.

"So, we're going to put in some chipotle powder," Mary Sue went on.

"I'm smoking chili, mon!" murmured the suddenly Jamaican Brady, holding his chili like a spliff.

The segment wrapped a few moments later on a high note of laughs. Once again, "the Girls" had worked their magic.

"THE Girls" is how their familiars address them, although they have many aliases. Professionally, they are Milliken and Feniger, which sounds rather like a law firm. To TV viewers, they are the "Too Hot Tamales." To Southern Californians, they are the Border Girls of Border Grill.

For Mary Sue and Susan, their partnership is both the core of their strength and a weak point, a two-edged sword. As much as they have found success in restaurants, television shows, radio shows, film, book series, and product lines, they have also been set back by poor decision making. The ability to come back again and again after disaster, common among most successful chefs and, in fact, most entrepreneurs, runs especially and happily strong in both Susan and Mary Sue.

It's not in the way they walk or the way they wear their hair. It's the way they talk: they speak as one person. Each finishes the other's sentences or questions the other. Talking to them is like an externalized stream of consciousness, a constant debate between ego and id. Talking to them, it becomes clear that the partnership of Mary Sue Milliken and Susan Feniger creates a critical mass whose sum far exceeds one plus one.

SUSAN Feniger is a diminutive woman who bristles with physical and emotional energy. Her shoulders sometimes hunch over as if she were pushing through a line of basketball players charging down court. As a child, Susan was an avid sports enthusiast.

"I started ice skating when I was three and skiing when I was six. I loved sports. I was a total tomboy." Sports may be part of what lies underneath the determined, persuasive, and focused attitude that Feniger exudes.

Born in 1953, Susan grew up in Toledo, Ohio, in a Russian Jewish household that revolved around her mother, who, she said, had "great taste buds." The seeds of a professional career in food, however, were planted outside the home.

"When I was in high school, I was very rebellious. I used to go to Goodwill to get my clothes and do everything I could to rebel against my parents." She wanted to make her own money, so she got a job in a restaurant when she was in high school. Penny, the woman who ran the cafeteria kitchen, was a real drill sergeant. Susan loved it. "I absolutely remember loving the energy, the camaraderie that happened in the kitchen from that point on."

She spent a term in high school living with a farm family in the Dutch countryside, where she gained a passion for growing foods. She started at Goddard College in Vermont but dropped out to work for a year as a furniture refinisher while living in a tepee. When that proved too cold, she moved on to Pitzer College in Claremont, California, to study economics and business—and to be with hometown boyfriend Josh Schweitzer, who was also studying there.

At Pitzer, she got a part-time campus job in the cafeteria and again fell in love with the camaraderie and strong characters of the kitchen staff.

"I loved the different types of people, some extremely educated who work in a kitchen and others who are not educated but who are great creative cooks. I love how it equalizes in many ways, the same way today, in our kitchen, there are people who are not educated, haven't gone to cooking school, and maybe haven't even finished high school, but they are great cooks."

By the end of her junior year, Susan had finished all the coursework in her major without taking a single elective. She still did not know what she wanted to do. Harry, the head cook at the cafeteria, suggested that she look into culinary schools.

"I couldn't see myself in a bank or being an economist. I finished my third year with all of my requirements done, and I convinced my economics professor to go with me to the head of the university to see if I could do my last year at the Culinary [Institute of America]."

The university agreed to the plan, and Susan moved to Poughkeepsie. At the CIA, Feniger was passionate about Chef Ferdinand Point. "I was so into Point and Auguste Escoffier. I wanted to read every single thing. I made the decision that I wasn't going to read any more novels: I was only going to read cookbooks for the next four years."

Susan decided that she had to catch up with French chefs, who start their apprenticeships at 16 or younger. "I wanted to work for great people, stay a year and a half, pick their brains, work as hard as I could, and then go to the next person till I was ready to open my own place. I was in such a frame of mind that I didn't care what I made, or what I did." So, just as in high school, she continued to work hard outside of her studies. Her first job was filleting fish from 6:00 am to 1:30 pm at Gadaletto's Seafood Market & Restaurant in New Paltz, across the Hudson from Hyde Park. Sometimes she drove down with the owners to the Fulton Fish Market on the Lower East Side of Manhattan. Her next job was at Harrolds restaurant in Brewster, New York.

With a B.A. in business and a Culinary Arts degree, in 1975 Susan headed to Kansas City. Her hometown boyfriend Josh Schweitzer was studying architecture at Kansas University. They married.

She decided to work for Gus Riedi of La Bonne Auberge restaurant, the top, five-star restaurant in town, but he did not have a place for her. To secure the job, she worked one month for free: Riedi hired her. Characteristically, Susan threw herself into the work.

"Riedi was a European chef with a great heart. He worked from 7:00 am till midnight every single day. I would meet him there at 7:00 am and work till midnight. I did every single process with him. I kept doing it even after I was put on the payroll—I didn't want to miss it."

Two years later, in 1978, as she and Josh drifted apart, she decided to move on, this time to Chicago. Aiming again for the top, at either one of the city's best two French restaurants, Le Français or Le Perroquet, she eventually landed herself a spot at Le Perroquet, a *nouvelle cuisine* restaurant. Le Perroquet was "a very intense kitchen," detailed, organized, and oriented toward teaching young cooks about traditional French country cooking.

At Le Perroquet Susan first encountered Mary Sue Milliken, who had been hired shortly before her. They became fast friends, hanging out together on days off. After a year on the job, Chef Mike Beck went on a holiday and left Susan and Mary Sue in charge of the kitchen during the day shift. They did all the ordering, wrote the menus, and made the sauces. The all-male night crew would come in and actually put dishes together.

"It was really exciting for us," said Mary Sue. "I would pick up Susan on a bicycle, and with her riding on the handlebars, we would get to the restaurant at 5:00 a.m., although we weren't supposed to be there till 8:00 a.m. We'd open the restaurant and receive the fish."

It was also about this time that Susan seems to have come to terms with her own sexual preferences. Never complaining about how she was treated as a woman, she did come to much grief at the male-dominated Le Perroquet when she let herself be known openly as a lesbian.

After working through each station in a year and a half, Susan decided to move on again. This time she headed for Los Angeles, where she landed a job with Wolfgang Puck at Ma Maison. At that time, Ma Maison was Los Angeles' hottest, most glamorous and exciting restaurant, owned and managed by Patrick Terrail.

"You could see every star pull up, every Rolls Royce. The valets would tell you who was there. It was pretty incredible for a Midwest girl to see," said Susan. Puck and then-girlfriend Barbara Lazaroff took Susan under their wing. She found Puck's relaxed style the opposite of Le Perroquet. "Wolf's kitchen was all about delicious food, but there wasn't nearly as much teaching going on."

Two years later, in 1980, Patrick Terrail set up a year-long, unpaid *stage* for Susan at L'Oasis restaurant in La Napoule in the south of France, run by his friend, Chef Louis Outhier. Do you want to go and work at L'Oasis in the south of France? Terrail asked her. Yes, I'll do anything—wash dishes, anything, she said. Joachim Splichal was there for a few months before Outhier sent him to open a restaurant in Los Angeles, where he remains to this day with his Patina Group. Outhier opened Susan's eyes to the further glories of French food. "I never had fresh *foie gras* until I worked there. I was at the *foie gras* station, so each time I made a serving I would cut off a piece for myself. I couldn't believe it: I ate a hundred pounds."

After L'Oasis, Susan headed to Paris, where she met up and stayed with friend Mary Sue Milliken, who was also finishing an apprenticeship. They helped out during the day for a month at a large catering house called Potel et Chabot, taking notes on dishes and technique. One night, the two of them resolved to open a restaurant together.

Borrowing money from her friend Mary Sue, Susan flew back to Los Angeles in 1981 to work at Ma Maison. Terrail celebrated her return: "She went over [to France], stayed for year, and became a major chef."

MARY Sue Milliken's childhood was surprisingly similar to Susan's. The youngest of three girls, she was also a midwesterner, born in 1958 in St. Clair, Michigan and grew up outside of Chicago, mostly near Lansing and East Lansing.

Her father had a doctorate in education and was superintendent of schools. He negotiated the first teachers' strike in the country, outside of Chicago. "It was very stressful—so stressful that he went right over the edge, because he had a drinking problem." Her parents divorced, and she moved in with an uncle for a while in Michigan and then back with her mother. Her mother struggled to raise the three children while teaching grammar school. Mary Sue credits her with stirring an early interest in food: her mother spent a small inheritance on a family culinary tour of Europe when Mary Sue was 12.

Like Susan, Mary Sue was driven and focused. By attending summer and evening school, she finished high school in three years and then moved to Chicago at age 17. She got her own apartment and a job at a bakery called Let Them Eat Cake, owned by a friend of one of her older sisters. Mary Sue credits baker-owner Greg Duda with inspiring her to become a chef.

"I met him when I was 16. He said, 'Come on over to dinner!' So, we got there at seven o'clock, but nobody was home. All of a sudden, he trundles up the sidewalk with two grocery bags. 'Oh, the bakery was busy today, and I couldn't get out of there. I'm so sorry I'm late.' He had appetizers on the table in like 12 minutes flat, and then dinner. And that day I said to myself, 'I want to cook like that!' "

Duda encouraged Mary Sue to apply to Washburne Culinary Institute, where he had gone to school. When she was put on the waiting list, he got her accepted for the following year. Mary Sue worked in his bakeries for five years, which grew from one location to seventeen.

Washburne was a vocational school with only 100 of its 3,000 students in the cooking program. Mary Sue was younger than most of the others, largely returning Vietnam veterans on the GI Bill. "I learned to hold my own with tough GI veterans in a man's world, and not only with chefs but plumbers and pipe fitters." She graduated in 1978 after completing the two-year program. For the first year after her graduation, she worked nights in the Hilton Hotel's kitchen on banquets. The following year, she worked at Maxim's of Paris in another all-male kitchen.

At graduation she had told the director, a Yugoslavian, that she wanted to work only at Le Perroquet. The owner, Jovan Trboyievich, was also Yugoslavian, and Mary Sue was duly invited for tea. When she told him she wanted to work for him, Trboyievich laughed. She recalled the conversation clearly.

"Jovan said, 'You would create havoc: my men in there are animals! All I can offer you is hatcheck girl.' I said, 'What?' and cried all the way home. So, I started a letter campaign, sending him a letter every day. He got worried and after a month he asked me if I were going to sue him. 'All I want is a job!' I said. Finally, he gave me a minimum-wage job peeling garlic and shallots."

As promised, the men were indeed tough. They wore steel-toed boots and tall hats and made the shy Mary Sue even shier, but Mary Sue ended up proving her mettle by working circles around everyone else.

Susan Feniger applied for a kitchen job two months later, in 1978. "I saw her, and thought, 'Oh my God, I hope he hires her!'" Mary Sue said. "And he did—we were such a great deal: minimum wage and better than anyone else in the kitchen!"

Mary Sue started at the bottom of the kitchen ladder, peeling shallots, and then quickly moved to pastries. When Susan was hired she replaced Mary Sue, and the two quickly moved up the kitchen hierarchy, from station to station.

After their short day-shift reign during the chef's vacation, Susan left for Los Angeles, and Mary Sue left to work as a chef for a new café owned by her mentor Greg Duda a few months later. When her relationship with one of the owners turned sour, she decided she wanted to go to France to study. Mary Sue, whose relationship to Le Perroquet's owner Trboyievich had taken a 180° turn from his initial offer of hatcheck girl, offered to introduce her to top chefs of Paris and help her get a job. They traveled to Paris together and spent lunch and dinner at three-star and then two-star restaurants, but all the chefs they met laughed at the suggestion of a woman in their kitchens.

Finally, they ended up at the two-star restaurant L'Olympe, run by a French-Moroccan woman, Dominique Nahmias, and her husband. "Jovan asked, 'Can you give her a job?' and she said, 'Come tomorrow.'" Mary Sue got $250 a month, enough to cover her rent. She took intensive French classes in the mornings and worked in the six-person kitchen in the evenings.

"Dominique would arrive at 8:00 p.m. in a V-neck white T-shirt and white skirt and stiletto pumps and start cooking. Here I had thought I had to be a man to be a chef, wear steel-toed boots and cut my hair short. This was the greatest thing for me. I like to be feminine. My passion for food was overruling my passion for life. All my role models before then had been men, really rough men," said Mary Sue.

Outside the restaurant, however, Parisian snobbery made Mary Sue miserable. To cheer herself up, she often called Susan, who was working at L'Oasis with Outhier on the Riviera. When the restaurant closed in August she went down for a holiday with Susan. When Susan quit her job she spent the month with Mary Sue, who was recovering from a kitchen accident in which she had chipped a vertebra.

Susan was ready to return to America and start her own restaurant. "We would buy a $2 bottle of wine, get the meal half-cooked, and go out for another bottle of wine. There was plenty of wine. On one of those nights—it's corny—but there was a rainbow outside. We were drunk, and we said we had to go home and do it—open a restaurant together. We wrote down names and what we would cook there."

Mary Sue lent money to Susan, and they both returned to America. Susan headed back to Los Angeles. Mary Sue, after cooking privately for an insurance mogul who doused everything she made with chili sauce at the rate of 27 bottles a month, telephoned Susan to let her know she had to get out of there.

IN 1979, Gai Gherardi and Barbara McReynolds founded L.A. Eyeworks on Melrose Avenue. They made the big time when Elton John donned some of their outrageous glasses for his tours in the early 1980s. The Jackson Five followed suit. By 1982, their store had appeared as "Chew's Shop" in *Blade Runner,* scripted largely by their friend Hampton Fancher. At one point in the first few years they had to lock their doors and let eager customers in and out by the batch to avoid stampedes.

Gai and Barbara decided to rent a small space next to their flagship store, once a furniture-refinishing shop, to control what would go in next. Both loved good coffee at a time when there were few places to grab a decent espresso in Los Angeles. So, they opened an espresso bar that served pastries, sandwiches, and cold dishes.

They had invited Susan to run the small café, called City Café, but she turned them down, opting for a more glamorous trip to France. When Susan returned to Los Angeles, she went back to work at Ma Maison. Wolfgang Puck had abandoned Ma Maison by then for his own new restaurant, Spago. He had asked Susan to come join him there. Susan declined Wolfgang's offer: she wanted to go out on her own.

Barbara and Gai again approached Susan about running their café. Barbara recalled, "She came in one day for a coffee and sampled the salad. I have to say that what we were doing was good, but it was a speck of dust compared to what Susan had to offer. I didn't have a clue who she was, or her background, or her potential. I just said, 'We need to work on our salad dressing here: would you come in and help us out?' "

Barbara says that Susan was intrigued by the L.A. Eyeworks team, who shared a philosophy of passion and brashness. They had opened their store on an industrial stretch of Melrose Avenue. Susan was intrigued by the gay and art world clientele already drawn to the café from the store next door. She started helping during day shifts, making a daily soup and special. Soon Barbara recognized Susan's culinary genius and promised to teach her what she knew of business and help her turn the café into a restaurant.

Barbara admits that the two businesses were very different from one another. "You can manage the optical business in a day with a managers' meeting once a month. It goes on. There is no urgency. The glasses don't rot. There are no cockroaches. In a restaurant, every day there is an emergency. The fish doesn't get delivered. The dishwasher doesn't show up. You are always in management meetings. It's very time consuming.

"I am as passionate about that business as Susan and Mary Sue," Barbara said, "I love that business. I love the idea of service, of making someone happy. Once they cross the threshold, there is an unspoken responsibility for them to have a good experience. I care about that 100 percent. Living the City culture and L.A. Eyeworks spirit, you want to see that go on."

Barbara and Susan also became a couple soon after Susan started working at the café.

Six months later, in 1982, Barbara and Gai asked Susan to run the place full-time. Part of Susan's acceptance was based on her experiences in all-male kitchens: "Being in the system with men just never felt equal and fair, so it's like 'I'm going to be my own boss, that's how I'm going to deal with this!' " She left Ma Maison and took over the café.

"I put a hibachi in the back parking lot, and I started running a grilled fish and a grilled veal chop special. On the hot plate I would do things like veal tongue with lobster sauce and pear, and everything else was like tuna sandwich or pasta salad. Everything else was cold. I did that for maybe six months, so we got a write-up in the *LA Times*."

Flushed by her first success and with the small café bustling with celebrities like Lily Tomlin and Divine, who were also L.A. Eyeworks customers, Susan called Mary Sue in Chicago and invited her to Los Angeles to join her at City Café. "I finally convinced her to come out for her birthday in February 1982. We went downtown to the market, and then it took us an hour to boil the water on the hot plate!"

Mary Sue said, "Susan called me and said, 'Come on out, and let's do this together.' So I came on out and said, 'But there's no kitchen! Here we've been working all these years, and you want me to come out and work on a hot plate?' But Susan said, 'Oh no, we're going to put in a kitchen, so. . . . ' Only it wasn't a kitchen: it was a four-burner stove!" Guests had to scramble past the chefs to get to the bathroom, and the chefs had to scramble in the bathroom to get to supplies stored there.

Despite the cramped, makeshift conditions for two chefs used to French kitchens, within months Mary Sue decided to stay—as a partner. "I made it clear that they had better include me, or I would leave. I wasn't going to work for Susan. They acquiesced." According to the Girls, L.A. Eyewear had cut a hard deal for Susan to become a partner: five years to buy in with cash. When Mary Sue joined the kitchen, she was offered the same deal. Ultimately, there were five partners in City Café, each with 20 percent: from L.A. Eyeworks, Barbara McReynolds, Gai Gherardi, and Margo Willits, who ran their international wholesale distribution; from City Café, Susan Feniger and Mary Sue Milliken.

THE chefs managed their employees in the less strict way Susan had experienced under Wolfgang Puck and Patrick Terrail at Ma Maison.

SUSAN AND MARY SUE AT CITY CAFÉ

Courtesy of Mary Sue Milliken and Susan Feniger

Mary Sue said, "Our partnership in 20 years has evolved through stages where I was the hard ass and she was great, and other times it was reversed. It's not good to stick to those roles forever. I find that she and I have gone through major changes in 20 years, emotional maturing. A lot of partnerships fail because you get stuck in these roles and one party is maturing and the other is happy staying where they are. Luckily, we haven't done that."

Mary Sue and Susan recall making only about $12,000 a year each, even though the restaurant was doing over 100 covers a night for its 39 seats:

Feniger: We were just working. It was Mary Sue and I. We worked breakfast, lunch, and dinner.

Milliken: Yeah, we only had Mondays off, and all we did on Mondays was go down to the beach and sleep.

Feniger: Yeah, so we weren't thinking about growing: we were thinking about getting rest on Monday.

Milliken: Because we were having so much fun!

Feniger: And we weren't even thinking about growing.

Milliken: It was about, "What are we going to cook tomorrow?" and this was so exciting—we can cook whatever we want!

The City Café space had been a nondescript espresso and sandwich bar; Susan and Mary Sue had transformed it into a cutting edge restaurant using fresh produce from local farms that was burgeoning in California at the time.

Both chefs also took working holidays in Thailand, India, and other countries, building up their repertoire of exotic recipes and adding Asian and South American ingredients to their French and American-inspired cuisine.

THERE was no getting around the limited space of City Café. Mary Sue said, "The kitchen was 12 x 12, and the storage space was above the bathroom, so you had to climb up a ladder. I would sit there, and Susan would pitch cans to me—or toilet paper. Diana Rigg was there one day. We were all excited, and there I was, standing on top of the table, when she walked in to go to the bathroom. I remember looking down at her, and thinking, 'Why can't I be on the floor instead of up here?' "

In 1985, Mary Sue and Susan and their L.A. Eyeworks partners decided to open a full-size restaurant. They found a carpet warehouse in a largely industrial section of La Brea Avenue. They jumped from 11 to 125 seats in 5,000 square feet. It was the Girls' first restaurant opening.

Even with the exposure to Los Angeles' wealthy patrons enjoyed at Ma Maison and then Spago, Wolfgang Puck had to scrape to raise money: Susan and Mary Sue had to scrape twice as hard. With the two of them almost always behind the stove, they had little front-of-the-house presence with which to lure potential investors. Nevertheless, they managed to raise $660,000 from friends and family for the new restaurant, paying off the investment in only two years. The chefs closed the old City Café for one month and went on a tour of Mexico; four months later they opened City Restaurant on La Brea.

It was an important step for the Los Angeles restaurant scene in the very fact that both chefs were women and their partners were women— "trailblazers" as Barbara Fairchild, editor-in-chief of Los Angeles-based *Bon Appétit* magazine, called them.

Meanwhile, Susan's ex-husband Josh Schweitzer had come out to Los Angeles and joined the firm of prominent Los Angeles architect Frank Gehry. To design the new City Restaurant, Susan called on Josh, who worked on it in his spare time. Eventually, Josh left Gehry to form Schweitzer-Kellen with fellow Gehry alumnus David Kellen.

Their design for City was spare and modern, rejecting the current idea of restaurant as gallery made famous by such Los Angeles icons as Michael's in Santa Monica. The walls were bare and cut by large windows, putting all the focus on the tables and the food. An exhibition kitchen, so popular at Wolfgang's Spago and other restaurants, was out of the question on the small budget of $660,000.

Leaving the walls bare, Josh tried instead to capture the intimacy of City Café. In the old City Café, guests literally had to go through the kitchen to go to the bathroom, so he made sure they would still have to pass by the kitchen, glimpsing inside through open doors. The chef's and manager's offices were accessible from a spiral staircase in the dining room, which meant that even if they weren't in the kitchen or the dining room they were visible to their guests.

The Girls decided that they wanted a tandoori oven in their new restaurant. "Coming out of a couple of totally dreamy cooks, we installed our own tandoori oven, which we had to research. It came as an unfired clay pot from India, held together by elephant hairs. When you put it in place, you had to build a structure around it and then fire the pot inside. You had to build a fire that had to reach 1,800° [Fahrenheit]. You glazed the inside with brown sugar and mustard oil. And then you had a tandoori oven! And then, having done all that, we didn't know how to use it!" said Mary Sue. So, they had wrought iron skewers made for grilling meats.

The negotiations to rent the City Restaurant space were primarily done by the L.A. Eyewear partners, rather than the chefs. Four months into construction Barbara fired the general contractor and assumed the job herself. Josh was hired strictly as an architect with little say in site selection.

The opening was chaotic, with few experienced staff involved. Both chefs worked around the clock, attempting to do the City Café on a much larger scale. "We weren't very organized in thinking what our roles were. We didn't change our roles very much," said Susan. After three months of nonstop work, one chef took nights and the other took days.

Press reviews raved about City Restaurant and its eclectic mix of world cuisines. It was packed from the start. "Feniger and Milliken are two of the most accomplished chefs working in the new American idiom, and now that they have a kitchen larger than a postage stamp, who knows what wonders will come rolling out of it?" wrote Ruth Reichl for the *Los Angeles Times* in 1985. "Feniger and Milliken cook with individuality, originality and joy, and the results defy imitation," wrote Rose Dosti a few months later in 1986 for the same newspaper.

More than a decade later, Ruth Reichl told the *Los Angeles Times*, "Unlike most women at the time, they weren't practicing a *cuisine de [grand]mére*. It was not just refined home cooking, food you'd expect to get in a mother's kitchen. These were technically well-trained chefs, doing the kind of cooking that, until then, only men were doing. And they had sympathy for non-European food. They did Third World cooking in a professional way. They'd been to Mexico and they'd been to India, and they came back and were doing things with ethnic food—incorporating spices and ingredients that were virtually unused until then in American cooking—it was amazing. It was important work and worth doing and worth knowing about."

Mary Sue and Susan returned from their month in Mexico with a new concept for the City Café space, which they called Border Grill. Border Grill and City Restaurant were only six blocks apart, so managing one restaurant and one tiny café was hardly a stretch, but by 1990 Border Grill too had outgrown the tiny café's space. Susan and Mary Sue, with their L.A. Eyeworks partners, opened a much-enlarged Border Grill on Fourth Street in Santa Monica.

The location presented itself to the chefs. They had acted as consultants to a group of lawyers who owned the City of Angels Brewing Company, a microbrewery and restaurant. Eventually City of Angels failed. The chefs decided to rent the space themselves since it was already set up for a restaurant and would need little investment. However, the restaurant would continue to pioneer that area: at times during its first years, Border Grill was the only restaurant for blocks on Fourth Street. Back in the early 1990s, Santa Monica did not appear to be at the cusp of today's affluence. Nearby Third Street Promenade had only just been completed and was not yet luring crowds of tourists. The restaurants moving into Santa Monica were opening several blocks to the south and west, on Main Street near Wolfgang Puck's Chinois on Main, including Schatzi on Main opened by fellow Austrian Arnold Schwarzenegger.

Josh knew the restaurant well, having been associate architect to the microbrewery. Since City Restaurant, with partner Kellen he had designed Rondo and then on his own as Schweitzer BIM designed Campanile, the restaurant of chefs Mark Peel and Nancy Silverton, which opened in July 1989. His redesign budget for Border Grill Santa Monica, however, was a meager $65,000.

"The idea for Border Grill was all art. The entire space is a big painting, playing on the idea that what you find in Central America and Mexico is mural art." Josh designed the furniture from ripped-up 2 × 10 southern yellow pine, along with uniforms and fixtures.

Josh hired English-Canadian graphic super artists Su Huntley and Donna Muir. By then, in 1990, Huntley and Muir were already famous for music (Sting's video *Bring on the Night,* and a Joan Armatrading album cover) and books (covers for Sylvia Plath and Kurt Vonnegut). Josh asked them to create huge murals based on Mexico's Day of the Dead, complete with giant devils against a dark ceiling.

"I look at it as a desire to express the idea of Mexican restaurant different from the way City Restaurant was expressed," Josh later said. "The idea of fun and food and music and drinking, it is a real festive idea. And even playing with the idea that we have these devil figures in there, the whole day of the dead, the celebration of death and just about anything—I love that idea, and I think this restaurant is supposed to be about that."

It was one of the first upscale American restaurants to specialize in Oaxacan cuisine, though of course with the special Milliken and Feniger twist of formal French training applied. "I think what Mary Sue and Susan bring to their style of cooking and restaurants is an exuberance that reflects their own personalities. They are colorful; their food is colorful and boldly flavored. And it's all a reflection of themselves," said *Bon Apétit*'s Fairchild.

MARY Sue and Susan were part of a self-conscious confidence that permeated the Los Angeles chef scene in the 1980s, a decade not only of celebrity chefs but of music videos and rockumentaries—the decade of *This Is Spinal Tap* (1984). Another chef-restaurateur who was caught up in the times was Michael McCarty, owner of Michael's of Los Angeles and New York and a cofounder with Julia Child and Robert Mondavi of the American Institute of Wine & Food (AIWF). McCarty made a rockumentary-like film based on footage of the 1982 AIWF gala dinner at the Stanford Court Hotel in San Francisco. The AIWF gala had featured Julia Child with ten rising regional chefs: Alice Waters, Wolfgang Puck, Mark Miller, Paul Prudhomme, Jimmy Schmidt, Larry Forgione, Barbara Kafka, Bradley Ogden, Jonathan Waxman, and McCarty himself (who trained in Paris). Many other Art-aspiring segments appear, including a long, very amateur Spago dance video with shots of Wolfgang and Barbara.

Local PBS station KCET shot a more professional documentary of the opening of City Restaurant, very much within the tone of McCarty's documentary (and even featuring McCarty as an interviewer). The documentary opened with shots of Fritz Lang's 1927 silent film *Metropolis* (i.e., "City"), then switched to modern-day Los Angeles, where it zoomed in on two women in chef's whites and sunglasses cruising the streets on motorcycles. Once past this amusing opening, the documentary bogged down with snapshots of Mary Sue and Susan interacting with construction workers, Mary Sue attempting to glaze the tandoori oven (but only managing to set her oven glove on fire), Susan walking the restaurant with an inspector.

The documentary provides insight on the Girls' appeal to public and press: their unusual dress, including bangles, cropped hair with offbeat highlights, attitudes daring for the times, and the unvoiced question of whether they were involved with each other. The spotlight shone more often on their exuberant personalities than on their food: young chefs making hip food in a cool restaurant. In fact, they were pioneers in building chef personalities and creating their own celebrity status, much as Wolfgang was doing at Spago. Even if the food was good and cutting edge—which it was—the spotlight was on Puck & Lazaroff and Milliken & Feniger as personalities.

City Café had enjoyed its own special self-conscious style. "One of the things about City Restaurant was to re-create that intimacy," said Josh about his design effort. To help re-create that at the new restaurant, "they had a closed-circuit TV at the bar—so diners could watch the kitchen line. In the beginning they were hamming it up all the time. They would be doing stuff like picking up duck bills and heads. People were caught up in their drinks, and they would look up and see this. It was pretty funny."

All good things come to an end, especially such heady, carefree days, and anyone in Los Angeles who was less than ready for disaster was soon to be hard hit. Mary Sue and Susan would be among them.

AFTER a few years of inexperienced general managers, Susan and Mary Sue hired Kevin Finch, first to run Border Grill Santa Monica and two years later also City Restaurant. Kevin was an experienced food and beverage director who had worked primarily in northern California. Having hailed from Los Angeles, however, he knew the chefs' reputations well.

Kevin recalled how the Girls were running the restaurants when he arrived. "They were totally chefs. Their financial reports were not designed to capture data. It was more like retail than like most restaurants. I had come from a good hotel, and hotels are good at financial data and organizing the data to let you know if you are making money or not. Labor cost is this, wine cost is this, beer costs is this," but that kind of data was missing from Border Grill and City Restaurant.

With the financial systems Kevin put in place, the chefs were able to focus on profit and loss for the first time. They were finally able to see where they were losing money.

Mary Sue said, "Barbara and Gai brought the business expertise. We didn't know much about business at all. And that's one of the real stumbling blocks for chefs. You know, you're really focused on food, you're really, really passionate—and then there's never a good time—and no one really likes it that much—for learning about business—all the things that go hand-in-hand with business: how to run it, the ups and downs, how to imagine the future, how to control costs, how to increase sales, none of that. So, for us, we felt that this was a good match. The eyeglass people had the business sense. They knew what a P&L was; we didn't."

Meanwhile Susan and Barbara had broken up, which added strain to the five-way partnership. Eventually, Susan and Mary Sue decided to dissolve the partnership with Barbara, Gai, and Margo. According to the dissolution, which became public in September 1991, L.A. Eyeworks would keep the Border Grill café on Melrose, and the Girls would keep City Restaurant and Border Grill Santa Monica. The chefs borrowed six digits from their Santa Monica landlord to the pay off immediate debt to L.A. Eyeworks and were then left with a buyout agreement in their contract based on current earnings.

The settlement deal with L.A. Eyewear created a severe burden on their resources. Mary Sue said of the experience, "In retrospect, if I were to do another buyout like that, I would base it on *future* earnings so, if you decide or want to leave, you have value in and should retain it."

Then the first of several *forces majeures* hit Los Angeles.

Force majeure is a contractual term that excuses a party from liability if an unforeseen event beyond control prevents the performing of its obligations. A *force majeure* would be a natural disaster, war, or the failure of a third party—such as a supplier or subcontractor. But, as Kevin Finch observed, contracts were never one of the Girls' strong points.

On April 29, 1992, four white LAPD cops were acquitted of charges of assault made upon Rodney King. Los Angeles exploded. By the next morning, 13 people were dead, 192 injured, and 40 of 140 fires were still burning out of control. Looting and violence continued. Mayor Tom Bradley declared a state of emergency, and Governor Pete Wilson sent in 2,000 National Guard MPs. By May 4, the U.S. Army and Marines had joined the National Guard in a city where 55 people had been killed, 10,000 businesses destroyed, and over $1 billion of property lost.

"The riots were up and down La Brea on either end of where City was. La Brea was definitely ravaged," said Mary Sue.

At 4:31 a.m. on January 17, 1994, a magnitude 6.8 earthquake centered at Northridge, California, hit the Southlands, with aftershocks that lasted for weeks in the magnitude 4.0–5.0 range. Fifty-seven people died and 1,500 people were seriously injured. For days, 9,000 homes and businesses had no electricity, 20,000 had no gas, and 48,000 had little or no water. It was "one of the costliest natural disasters in U.S. history" and "the most damaging earthquake to strike the United States since the San Francisco Earthquake of 1906," with damage initially estimated in March 1994 at over $15 billion.

After the business day concluded on Tuesday, December 6, 1994, the government of Orange County, California, filed for Chapter 9 Municipal Bankruptcy, a figure that would eventually spill over $2 billion, the "largest governmental fiscal failure in U.S. history," according to the *Los Angeles Times*. Within 20 months, Los Angeles' unforeseen losses would exceed $20 billion.

L.A. Eyeworks had reacted to the Rodney King riots almost immediately, closing the original Border Grill café less than 60 days later, in July 1992. Along with the economy, Barbara McReynolds cited specifically "exorbitant workers' compensation insurance costs" as the key factor in the closure. At the same time, she claimed that the L.A. Eyeworks partners would open a new restaurant in the café's spot. So, L.A. Eyeworks fired all 20 employees at Border Grill café and offered 50 percent of the partnership to a new investor. The deal never materialized, and L.A. Eyeworks returned the café space to the landlords.

After the riots, City Restaurant and Border Grill Santa Monica also started to slide into the red. City was in worse shape than Border Grill. City Restaurant, the former carpet warehouse, had a steep rent. The area was still a largely industrial stretch of La Brea Avenue, making it a "destination" restaurant whose clientele had to be drawn to the neighborhood specifically for itself. After the riots and the earthquake, people did not venture far from their own neighborhoods.

Unable to meet payments to their former partner, the Girls realized that they might lose their entire business.

First they renegotiated their rent for both City Restaurant and Border Grill. They had a great lawyer, another of Susan's Pitzer classmates, Wendy Glenn, who, along with Josh and, later, toy industry executive Bruce Stein, formed a nucleus of advisors to the Girls. Then they called up Rich Melman, whom they had met when they were inducted into the D'Artagnan Cervena *Who's Who of Food and Beverage Professionals* at the

James Beard Awards back in 1985. Melman, one of America's most successful restaurateurs, owns the Chicago-based Lettuce Entertain You, Inc.

Mary Sue said, "We called Rich up and said, 'We are really worried. We are losing money.' We had limited partners who had no liability, but we were personally liable to our partners for the rent and the debt. Border Grill had opened, and we were not doing well there either, so we had debt associated with Border Grill, too."

Melman sent a crack team, CFO David Swinghamer and head of business development Gerard Centioli, in exchange for future consulting on his restaurants. For two days, Swinghamer and Centioli pored over the books for the two restaurants. They found that the chefs were bleeding $1,500 a day just staying open for lunch. They closed for lunch and stopped the bleeding. Swinghamer and Centioli also recommended they sell one of the restaurants.

Privately, operations director Kevin Finch agreed.

"Border Grill was making money: City wasn't. Like a lot of restaurants of the 1980s, City had a reputation as being expensive, esoteric, with a lot of attitude, and notorious for a snotty *maître d'*. In the early 1990s, the ad agencies went out of business. The movies became accountable. Trump went out of business. Michael's almost went out of business. It was a very hard time in the restaurant business. There was a transition in the nineties to less expensive, more cheerful, more upbeat restaurants instead of mean-spirited and well dressed. The energy was in casual Italian: we couldn't figure out how to adapt City. Goat cheese quesadillas didn't make sense anymore," recalled Finch.

Then local restaurateur Ron Salisbury, president of Restaurant Business of La Habra, California, offered to buy the lease for City Restaurant. The reduced-rent lease was extremely attractive to Salisbury, who was looking for a property close to his home.

The Girls made the decision and parted with City Restaurant in March 1994 to save their company.

The closure of City had immediate, everyday consequences. Kevin had to leave, as they no longer had two restaurants to underwrite his salary. Furthermore, without their former business partners, whom they had relied on for running their businesses, the chefs were forced into more administrative work themselves. Even with just Border Grill in Santa Monica, they found themselves further and further from the kitchen.

"This is the problem with great chefs: they get pulled out of the kitchen

Courtesy of Mary Sue Milliken and Susan Feniger

EXTERIOR OF CITY RESTAURANT

and bogged down with the management and administrative aspects of running a restaurant, and then there are so many of them that they don't spend time doing what they do best—and what they don't do best is the administrative side of things," said Swinghamer. "They might be OK at it, but they don't excel at it. All of a sudden, the food suffers a little bit, because they aren't in the kitchen as much, which affects the sales, and all of a sudden it starts crumbling."

During the 1980s, Susan had drawn many people into her world: high-school sweetheart Josh, comrade-in-arms and business partner Mary Sue, college friend and lawyer Wendy Glenn, companion and business partner Barbara, and others. They were intertwined in each other's lives—particularly Josh and Mary Sue. Susan told Mary Sue from the first time they met, "You gotta meet my ex-husband. You guys would be perfect together." Not too long after they meet, Josh and Mary Sue began to live together and eventually married. Susan is godmother to their two sons.

In the early 1990s, however, the Girls suffered great losses: their business partner L.A. Eyeworks, their employees at City, and their first restaurant itself. In addition, Susan had lost her companion Barbara. In those dark days of 1994–1995, Susan retreated into work at Border Grill in Santa Monica: both chefs underwent a mourning period.

Mary Sue said, "It was a horribly difficult, excruciating decision, just like cutting off your arm. City was groundbreaking. It had put us on the map. It was really, really hard [to close it]. It took a lot out of me, for sure."

As Kevin said years later, "That was a big blow, because City was their baby. City was like their firstborn child, not Border Grill. It was their first one, and it made them stars."

Instead of crumbling or wallowing in grief, Susan and Mary Sue shifted into new roles. Mary Sue had become increasingly fascinated with research, education, and performance, despite her stage fright. Susan became even more committed to staying as close to their restaurant kitchens as possible. "I don't want to be in meetings, in front of my computer. If I never did a cookbook, I could care less. For me, cookbooks, TV, articles, all that stuff for me, well, I would rather take care of the restaurant."

In 1994, Kevin saw Susan as completely tied to the restaurants. "Susan is totally a restaurant person. In fact, she is the strongest restaurant person I have ever worked with in my life. She is phenomenally talented in the kitchen. In a busy restaurant she can jump in anywhere and make herself useful. She is passionate about day-to-day cooking, tasting everything, nudging cooks. She is a restaurant animal. And it's not just the kitchen: she is a gifted front-of-the-house person, too, really talented. She has always spent time greeting guests, connecting with them. She gets her energy in some ways from interacting with guests."

Kevin saw Mary Sue as a much different person. "Mary Sue is more of a food person than a restaurant person. She is not drawn to the restaurant like Susan. Her interests are in food, in all the intellectual and artistic elements of food. Some of it has to do with restaurants, and some doesn't. Mary Sue is not driven to open up a restaurant in the morning and train cooks, while Susan is. Susan is part of the fabric of a restaurant."

"It makes them a powerful team," he said. "It's good to have that element of someone interested purely in food. It keeps them fresh."

The wonderful thing about real working partnerships is that when one cannot carry, the other can take over. Susan had been carrying them for years. It had been restaurant life nonstop. Now it was Mary Sue's turn to lead. Strangely enough, it was Mary Sue's forays into media, founded on a passion shared with Susan for teaching, that would make them one of the hottest household names in the cooking world.

FROM the start of their partnership, Mary Sue and Susan taught cooking in their rare spare time. They began to teach at Ma Cuisine, the cooking school at Ma Maison, and have continued throughout their careers.

Teaching forced them continually to reconsider their own philosophies about food and cuisine and their roles in their restaurant kitchens. "We were able to verbalize our philosophies about food to an audience, and let each other know, and get committed to them," said Mary Sue.

Although they were based in the environs of Hollywood, they only became enmeshed in "The Industry" in 1988, when Susan and Mary Sue cofounded an annual fund-raising event with another of Susan's college friends, Sharon Monsky. They called it *Cool Comedy/Hot Cuisine*, featuring the Girls' spicy foods and great comedy acts. Over the years, comedians who appeared included Robin Williams, Dana Carvey, Lily Tomlin, Louie Anderson, Rita Rudner, Howie Mandel, Rosie O'Donnell, Ellen DeGeneres, the late John Candy, and Bob Sagat.

The beneficiary was the Scleroderma Research Foundation, founded in 1987 by Monsky and the only organization in the nation dedicated exclusively to finding a cure for a little known but widespread disease, scleroderma, a chronic, degenerative, autoimmune disease that attacks the body's connective tissue. Sharon Monsky suffered from it herself. The Girls found out in 1985, the year after her diagnosis; since then, they have raised some $14 million. Sharon passed away in 2002, but the chefs remain committed to SRF in memory of their friend. "We raised over $1 million in 2002 from one dinner. We started off in their restaurant, and now we have to hold it in a major hotel," said foundation vice president Charles Spaulding.

It was Mary Sue's interest in cookbooks, however, that edged them further into showbiz. With Susan's help, in 1989 Mary Sue published their first cookbook, *City Cuisine*, cowritten with Helene Siegel. Siegel remembers having to meet them at City Restaurant during the lunch rush to take notes as they tested recipes for the book. Recalled Siegel, "I was in the kitchen with my little pad chasing them around. It was total chaos." Nevertheless, the book they produced defined the Girls, setting down recipes from their work in other restaurants, family recipes, and new recipes at City Restaurant.

In 1994, the threesome turned out *Mesa Mexicana*. Books continued to appear: *Cantina* (1996), *Cooking with Too Hot Tamales* (1997), *Mexican Cooking for Dummies* (1999), and *Mexican Cooking Essentials for Dummies* (2002).

The last link in the chain came as an invitation in 1992 for the Girls to be included among 16 chefs on *Julia Child—Cooking with Master Chefs* produced by A La Carte Communications Geof Drummond. Now they had a serious TV credit. Their episode was shot in Mary Sue's home for a session of "contemporary Far Eastern vegetarian cooking." Child introduced them as "a lively pair of teachers."

Mesa Mexicana had just been published in 1994 by William Morrow, and their publicist had placed the two chefs on David Rosengarten and Donna Hanover's Food Network show *Food News and Views* in the fall of 1994 to plug the book. That was when they came to the attention of Reese Schonfeld, founder and president of the Food Network.

Schonfeld, a veteran newsman, already had under his belt one successful, national cable channel, Cable News Network (CNN), financed mainly by Atlanta businessman Ted Turner. In 1992, he started work on what would become the Television Food Network. It took 18 months to develop the concept, lay out the framework, and finance it; when it suddenly crystallized, Schonfeld had three months to create the content. The Food Network scrambled for talent, especially female chefs who, the network thought, would appeal to the mostly female audience they were targeting. After their appearance on *Food News and Views*, the Food Network invited the Girls for *Chef du Jour.*

MARY SUE AND SUSAN WITH JULIA CHILD

Courtesy of Mary Sue Milliken and Susan Feniger

Wife and producer Pat O'Gorman invented *Chef Du Jour* as "the perfect screen test for a new network," according to Schonfeld. "We brought in chefs from everywhere. They did five shows in two days. We watched their progress: either they improved in two days or they didn't. We ran all the shows anyway, but some we really liked."

The Girls ran the gauntlet like everyone else: they shot their five episodes in two days and had them run the following week. Schonfeld suggested that they turn it into a regular show on air, and they accepted.

Pat O'Gorman remembered that, unlike other chefs, the Girls needed little coaching and were immediately comfortable in front of the television cameras. "A lot of other chefs saw themselves as being special. Like 'I will show you what I can do, but I don't think you can do it.' Susan and Mary Sue always had fun. They didn't make cooking a mystery. They had a passion for cooking. It was so obvious. People loved watching them; they fell in love with them. Those two really had a love affair with the camera."

Schonfeld was a tough negotiator who fought and won the right to co-own the title, "Too Hot Tamales," which Mary Sue and Susan had come up with. They signed the contract August 1, 1995, and three weeks later started filming in New York. They flew to New York every five or six weeks for a grueling schedule filming as many shows as they could fit in. The Food Network proposed the show title *Girls South of the Border,* but a friend of Susan's came up with *Too Hot Tamales.* They tried it out for a week and liked the sound.

Too Hot Tamales featured the Girls making dishes in a mock Mexican kitchen, bantering with each other while teaching about ingredients and cooking techniques. They looked young and hip and made cooking look easy and accessible.

They came out with a line of chilies especially for the show with Shep Gordon's Alive Entertainment. They published many of the recipes from the show in a book, *Cooking with Too Hot Tamales.*

According to Martha Wright, former newsletter writer and PR manager for the Girls, *Tamales World Tour,* came about because the head of programming, Eileen Opatut, thought their emphasis on Latin food had played out and was too limited. The idea was to tap into other cuisines that had inspired Mary Sue and Susan, chiefly Thai, Indian, and French.

Mary Sue was largely responsible for writing the shows, testing the recipes, and choosing the material. The chefs invited their cookbook collaborator, Helene Siegel, to help write the shows, but she turned it down as the money was too modest, so they turned to other writers and assistants, particularly Martha Wright.

Reruns remained on the air for several years, and they were on air from 1995 to 1999. Altogether they filmed 296 episodes before *Too Hot Tamales* and *Tamales World Tour* were canceled in 1999. The Food Network had changed CEOs several times during the show's airing, ending for them with the presidency of another newsman, Eric Ober. Both shows were very popular, but those close to the Food Network say that they were moving away from education toward more entertainment.

Though *Too Hot Tamales* certainly did try to instruct, the show was far cry from purely educational programming. There was the banter between the two chefs that made for a lively show. Susan, for all her reluctance to do media, was very playful on camera, with Mary Sue her constant foil.

"The great thing is having Susan; I wouldn't have done any of this by myself," Mary Sue said. "It's more interesting for whoever is watching. There is a dialogue. Now, the reason that so many people don't have partners is that it's a lot of work. You don't get your way all the time. You have to have arguments, difficult things. Emeril or Wolf can say, 'This is the way it's going to be'—they don't have Susan to answer to!"

Logistically, the shows could be more interesting because with two chefs one could be talking while one was preparing or doing something else. Also, as Mary Sue put it, "People could really relate [to our show]. Things had to look like they really did in somebody's cupboard. You know, nobody has a bunch of little petri dishes that they cook with—that drives me nuts!"

By 1997 Susan was itching to open a new restaurant. Mary Sue, with two children and a heavy media schedule, was still spooked by the closing of City Restaurant and reluctant to open anything new. They reached a decision on a cross-country flight to New York to tape more episodes of *Too Hot Tamales.* Susan said, "This is not enough for me. I don't want to do only TV and books. My heart isn't in it. We have to figure it out, either do it together or, you know, we have to figure out what we want to do."

Bolstered by their TV success, Mary Sue acquiesced, and Susan pursued a new restaurant with a vengeance. She fell in love with Los Angeles' quiet downtown. Trying to follow the success of converting the cheap

Santa Monica space into a restaurant, she found a space that ironically had been years earlier the space of City's successor, Sonora restaurant.

Recalled Swinghamer, who had become one of the chefs' informal advisors, "Susan ran the deal by me. I said, the deal makes sense to me from a deal point of view, but I can't tell you if you are going to do great sales there. Only you know that, and you know L.A. better than I do."

The chefs opened their new restaurant in 1998. They invested the three years they had spent exploring the foods of Latin America on their second television show, *Tamales World Tour,* in this new restaurant, Ciudad or "City" in Spanish, which reflected both their earlier restaurant and their new fame as Latin American experts.

With most of their new customers coming from their television shows and only aware of Border Grill, however, they needed to link Ciudad to their other restaurants.

"It was an upscale version of what they are doing [at Border Grill]," said Josh. "It was 'City,' applied in a Latin way. It had a more refined quality to it. It was inspired by the Latin America of the 1960s, with a cool, jazzy, samba quality—and that to me was what the design should speak of."

With a $650,000 budget, the same amount raised for City Restaurant, Josh brought back muralists Huntley and Muir to take off from their Border Grill murals with similar color schemes of mustard and ochres for Ciudad. "We used the [same] tiles and murals, and bold colors and design. I did the design for plates at Ciudad first before I went back and did it for Border Grill."

The Girls brought back Kevin Finch, who had been running the City Walk restaurants for Universal Studios and was then managing at Universal Restaurant Group. Kevin was willing to return—as long as he became a partner and got equity in new ventures. So, in 1997, they formed Mundo Management to run any new restaurants the three partners got involved in. Each new restaurant is a separate limited liability company, managed by Mundo. Kevin brought with him Carollynn Bartosh as head of public relations.

Kevin, who is fluent in Spanish and had traveled throughout Latin America, has claimed that the idea for Ciudad was his, while Susan has said that it is hers.

"Ciudad was intellectually really cool, more expensive to run—and has never been quite a go," said Kevin. They found it difficult to cut into the happy hour business of nearby restaurants, and downtown Los Angeles died around 8:00 p.m., leaving the restaurant struggling to develop a following. It was hard to convince their customers to pay double or triple the price for dishes that sounded like cheap Mexican classics, enchiladas, or tortillas, Kevin explained.

In 2000, Samuel Goldwyn Films asked the Girls to work as real-life chefs behind two fictional chefs in the remake of Ang Lee's *Eat Drink Man Woman.* Goldwyn had rights that included a remake. Project leaders John Bard Manulis and Lulu Zezza had Vera Blasi rewrite it to appeal to America's fastest growing ethnic group, Latinos, and so *Tortilla Soup* was concocted.

The film cast Hector Elizondo as patriarch and owner of a classical Mexican restaurant who has lost his sense of taste but is still trying to rule his three daughters. The middle daughter, played by Jacqueline Obradors, dreams of creating a more modern, Latin cuisine. There are seven meals in the movie, including a restaurant scene.

Zezza called Carollynn Bartosh, told her about the project, and sent her the script for a first read. "With this one, I was really excited," said Carollynn, "because it was completely *made* for them. . . . Classically trained chefs, food from Mexico—completely Border Grill, while Ciudad is that same classical training with that contemporary edge, means it was a great branding opportunity as well as a great showcase for the Girls."

Mary Sue had a different take. "At first, we had no intention of doing the food for *Tortilla Soup,*" Milliken told the *Richmond Times Dispatch.* "We sure weren't going to make any money for it. The budget for the whole film was only $2 million. Then it suddenly dawned on us that if we didn't do it, they'd have to get somebody else and the food wouldn't be authentic. It would be all wrong. The two styles of food in *Tortilla Soup* are what we're all about."

There were several food movies in the previous year, though few with any chefs. *Chocolat* (2000) had no chocolatier—though it did have Juliette Binoche, Alfred Molina, Carrie-Anne Moss, Lena Olin, Leslie Caron, and Judi Dench, not to mention Johnny Depp. *Woman on Top* (2000), with a screenplay also by Vera Blasi, featured Penelope Cruz as a Brazilian chef suffering from motion sickness. *What's Cooking* (2000) went light on food and heavy on the intersecting lives of Joan Chen, Julianna Margolis, Mercedes Ruehl, Kyra Sedgwick, and Alfre Woodard. *Dinner Rush* (2000) with Danny Aiello dealt with the New York restaurant scene rather than food. Then there was *Big Night* (1996), which added a food stylist to a cast starring Stanley Tucci and Tony Shalhoub. *Like Water for Chocolate* (1993) did much to start this spate, including *A Walk in the Clouds* (1995).

"Mary Sue and I were at some appearance," Carollynn said, "and Susan was on the set from 6:00 a.m. until 11:00 at night. It was in Encino. It was hot. It was summer. There was this little cooking tent outside with a fan, but it was 105° without the fan. Susan used to tell me, 'Carollynn, this better be worth it.'"

"It was a tough, tough shoot," lead Hector Elizondo told *New Times Los Angeles*. "The temperature was up to 120 degrees. Feniger and Milliken were creating food for the table and had to keep everything looking fresh. . . . The first thing I was impressed with was how the kitchen's rhythm was like that of an orchestra. You could feel the music, the pots, all the dishes going at the same time. Susan and Mary Sue were immune to heat. I couldn't touch the roast peppers, but their hands were like asbestos. And they can chop without looking."

The Girls had to teach the actors how to act like chefs: how to chop and handle food, how to mix ingredients, and how to cook the food that was presented. Manulis assigned one chef to each of the two cooking actors to take full advantage of developing their characters.

"Milliken and Feniger have each a distinct style, and we have two chef characters, that is part of the script—the part we had to make tangible. One of the ladies worked as Jacqui, and one as Hector. That was really handy," Manulis said.

Naturally, Border Grill, with its more traditional Mexican cuisine, represented the father's cuisine and Ciudad, with its innovative, pan-Latin food, the daughter's.

The chefs set up a tent kitchen beside the house where the movie was filmed and arrived early to prep the food for each day's scene. They would make sure everything looked authentic and then leave it to their staff to manage the food for the day.

The chefs quickly discovered how different food for a movie had to be. Associate Producer Lulu Zezza recalled many meetings before shooting started to get the dishes dramatic enough for the film.

"The fun part was the design of the food. We were concerned early on that the dishes look different for Hector and Carmen. We needed colors, architecture. After all, if you can't smell it, it has to look *really* good. We had to think about how it was going to play."

There were classic moments of near disaster behind the scenes. In one of the final shots, a suckling pig dominates the family dining table, but as Manulis recalled, the pig sat too high for the table-level camera to see over. They had only two pigs for the whole shoot, so there was no leeway for experimentation, much less failure. Fortunately, they had real, expert chefs on call. "Susan said, 'Give me a knife!' She took the pig and cut off the bottom half lengthwise, which lowered the pig on the table," Zezza said.

Reviewers had a field day playing with the food.

One wrote, "The camera lingers over such dishes as tangerine glazed lamb (courtesy of celebrity chefs Mary Sue Milliken and Susan Feniger of L.A.'s Border Grill and Ciudad restaurants) like a lecher over a glistening naked body. I knew I shouldn't have seen this movie on an empty stomach."

Many agreed that despite names like Hector Elizondo, Raquel Welch, and Elizabeth Peña, the food was the star of the movie. "The audience at a recent screening oohed and ahhed as Martin presented little Yolanda (Constance Marie) with tiny tomatoes filled with guacamole. You just want to reach right onto the screen and pluck one off the plate."

As shooting got underway, Mary Sue and Carollynn met with Sam Goldwyn, Jr., and Meyer Gottlieb, the president. The Goldwyn executives were focused on crossover into the large Latin audience in the U.S. Carollynn offered to get them entry into the food world and wound up in weekly meetings with the movie's advertisers, distributors, and promoters.

In hindsight, all the parties now know they need more lead time for marketing opportunities in food. Carollynn saw the finished film only in May for what was originally a June release, which gave her little lead time to approach magazines for sponsorship opportunities for products by companies like Kitchen Aid and All-Clad. Though the film was eventually released in August, most food magazines are "put to bed" some three months in advance. The Girls had missed big sponsorship promotion deals. Reviewers noticed, too, such as the *Pittsburgh Post-Gazette:*

> We loved Hector Elizondo ("Chicago Hope," "Pretty Woman") as the widowed father—heck, I'd marry the guy just for his kitchen equipment.
>
> We did wonder if a chef who runs a restaurant would really devote every weekend to cooking for his family, but isn't that what love's about?

"Look at that stove!" Ace whispered.

"Did you notice the refrigerator?" I whispered back.

All Carollynn could do was chase publicity. They barely made the annual Aspen *Food & Wine* Classic event, without even time to be listed on their roster. She worked with Sur La Table and *Bon Appétit* magazine on events in Dallas and Los Angeles that featured screenings, meet-and-greet's with the Girls, and receptions at Sur La Table retail stores. She also worked on screenings and meet-and-greet's at Share Our Strength benefits in Denver and Phoenix. Those events happened before the national opening on August 14, 2001. Sur La Table also sponsored a national sweepstakes to both restaurants to taste the food of both restaurants as seen in the movie.

True, the film's closing credits led with "Food and Menus Created and Designed by Mary Sue Milliken and Susan Feniger," an unheard-of honor and opportunity for the Girls that was noted by newspapers, but since the film was hard hit by 9/11 the exposure was less than hoped for. Also, at the box office the film was more successful not in the anticipated Latin neighborhoods but in more affluent, white neighborhoods and art house theaters—the same demographic as Sur La Table's.

Gottlieb suggested an accompanying cookbook, but Mary Sue and Carollynn vetoed it as "too heavy-handed" for such a light-hearted movie. This attitude ignored the success of a number of cookbooks cum movie documentaries, such as the book accompanying *Room with a View* by producer Ismail Merchant called *Ismail Merchant's Florence: Filming & Feasting in Florence.*

This attitude also ignored the potential success for packaging their *Tortilla Soup* recipes as a potential "best of" collection. Less than two years later, Wolfgang Puck published the *Live, Love & Eat: The Best of Wolfgang Puck* cookbook.

They opted instead for the inclusion of ten recipes on the film's music CD. Distributed by Virgin Records, with music by Latin jazz artists including Cuba's Eliades Ochoa (*Buena Vista Social Club*) and Venezuela's Los Amigos Invisibles, the CD was available online, at record retail stores, and at Sur La Table retail stores. Amazon.com mentions "what must be a soundtrack first, a series of individual menu cards relating to the film are inserted with the liner notes"—right there, one can tell that few people would be looking in the CD of a film soundtrack for food recipes.

Overall, the Girls were just not ready to handle the marketing minutiae that go into making a film profitable. People noticed, too. *Daily Variety* reported, "Ironically, after watching the intensive preparation of gourmet Mexican food for 90 minutes, the tortilla chips and variety of salsas at the after-party in the DGA (Directors' Guild Association) lobby were sadly unsatisfying."

Susan had a lighter take on the experience. In anticipation of any future movies, she said, "Mary Sue is working on the software for her new invention, 'Smell-a-Vision.'"

The movie's release in August 2001, a few weeks before 9/11, almost guaranteed that it would fare poorly in the box office. Americans were staying home the next month to watch the horror of 9/11 again and again on their televisions rather than going out to see films in theaters. *Tortilla Soup* only grossed $4.5 million in ticket sales. John Manulis, now head of VisionBox, a postproduction company, believes that *Tortilla Soup* did quite well in the video market at over 300,000 units, distributed by Columbia Tristar. "It is also one of the most successful American independent digital films, outside of *The Blair Witch Project*," he said.

BY the time they had wrapped up shooting for *Tortilla Soup* the Girls were publicly discussing a new TV series. They were working with 44 Blue Productions to sell the show to Los Angeles's main PBS station KCET. The show was tentatively titled *Border Girls*.

The TV show would help them to leverage their relationship with Whole Foods, a natural food store that was in its second decade of expanding and acquiring similar and complementary companies across America. Mary Sue and Susan began to work with them in 1999, after several years of running into Elizabeth Carovillano, Whole Foods Market marketing director for the Southern Pacific region, at charity events, community fund-raisers, and conferences on organic sustainability. The Girls could help Whole Foods reach out to the foodie community with gourmet, artisanal, and their own unique products, in addition to Whole Foods' own organic and natural products.

In October 2000, the Girls cooked a Whole Foods dinner in honor of Sandy Gooch, whose Los Angeles natural foods store had been bought out by Whole Foods in 1993. By the end of that winter, in February 2001, they were holding cooking demonstrations under the Whole Foods banner.

The chefs developed products that would be prepared in the Whole Foods commissary that serviced Southern California, Arizona, and Nevada. The products would include burritos, salsas, quesadillas, soups, hummus, and marinades. The chefs would do in-store demonstrations, promotions, and commercials, and their writer, Helene Siegel, would provide content for the Whole Foods store flyers.

The products would launch in 2001, branded under the name "Border Girls," because the Food Network would not release the name "Too Hot Tamales" for their use.

Then KCET passed on the TV project, after much debate and also difficulties the Girls faced in raising financing. There would be no *Border Girls* TV show. Whole Foods was left with a new problem of continuing to launch the brand themselves, rather than piggybacking on the TV show.

A Border Girls Tour 2002 promotion for Whole Foods ran successfully in Los Angeles for six months, and the relationship was on track to go much further than a line of Mexican foods. Whole Foods was looking to hire the chefs to be experts on all gourmet foods, rather than just health or all-natural food.

Said one person knowledgeable of the deal, "The thing about celebrity chefs is that there are a lot of other celebrity chefs out there, and they [Whole Foods] could get them for free to promote their stuff. The question came up internally: why should they be paying Mary Sue and Susan when they can get other chefs to come in for free?" Others felt the Whole Foods deal fell apart because the Girls had no TV name to use, either the past "Too Hot Tamales" or the passed-over "Border Girls" series.

Mary Sue and Susan were unable to sell their product line or promotional abilities to the rest of the corporation's regions, and the whole plan was downscaled to just the Southwest region for the product line.

MEANWHILE, Susan kept pursuing other locations for new Border Grills. She considered San Diego and Orange County but was drawn to Las Vegas. Mary Sue had no interest in expanding to Las Vegas, so as with Ciudad Susan was left to pursue a new restaurant on her own.

She was first approached by the Venetian Resort Hotel Casino but turned down an offer she deemed ungenerous; also, she wanted to avoid unionized labor, which she understood had dogged other restaurants. Then, a local, well-connected lawyer named Jay Brown, who was working with the Venetian, introduced her to the Mandalay Bay Resort Group. Brown also introduced her to American Vantages Company, which owned 49 percent of Mandalay Bay and was willing to back Border Grill. Susan talked the deal over with Mary Sue and Kevin, and they made the deal. As with the hotel, American Vantages Company owned 49 percent of Border Grill and the Girls 51 percent.

The hotel casino built out the restaurant with $800,000 of its own money; the investment company put in $2.2 million. That amount was nearly four times what they had previously spent on a restaurant and was their first restaurant in a new building. "That is an area, negotiating deals—we are very weak there. It is not a strength of mine, and certainly not of Mary Sue and Susan," noted Kevin.

Border Grill opened in June 1999. Initially, Mandalay Bay proved to be a terrible location at the end of the strip. The restaurant was next to a planned convention center, as yet unopened, and a shark exhibit, also a year from completion.

"I think they probably needed to fill a spot that no one wanted," admitted Susan. "For the first two and a half years, everyone thought we had the worst location." Without foot traffic, it was difficult to lure customers to their own remote location. According to Mary Sue, they did renegotiate a good rent and utilities deal.

Said Kevin, "First we did badly. It's a tricky location. One of the things is that we became a bad team in planning restaurants. We all disagreed. We had these funny loyalties with Josh, Mary Sue, and Susan, and me. We ended up with no one happy with the restaurants."

In the midst of this division, Josh had to wrestle with the physical identity of the new restaurant. Much of the character of Border Grill in Santa Monica was based on the age of its building, the low budget, and the preexisting microbrewery. "There is not that funky floor, and I wasn't interested in replicating. So, how do you make it so you can have that same fresh, fun feeling in a restaurant that is going to be way more polished?"

The chefs were hard clients, but ultimately Border Grill Las Vegas wound up with the murals and the strong colors of Mexico in the style of the Santa Monica flagship restaurant but with huge windows opening onto walkways and outdoor seating that create a more polished, open, and light space.

On top of everything else, Border Grill's operations in Las Vegas were jinxed from the beginning. Their first and second executive chefs were hired and fired in short order. Meanwhile, as more high-end restaurateurs and chef-restaurateurs joined the gold rush of restaurant openings in Las Vegas, they found themselves losing staff to higher paying restaurants and winding up with less talented staff in the front of the house and the kitchen. Kevin spent nearly half his time there trying to put out fires, along with Susan and PR manager Bartosh. In Vegas terms, it seemed that they just kept rolling sevens, Kevin said.

The third time proved the charm when in May 2000 they hired a more seasoned chef, Chris Mortenson. Married to children's book author and illustrator Lisa Kopelke, Chris was very able to resist the lures of Las Vegas and grow the restaurant. Border Grill had lost money in the first year and a half, but with Chris in the kitchen and the shark exhibition and convention center opened, it finally began to pull in customers.

TOWARD the end of 2001, the Girls opened a third and fourth Border Grill, one on September 28 in Pasadena, California, and the other on December 18 in the Green Valley Ranch, less than 10 miles south of the Las Vegas Strip.

Pasadena was Kevin Finch's idea, set in a suburban mall with 400 high-rise apartments, a spa, a supermarket, and a gym. Border Grill was on the second floor, without sidewalk traffic. Kevin left the partnership, however, before Pasadena opened its doors. Kevin had complained about Ciudad's more modern décor and a design for customers less comfortable than he himself demanded. The same was planned for Border Grill Pasadena. Increasingly, his role in the group had been questioned.

"We were emotionally ready. We were burned out fighting each other. . . . The energy wasn't good." Kevin suggested getting a marriage counselor to resolve their differences. Mary Sue found them a rabbi from the San Fernando Valley who led them through the process, saving them large sums in legal bills.

Border Grill opened in Pasadena without Kevin, but it struggled to draw in customers and failed to grow as expected. Sales were flat, and the restaurant just broke even. Chef Joachim Splichal had opened one of his

Pinot Bistros in Pasadena, only to witness the only failure in his Patina Group. (Splichal's site was later taken over by Jennifer Lopez, whose Madre's restaurant also had financial difficulties in its first year.)

"Honestly, I think we have done a great job," said Susan. "We have done a ton of marketing. We have got our strongest chef and GM there. It's not street visible. We are doing better than all the others except P. F. Chang's. I don't know how the others stay open. If our restaurant does a little better for a year or two, it's worth hanging onto."

LIKE Pasadena, the Border Grill in the Green Valley Ranch Resort, Casino & Spa turned out to be a poor location.

Station Casinos, the owners, had approached Susan with the promise of a new resort for the local population that would change the orientation of their casino business to a more upscale clientele. The Green Valley section west of Henderson is home to an affluent population of executives and upper management from the casinos of Las Vegas, as well as retirees. Susan was impressed that the chain had also lured Il Fornaio, a successful restaurant group reasonably comparable to Border Grill in geography and stature. Coming off one relatively good opportunity with a Las Vegas casino, Susan was eager to put Border Grill in a nearby location. Financial backing for the Border Grill in Green Valley fell apart after 9/11, but the Station Casinos stepped in to help.

The resort and its restaurants made a splash opening a week before Christmas 2001, despite the national gloom following 9/11; among the hardest hit industries was the restaurant industry. The opening was studded with celebrities: Cindy Crawford, Charlize Theron, Chris O'Donnell, Kate Hudson, Christian Slater, and Lenny Kravitz, not to mention U.S. Senator John Ensign and Governor Kenny Guinn. Music featured Slash from Guns 'N' Roses.

Despite the fanfare, however, Border Grill did not fare well. Within a few months of its opening, the Girls faced a second dilemma involving closure: either lower the cost and quality of the food to keep the restaurant open, or shutter it quickly to avoid further losses.

According to one industry expert familiar with the site, the space offered them was impractical. "Whenever you choose a location, it's got to be a good space: you have got to have good flow-through. That space was disjointed from the start. I don't care what you put in there, it's going to be a challenge. You have one front room to the left, an awkward bar in the middle, and then you have this other sprawling dining area to the right. I never liked that space—for any concept."

Said an analyst, "If you actually look around the hotels in Las Vegas, Mexican isn't a big concept. The Mirage has one called Ricardo's—it's really low-end. Mark Miller has Coyote Café—it's a little Mexican, but I wouldn't put it in the same category. So, you first have to look at the city, and it's not a great concept for Las Vegas. Then, when you go into an environment like Green Valley, it's a local's market, and locals have a million taco joints where you can get a good dinner for five or six bucks. So, it's tough trying to appeal with a high-end Mexican restaurant. You can't say that just because Border Grill is successful in Mandalay Bay in Las Vegas it's going to be successful at a local's casino as well."

It was just at this time that longtime friend Sharon Monsky died of scleroderma, and a number of classmates from Pitzer gathered for her funeral. Susan ran into fellow Pitzer graduate Bruce Stein, who had since risen up through the toy industry to become president of Mattel and who then became another informal advisor to the Girls.

He urged them to close Border Grill in Green Valley.

"In Green Valley, the casino wanted them to dummy down their menu. That compromises the brand, and once you do that to your brand you never get it back," Stein said.

The Girls closed Border Grill in Green Valley in June 2002. The hope for clientele of wealthy locals had not materialized. Station Casinos went out of its way to help them out of financial obligations.

THE post-9/11 world brought much hardship to the Girls. In addition to closing the Green Valley restaurant, Border Grill in Pasadena was barely making ends meet, despite the high performances of both chef and general manager, while the *Border Girls* project was finally acknowledged as officially dead.

Also, Susan lost her mother as well as her close friend Sharon Monsky.

Since 9/11, they had been rethinking their businesses and goals. Susan was set on following through with expanding Border Grill to more units in Southern California. Mary Sue was content to hold onto the restaurants they already had. Still, business troubles have allowed no time out while they have been rethinking.

Early in January 2002, the Girls hired Rick DeMarco as COO. DeMarco had been vice president in charge of operations at California Pizza Kitchen for 10 years, then at the House of Blues, and lately for a fledgling Chicago-based restaurant group, Stir Crazy, that was trying to expand beyond three restaurants.

DeMarco's first task was to help the Girls put their house in order. This meant putting all four restaurants—Border Grill Santa Monica, Ciudad, Border Grill Las Vegas, and Border Grill Pasadena—on the same system with a shared recipe book and shared information for the first time. Corporate chef Kajsa Dilger had finished the corporate recipe book by the end of 2002, a tool for quality control.

While Rick was putting their house in order, they needed to rethink expansion of any kind. Expansion means financing, and financing had been tough.

Before 2001, the sums that the Girls raised for their restaurants were modest in comparison to other Super Chefs. Even in Las Vegas, the financial commitment was minimal thanks to the deal's financing. Pasadena and Green Valley were different. Within the same year Milliken and Feniger had to raise huge sums in a more difficult financial environment because of the dot.com failures. Raising money fell primarily to Susan as the keener of the two for new restaurants.

Susan called Swinghamer to evaluate two different offers of financing for Pasadena and Green Valley. The first was in exchange for 25 percent of the rolled-up Border Grill group. Swinghamer advised them to turn it down because they were not ready for a roll-up and the terms were not attractive enough.

The second deal from a large multiconcept restaurant company involved an investment by the company in Border Grill and the Girls consulting for the company's restaurants. They would be joint venture partners retaining significant ownership. Swinghamer said, "That company was really buying their culinary expertise and culinary reputation."

The Girls asked Swinghamer to advise them, including valuing their company and sitting in on meetings with the buying company. The company had its own Mexican concept restaurant but at a lower price point than Border Grill.

Robert Del Grande was going through a similar decision about the same time. Del Grande's flagship restaurant, Café Annie, has been one of Houston's premier spots for two decades. During the Houston oil bust of the mid-eighties, he came up with a quick casual dining concept that by 2002 had become a 13-unit chain called Café Express.

In February 2002, Wendy's bought a 45 percent stake in the Café Express chain, representing an investment of $9 million to fuel expansion to 50 units by 2005. In addition to growth capital, Wendy's offered expertise in site selection, restaurant operations, and marketing. Del Grande kept the Schiller Del Grande Restaurant Group out of the deal and spun the Café Express Group off from its other restaurants. Del Grande is president of the Café Express group, and all his people run it with him.

After Swinghamer valued the chefs' holdings and listened in at the meetings, he announced his decision: the deal was to their advantage. "Bottom line, the deal was fair, maybe more than fair," Swinghamer recounted. "And also you could have another outlet, not only the Border Grills, which you want to grow, but one that balances out the whole thing—a kind of place in L.A. that is hip and cool, a home base that you go to, a single unit." This could be an updated version of City Restaurant, allowing the chefs back into the world cuisine that made them famous.

He appealed to their great love of education, challenging them to make cheaper food taste better. The Girls were unconvinced. Mary Sue decided immediately that the deal would compromise their values. "I don't regret it a bit, but we may consider the deal at a later time," she says. Susan took longer to reply, as she was the one frustrated with the search for money for the two new restaurants.

The Girls moved on.

Conservatively, their short-term aim is to regroup and then open another restaurant, presumably a Border Grill, in 2004 somewhere in Southern California and to continue expanding the Border Grill concept to around 10 restaurants.

The Girls continued deliberation. The previous year, 2002, had changed Susan's thinking. "I think that Border Grill isn't a P. F. Chang's concept, while two years ago I thought it was. I still think we could do 50 of them, but not 100," she said.

While the Girls were suffering losses in 2002, Steve Hanson, New York-based restaurateur and owner of B.R. Guest, was just getting into action. Hanson hired chef Scott Linquist, who had worked for several years at Border Grill.

In September 2002, Hanson opened his new concept, Dos Caminos. B. R. Guest stated "the 'classic authentic Mexican with a modern touch' from executive chef and partner Scott Linquist and his top lieutenant, Ross Gill, is generally a nuanced and vibrant play on traditional themes." This could easily read as a description of Border Grill.

In May 2003, he opened Dos Caminos 2 in the Soho neighborhood of New York, under Scott Linquist. Many more units are planned for New York City. Rick DeMarco noted that Dos Caminos puts at least some damper on any plans to open a Border Grill in New York.

Hanson plans to open soon in Las Vegas, Scottsdale—and Los Angeles. While the Girls wrestle with their Border Grill concept, a business-savvy restaurateur has decided to jump into the Mexican cuisine space with a very similar concept.

Hanson himself is but a late entry into a restaurant sector increasingly crowded by lower-end challengers like Taco Bell (Yum! Brands), Del Taco, Baja Fresh (Wendy's), and Chipotle (McDonald's), and veterans like Chi-Chi's (Pantium), El Torito (Acapulco Acquisition Corporation), Chevy's Mexican Restaurant, Rubio's Baja Grill (Rubio's), El Chico (Consolidated Restaurant Operations)—and Café Express (Wendy's).

THE Girls are human and have not always taken their own advice or the advice of others. Mary Sue once said, "A restaurateur is like an entrepreneur at the end of the day. The site selection for a new restaurant or the lease negotiations—you have to be willing to take responsibility, try to get the best expertise. Of course, Susan and I finally after several years figured out how to get more support, like hiring people who've actually done it before." Yet, they often admit that they have chosen support poorly.

Sometimes, they seem to have missed the lesson altogether: asked about the difficulties with the Border Grills in Pasadena and Green Valley, Susan once said, "It didn't have anything to do with us; they were both bad locations," whereas, in fact, as restaurateurs it was their responsibility to choose good locations.

At other times, they have learned only the lesser lesson. After opening in several locations that would only pan out later, Mary Sue has said, "The moral is, open when you have enough money to weather some time," when the more hardnosed commercial lesson would be to simply opt for a location that is profitable from the get-go.

Ultimately, as Mary Sue once said, "You get great advice, but it's time consuming and contradictory. Then you got to sift through it all, and even then we make mistakes."

Friend and advisor Bruce Stein advised them to return to television before expanding Border Grill. "Here is the challenge that faces them. They had a four-year run on the Food Network. That was the point in time when they really needed to leverage where they are. If they go to try to leverage it with other market techniques or product extensions like infomercials and things that I really thought would be great for them, it's hard to explain to someone that the show was on five years ago. Everyone wants to piggyback on something that is at its apex."

Time is running out on TV options because of age. One insider said, "Part of their personae was always young and hip. How do you do that when you aren't young anymore, and hip is always associated with youth? Part of the problem was that whole TV persona thing. With Julia Child, it didn't matter that she got older, because she wasn't about being young and happening." The only solution is to develop a new persona, a new kind of television show that does not rely on youth.

Rather than try to recapture the success of their Food Network shows, the chefs have turned to Buena Vista Television to pilot a lifestyle show.

Said Holly Jacobs, Buena Vista Television's vice president for programming and development, "What we look to develop is a morning talk lifestyle show, that covers a really broad arena—all kinds of service elements for women. It's every arena, from cooking to decorating to finding things on a budget, everything. We think that Mary Sue and Susan are very accessible, comfortable women who lead regular lives."

This was exactly the kind of show that Stein was looking for. "They are no longer young, upstart 20-year-olds. They are mature chefs who can appeal to a family. The idea of bringing family cooking into this mix better suits them, because of the nature of the product and their character."

Said Jacobs, "What we are trying to do is take two women who are best known for cooking and expand their brand to a much broader arena. We are actually not focusing on their skills as chefs and restaurateurs: we are focusing on the fact that these women have a passion for food and lifestyle and decorating and design and presenting that information to women. We are expanding beyond how people know them. This will be the first time that *they* are expanding into a broader arena." The two chefs are reinventing themselves and reaching out to a new audience.

"We are looking to find an interesting way—we're looking to find an advertiser-friendly show, where there may be opportunities for new revenue streams with spot placement and all kinds of things," Jacobs continued. "We're hoping to do interactive television, where viewers would be able to watch and they go buy what they see, when appropriate in some segments." That kind of advertising-driven aspect was wholly missing from *Too Hot Tamales.*

"We really think there is a place in the marketplace for an almost 'anti-Martha Stewart' where it's not complex elements to make something wonderful in your home. These are the women who are going to be the ones to do it," she said.

Buena Vista produced a pilot targeting first-run syndicators during 2003. If enough syndicated stations are interested in buying the show, then it will go into production. That means the show has to please the tastes of the whole country, rather than a small group of executives.

Bruce Stein has said, "What makes me most optimistic about their business today is that the category they are in is more popular than when they started. Latin, both authentic and modern Mexican, as a sensibility has grown. I am optimistic about that. I would feel different if it had matured as a concept, like McDonald's or California Pizza Kitchen, but they have a riper opportunity."

Stein has encouraged the chefs to bring in more cultural events from the Mexican and Latin American communities and tie those up with what Border Grill represents. "I still think you have to try to promote what is unique. Part of their position should be the expansion of the Latin Culture position. The food brand exists. People still remember them, but how do you make that current, how do you bring media into it?"

SINCE their split with L.A. Eyeworks, the Girls have never found a third force to counterbalance their partnership. They hired Kevin Finch twice and lost him twice. Rick DeMarco left the Girls in 2003 in the wake of the Green Valley closure and Pasadena's poor performance.

DeMarco predicted that, even with a successful new television show, and moving at lightning speed, it may be eight months to a year before they expand further and need a COO. Even though sales were up in the remaining restaurants, they were not generating enough to justify his salary. His parting advice to the chefs was to do their location homework.

"You need to find not just a real estate broker but a real estate consultant," DeMarco said. "It's worth it to pay for the homework. Chefs often they go into this thinking 'trendy and cool'; sometimes that works. It can be effective if you have a big enough name to draw people, but if you don't it's a roll of the dice."

Josh sits on the sidelines; he is too close to both of the Girls to risk his relationship with either for the sake of business. Besides, who could ever match up to the expectations their own partnership has created? Is there anyone who could survive barging into their partnership?

Speaking about the Girls, Wolfgang Puck said back in 1985 that to become a successful chef, "I think it's maybe 10 percent talent and 90 percent tenacity. You can ask Mary Sue and Susan. Probably they work 18 hours a day, and I think that's what it really takes."

Today, the Girls work as hard as ever. They have outgrown the tiny kitchen of City Café to oversee a broad empire of restaurants, products, cookbooks, radio, television, and film. Their fortunes have risen and fallen and risen again and fallen again, and still they work and are rising again. This time could be the charm.

With interests so wide, they are able to move forward by embracing each challenge and constantly devising new solutions. Even in their most amateur media moments, they shine with enthusiasm and comfort with their practical approach to the practice of cooking.

Perhaps Julia Child hit closest to the mark when she called them "a lively pair of teachers." Through teaching—in the kitchen, at live appearances, in cookbooks, on the radio, on television, and in film—Mary Sue and Susan are able to share the joy they experience in cooking. Perhaps the only real limit of their empire is the variety of media the world affords them.

Mary Sue said about the opening of City Restaurant:

> We didn't know really. We actually never had been through an opening, and our opening was as rocky as it could be. We were in the kitchen about 52 hours before we started taking money. None of the staff was really trained: it was just us. We knew what we were doing—and we barely knew what we were doing. It was pretty hard, but basically all we really did was to try to do what we did at City Café on a bigger scale. It wasn't really well thought through: we just did it. OK, we thought, we will both work double shifts until we can stop—and who ever dies first gets a day off!

That was 20 years ago. They are older and wiser, and still they are not chefs for the money. If they had decided to chase the almighty dollar, then perhaps they might right now have a nationwide empire, with Latino and other ethnic concepts. After all, Border Grill was conceived as a roll-out concept long before Wolfgang Puck Express was conceived of and even longer before Wolfgang identified fast casual as a cash cow. When asked whether they watch the moves and expansion of others, particularly Wolf, Susan has replied, "No, I haven't. We are so by the gut that we don't really watch him."

Wolfgang has been watching—not other chefs but fashion designers such as Pierre Cardin, Ralph Lauren, and Giorgio Armani. He has noted that, like fine dining, *haute couture* is necessary to establish quality and reputation, but that the money is in *prêt-à-porter* for fashion and in casual dining for food. Interestingly, some designers have become restaurateurs. Giorgio Armani, for instance, has partnered with Nobu Matsuhisa in Armani/Nobu in Milan and has put cafés in over ten of his Emporio Armanis, in addition to his flagship boutique and numerous retail stores.

While the Girls may not have been watching, Josh has been. "If you look at Wolfgang Puck, he has Spago and then all the cafés. Spago is like *haute couture,* and the cafés are like ready-to-wear. I think that right now Mary Sue and Susan just have ready-to-wear. They *could* have done a line of City Cafés and done a whole lot of those Border Grills." And City Restaurant or its successor would have been or could be their flagship.

The Girls have both confessed to naivete as they set out on their own. Many might say that they have retained, even cultivated a naivete as the price of continued creativity. They remain chef-artists. Their brains are focused on their art, which expands continually beyond food and restaurants, but they do not seem to have always used their heads as wisely when it comes to business.

Yet they survive. And thrive. They have faced business adversities that have crushed many others. To this day they have name, reputation, and restaurants, not to mention cookbooks, radio and television shows, and personal appearances that always include teaching.

They know their strength lies in neither brains nor brawn; as Susan said, "It's a question of where your heart is."

5

TOM COLICCHIO

Courtesy of Lori Silverbush

"All millionaires love a baked apple"
—Ronald Firbank, *Vainglory* (1915)

BASEBALL. On a cold May evening in 2003, the wind was gusting during a baseball game in New York City. Nonprofessional teams were playing, a Downtown team in black versus Uptowns in red. The game was already in the fourth inning, and the star hitter for the Downtowns had not even shown up yet.

Spectators clutched a hot dog in one cold hand and a hot pretzel in the other—only the dog was a Japanese Kobe beef dog in a sourdough bun, the pretzel a rosemary-speckled affair of dough, both courtesy of Tinker Boe of Mood Food. The game was not at Yankee or Shea or any stadium at all but in North Field No. 6 in upper Central Park at East 102nd Street.

As for the players, they were not part of any baseball league. In fact, they were in a different league altogether. They were some of New York's finest chefs and from the biggest and best-known kitchens in America and perhaps the world—New York City.

Steve Jenkins of Fairway and author of *The Cheese Primer* was pitching for the Uptown team, which also included Charlie Palmer (Aureole), Marcus Samuelsson (Aquavit), Cornelius Gallagher (Oceana), Andrew Carmellini (Café Boulud), Gabriel Kreuther (Atelier), Patricia Yeo (Pazo and AZ), Rick Moonen (rm), and John Villa (Patroon and Pico).

For the Downtown team Dan Barber of Blue Hill was pitching, relieved in the seventh inning by Mario Batali of Babbo, and their teammates were Aaron Sanchez (Paladar), Michael Otsuka (Verbena), Anita Lo (Annisa),

Mike Anthony (Blue Hill), Marc Meyer (Five Points), Harold Dieterle (The Harrison), Jimmy Bradley (the Harrison, the Red Cat, and Mermaid Inn), Alfred Portale (Gotham Bar and Grill), Matthew MacCartney (Craft), Katy Sparks (Katy)—and Tom Colicchio (Craft).

The game had seen no scoring until the third inning, when Downtown had scored 4 to Uptown's 1. By the fifth, the score was 6 to 4 Downtown.

During the fifth inning, a man in a black Downtown uniform No. 44 could be seen walking across the field. Stocky, strutting at a steady speed, he picked up a bat, walked directly to the plate, and signaled he was ready to play ball.

Tom Colicchio had arrived.

Steve Jenkins unleashed his first pitch right away. Colicchio eyed the incoming blur, then connected bat to ball. A fielder fumbled the catch, which sped on across the field, and Colicchio ran two men in for a three-run homer. Amidst the high-fives and congratulations of his teammates, he crowed innocently, "Hey, it was a just a fly ball!" By the end of that inning, the score was 10 to 4 Downtown. Colicchio took up his position as first baseman.

When Mario Batali came in to relieve Steve Jenkins on the mound, fans discovered one skill outside the range of the multitalented Mario. Despite demonic shorts and spiffy orange high-tops, Batali pitched so poorly that even first-time player Marcus Samuelsson got a hit off him. Downtown could afford the points, though, and the final score was 16 to 12. True to hot-tempered fame, the chefs broke into a minor dispute over the score, with the Downtown team claiming 18 points, not just 16.

This was one of many chef events that dot the calendar these days in America's larger cities. This particular game was sponsored by *Food & Wine* magazine, which is owned by the American Express Publishing Group. *Food & Wine*'s editor-in-chief Dana Cowin had thrown out the first pitch. American Express Publishing's president Ed Kelly had played for the Uptown team, chief marketing officer Mark Stanich for Downtown. In fact, the event was billed as *Food & Wine* Chef Softball, with proceeds to go to City Meals on Wheels.

As it turns out, Tom Colicchio, like many chefs, had been a serious sportsman in his youth and had opted not to pursue a career in baseball only because of his short stature. Growing up in Elizabeth, New Jersey, in striking distance of New York City, his family was second generation from Valatta, a small town in Campania, east of Naples in Italy.

"Everyone knew Tommy Colicchio," says Tom's cousin Phil Colicchio. Tom, second of three brothers, grew up with his immigrant father's sense of working hard and getting ahead, though that did not always translate into learning at school. On Fridays, he and his brothers accompanied his father and his uncle, who was on the local softball team called the Sticky Fingers, for a game followed by a huge spread at the local bar, Spiritos, which claims to have the best meatball sandwiches in New Jersey.

All the Colicchios love sports. Tom considered going pro in baseball. One of his brothers (also Phil) is a high school basketball coach. Besides baseball, Tom himself plays basketball regularly, golfs, and is an avid fly fisherman. He still gets in a baseball game like the *Food & Wine* event whenever he can.

TOM was born in 1962 and grew up in the working-class town of Elizabeth. His father, also named Tom, ran a barbershop for awhile and then when even working-class men switched to hair salons, worked as a correctional officer. His mother ran a high school cafeteria. She was a good cook, but good food was simply part of family tradition, nothing remarkable. He tasted food at friends' houses and realized that he ate better than most of them.

Along with his cousins, young Tom took his turn helping his uncle sell fruit and vegetables to Italian immigrants during the winter months. Though it didn't mean much more than a few dollars in his pocket at the time, he did observe how carefully the customers shopped for fresh produce rather than go to the local supermarket.

His first real job as a cook was at a local swim club called the Gran Centurion, where he was a short-order snack bar cook.

"I was getting $250 a week under the table in cash. I worked in a pair of cutoffs. It was awesome. I made grilled cheese sandwiches, minute steaks, grilled sausages, and stuff like that, but the great thing about being a short-order cook is that if you are a line cook you *are* a short-order cook. When you are actually working the line, especially then, when you are sautéing everything, it teaches you how to work the stove."

Colicchio did a short stint at Burger King before getting his first real restaurant job at a local institution that had opened a second location in Elizabeth called Evelyn's Seafood Restaurant. He was 18.

Meanwhile, he had discovered French food as a sophomore in high school. Having read about a restaurant in *Gourmet* magazine, he took a girlfriend after seeing *A Chorus Line* on Broadway to Pierre Au Tunnel in New York's theater district, where he tried the *coquilles St. Jacques.* After finishing high school, Tom took a job at the Chestnut Tavern in Clark, where for a year he learned to butcher whole animals. Then he got a job as a line cook at the Old Mansion, where two Culinary Institute graduates had been hired. He followed that with a six-month stint at the Seacaucus Hilton.

Though it is common for line cooks and even *sous chefs* and chefs to apprentice themselves in kitchens rather than attend culinary school, it is less common that a chef reach Tom's stature without a degree. Puck won a national cooking championship while only of high school age. Palmer, English, and Feniger studied at the CIA, Milliken at Washburne.

Tom considered school several times but found he did not have the money or the desire. Nor did he have enough money to apprentice in France at the beginning of his career. So, like many highly talented working-class Americans, he took a very practical approach to mastering his field: he read. Tom read what is perhaps the greatest cooking manual ever written, Jacques Pépin's *La Technique.*

Pépin's book became the centerpiece of the self-education of Tom Colicchio: he paraphrased it in his own first book, *Think Like a Chef*: "Don't read this as if it were a book, treat it as an apprenticeship."

Tom also read from David Liederman's book *Nouvelle Cuisine in America* and started to look for a *nouvelle cuisine* restaurant in New Jersey. He answered an advertisement for a *sous chef* at 40 Main Street, a storefront restaurant in Milburn, to help cook "new American cuisine." The restaurant's chef Jim Smith introduced Tom to cooking whatever was available in the local market.

Tom also met Jerry Bryan (now chef at Coastal Grill in Virginia Beach), Bill Rogers (now chef at Noho Star in Manhattan), and John Schaefer (now executive chef at Colicchio's own Gramercy Tavern). With a kitchen crew of four American cooks, 40 Main Street was typical of the movement among native-born chefs to discover local ingredients in a menu that changed daily.

After a year at 40 Main Street Tom headed for Manhattan, where he landed a job at Alfred Portale's Gotham Bar and Grill. Portale's creations epitomized the "architectural food" of the 1980s, which rose up off the plate in three (and some would claim, four) dimensions. Copycats matched Portale's physical food heights, but few if any ever made them as delectable, much less edible, without landing the construct off the dish and off the table.

A week later, Tom was apologizing to Portale: he had an offer he could not refuse from the Quilted Giraffe. Barry and Susan Wine owned the Quilted Giraffe (1975–1992). If Gotham Bar and Grill represented the heights—literally and figuratively—of architectural food, the Quilted Giraffe represented some of the most lavish and creative American food of its time. The *New York Times* called it "a temple to gastronomy," and *Bon Appétit* cited it as "one of the most influential restaurants of the Twentieth Century."

While Jeremiah Tower at Alice Waters' Chez Panisse was delving into the essence of American cuisine in California in the mid-seventies, Barry Wine at the Quilted Giraffe was interpreting *nouvelle cuisine* in New York. In the eighties, the Quilted Giraffe went beyond *nouvelle cuisine* to help introduce Japanese cuisine to America. It also became a place where culinary stars were discovered.

The Quilted Giraffe charged some of the highest prices in America; lunch for two was $80. Hamburgers cost $22, beggar's purses were filled with caviar, and pizzas were topped with raw tuna. The Quilted Giraffe started the trend in tasting menus individually tailored to the diner. It was also among the first American fine dining restaurants to spin off a casual version: the Casual Quilted Giraffe opened in 1985.

The offer Tom could not refuse was a one-week tryout on the line.

Barry Wine set up his kitchen on a clock system: cooks had 9 minutes to cook a dish once it was assigned. All cooks had a digital clock at their stations to monitor their progress. Once the food was ready, it was handed to Wine, who assembled the food on a dish, or "plated" it. If the food was 30 or even 10 seconds late, Wine would scream.

Tom ended up cooking next to the departing *sous chef*, who was fumbling. Wine kept yelling at Tom, "Hey, what are you doing down there! You are messing everything up!" On the last night of his tryout, Tom told the other cook to get out of his way. "If I am going to fail, let me fail." He got the job.

This by-the-clock method of cooking was part of a radical change in cuisine. Before the Quilted Giraffe, chefs would send a waiter or even the captain into a dining room with small pots of sauces, heated on Sternos® at the table. Little was cooked fresh for the customer: practically everything was cooked in advance because most dishes needed a long preparation time. What Wine did was to prepare everything freshly and quickly. "Barry just figured he couldn't screw up anything in 10 minutes," said Tom.

Barry Wine was another self-taught chef who had started his career as a lawyer. A culinary tour of France in the early 1970s introduced him to *nouvelle cuisine* and convinced him to replicate it in America. He started the Quilted Giraffe with his first wife Susan in their New Paltz home in 1975. Once he had his systems in place, in 1979 he moved the Quilted Giraffe to Manhattan's Upper East Side. It quickly drew acclaim.

He searched for great local ingredients, and he grew himself what he couldn't find. He offered his guests the first "free-range chickens." Taking full advantage of the airfreight revolution, he served then-unheard-of luxuries out of season, such as raspberries in midwinter.

Wine recollected, "One of my approaches was the only way I was going to get what I wanted was to hire, in effect, amateurs. If you had worked in Anthony Bourdain's kitchen, I didn't want you. If you had been a waiter at Tavern on the Green, I didn't want you. There was extraordinary animosity between cooks and waiters. Someone like that would bring the assumption that they were being oppressed by management and that they should steal. Tom was the first real cook who did my kind of stuff."

The rest of the staff were second-career chefs: lawyers, bankers, and other professionals. Wine realized that if he was going to cook dishes in 9 minutes he needed an expert at the stove. Tom's short-order cook background and his experience in other kitchens meant he was faster and more adept at handling a multiple-burner stove.

Within four months, 24-year-old Tom was *sous chef*. And by then Tom had given up any more thoughts about going to culinary school. Though Tom has resisted identifying a mentor in his chef's career, Barry Wine comes closest, being chef of the first very serious restaurant in which he worked.

By 1986 Tom was starting to talk with Jerry Bryan about running their own restaurant, when Dan Cannizio, owner of 40 Main Street, called. His chef, Jim Smith, had left the restaurant abruptly and Cannizio offered him the executive chef position. He took it on condition that he would be cochef with Jerry Bryan.

With Jerry, Tom changed the menu of 40 Main, introducing some

Quilted Giraffe dishes along with a modified clock system. The two would drive early in the morning to the Fulton Fish Market in Manhattan and end up in the Jersey City offices of D' Artagnan, run by Ariane Daguin and George Faison. D'Artagnan was one of the first companies to sell American-produced *foie gras*. "We called them Tom and Jerry, like the cartoon," recalled Daguin. Tom and Jerry were fascinated by the new produce that was being grown by farmers in the surrounding states.

Bill Rogers, who had worked as a waiter under Jim Smith, started working part-time in the kitchen helping Tom and Jerry. "Jim's food was OK. It wasn't bad. It was properly prepared—he wasn't a hack. He was doing mainstream stuff like veal with blueberry sauce. Tom and Jerry had worked in Manhattan, and they brought a new way of looking at food to New Jersey, food people hadn't seen before in terms of simply prepared stuff. It was more about flavor than blueberry sauce."

Although they were cochefs, Tom and Jerry fell into different roles. According to Tom, he took care of the menu and Jerry ran the kitchen, hired staff, and organized schedules. "With Jerry, I had all the creative input, and he ran the business of it. He is a real technician and a really great cook. We had some of his dishes on the menu, but I was more the creative person. He ran the food costs and hired all the cooks and stuff like that."

Tom ventured into the dining room to meet guests, while the shier Jerry stayed in the kitchen. "Tom has an incredible ability not just to cook but also to intermingle with the customer," said Bryan. "He made incredible contacts. We used to call him 'Hollywood Colicchio.' Tom was the man for the job. I didn't feel I could do it."

The restaurant had only four people in the kitchen, two of them on chef's salaries. The 14 owners were not happy about how little they were making and decided to get rid of one of the cochefs. Cannizio approached Tom, who said he would not stay if Jerry left, and then approached Jerry, who answered the same way. They both left after one year. Jerry went to California and did stints at Wolfgang Puck's Spago and Chinois on Main. Tom was invited back to the Gotham Bar and Grill under Portale.

Portale asked him to come in as *sous chef* with the aim of making his current kitchen staff think someone new was going to take over. He wanted them on their toes. It put Tom in a terrible position of being hated by the entire staff. He thought for a while about driving out to Seattle. Instead, he went to France.

Ariane Daguin set up a *stage* with her father at his restaurant L'Hotel de France in Gascony. The food was rustic and rich and the ingredients were impeccable and exotic for the American chef, like wild game. Tom didn't speak a word of French and became the butt of jokes among the French *commis* (apprentices) in the kitchen. A month into his *stage*, another American chef named Kerry Heffernen showed up and rescued Tom from the good-hearted abuse.

Back in New York in 1987, Tom worked for Thomas Keller at the newly opened Rakel, first as line cook and then as *sous chef*. What struck Tom was how there was no discussion among the cooks of movies or parties or anything other than food. This allowed for real collaboration between executive chef and *sous chef*.

"It happens in all kitchens: you are a *sous chef*, you create something, and you think it's your dish. The thing is, it was developed in the chef's restaurant. Everything that comes out of that kitchen is because that is the way the chef set it up. The cooking style is the way he cooked. The ingredients are the ingredients he wanted. The style of plating is the style he wanted. So, even though you say, 'Well, I came up with *that* dish,' it is only because you were put in a creative environment that allowed you to do that—and it was that chef's environment. I think a lot of young chefs don't understand that."

After Rakel closed in late 1987 in the wake of the Black October stock market collapse, Tom ran into chef-restaurateur Dennis Foy at the christening of Ariane Daguin's daughter. Tom had met Foy years earlier when he had applied and been turned down for a job at Foy's Tarragon Tree in Chatham, New Jersey. At the christening party, Foy told Daguin's partner George Faison that he was having a tough time staffing his new restaurant in Manhattan. Faison pointed out Tom in the crowd and said he should get him to head up his new restaurant.

In the meantime, Jerry Bryan was moving to Virginia to open a large-volume restaurant with an untrained crew. He asked his buddy Tom to come down a week before the opening. A few months later Foy came down and offered him the job of *chef de cuisine*. Tom's father had just been diagnosed with lung cancer. For family-oriented Tom, the decision was simple: stay near home with Foy's job. Besides, John Schaefer, who had done a *stage* with Tom at 40 Main Street, was already working there.

MONDRIAN, located in midtown Manhattan, was the first restaurant for New Jersey–based chef-restaurateur Dennis Foy and investor Robert Scott, a managing director at Morgan Stanley. Foy and Scott had begun planning the restaurant in 1986, which they opened in 1988. They chose "Mondrian" after the Dutch Neoplasticist artist Piet Mondrian (1872–1944), because his last studio was located at 15 East 59th Street, a few doors down the street.

"In the intervening period we had the crash in '87, which impacted the environment in fairly 'meaningful' ways, but we were committed to this beautiful club-like atmosphere," recollected Scott.

"I quit after two weeks," Tom recalled. "It was not the way I wanted to run a kitchen. Dennis was an ex-marine, and he ran a kitchen like a barracks. I am not into yelling and screaming and being in your face. Outside the restaurant, he's a delightful guy, fun to hang out with. He loved to party and have a good time. Still, he didn't run the kind of kitchen I felt comfortable in." Also, Foy's food at Mondrian was a far cry from the kind of fare that Tom had been cooking at Rakel.

Foy talked Tom into staying by offering to let him add his own dishes to the menu and giving him more leeway in running the kitchen. The restaurant started to get better reviews, thanks to Tom's dishes. David Rosengarten, who gave his highest rating to Mondrian in his newsletter *The Food and Wine Companion,* recalled "a kind of fish, striped bass, a meaty, flaky fish. He laid extremely thin slices of typical southern French vegetables over the fish—tomato, eggplant, and maybe some zucchini—and all laid under the caul fat so all of it would roast slowly and melt together. They were magical things. You put your fork into it, and it all slid off, a lush, velvety, sexy hunk. Listen, 10,000 chefs could put together *hoisin* sauce, butter, and cilantro so that I would never notice, but when somebody hits something with just the right texture and feel, like Tom did in that dish, it drives me wild."

Insiders say that a journalist told Foy that Tom's dishes were the best being served. Finally, Foy asked Tom to take over the kitchen. At that point, Tom started to go into the dining room to meet guests and talk to journalists. Foy remained in the kitchen—creating tension.

Tom confessed, "I think it was the best food I've ever done in my life, and probably because I was not bogged down with running a restaurant and running a business. I was just in the kitchen 24/7—just a really exciting time."

The New York Times welcomed his presence with these words, "Thomas Colicchio has an impressive pedigree . . . The economy has not improved, but Mondrian certainly has, and I wouldn't be too fast to make any bets about its demise."

After *The New York Times* gave the restaurant two stars, almost exclusively on the basis of his dishes, according to Tom, he decided to leave for good.

He went to France on another *stage* set up by Ariane Daguin, this time with Michel Bras at his two-star restaurant in Laguiole. Tom described his food in *Think Like a Chef*. "In addition to using the wild greens he found out and about, he was one of the first chefs I ever saw to experiment with herbed oils as an alternative to more traditional sauces. Michel believed in cooking things slowly." Slow cooking became one of Tom's preferred methods.

After a month in France, Bob Scott called Tom asking him to come back to Mondrian to take over the restaurant officially. Upon his return, he found out that the restaurant was in terrible financial shape.

"We couldn't make money on it. The deal was a bad deal. We paid $34,000 in rent a month for an 80-seat restaurant that cost us $3.5 million to build. We never did more than $3.2 million a year; the numbers did not add up," recalled Tom. Foy bowed out of the restaurant for personal reasons, selling his shares to the other partners.

In addition to its high rent, the restaurant was located in the old Playboy Club on 59th Street between Madison and Fifth avenues, a street full of bridge traffic and very little to draw customers to stop. The restaurant, designed by Philip George, who had also designed Le Bernardin, had wood paneling and recessed ceilings that made it resemble a steak-and-lobster restaurant more than a place for fine, French-inspired food. Tom also inherited the surly service that existed under Foy. "Once you have a culture on the floor, it's very difficult to change it," said Tom.

Despite the obstacles, with Tom in control of the kitchen, the *New York Times* awarded the restaurant three stars in 1990: Tom was 28 years old. In 1991, Tom was listed as one of the top ten chefs in America by *Food & Wine* magazine.

"I didn't let it go to my head. I come from Elizabeth, New Jersey: there is no pretense about that. I was just shocked that people noticed."

The investors offered to pump another half-million dollars into Mondrian, but Tom refused. Mondrian closed in 1992. "When it was clear that to continue to invest to keep the restaurant going didn't make sense, he was pretty hardnosed, so it was fairly easy for the two of us to decide that we should close the restaurant," recalled Bob Scott. "I would say that is the one thing today about Tom: I think he is a pretty unique combination of a talented chef and a good businessman."

Mondrian received a premortem eulogy from Bryan Miller in *The New York Times:* "If Mondrian indeed is expiring as scuttlebutt periodically has it, the city's fine dining scene will be poorer for it. Should such a sad day arrive, I certainly wouldn't want to miss the food at the wake."

With Mondrian slated to close, Tom made a decision to pay off creditors rather than file for bankruptcy. With about $200,000 worth of debt, he asked the restaurant's lawyers how much a Chapter 11 filing would cost in terms of lawyers' fees, filing, and payments. They put the estimate at $100,000 plus interest. He turned to Bob Scott, explaining that he would definitely be in business somewhere else and would need to work with these suppliers again.

He asked and got $100,000 to pay them off. He returned all the unused wine to wine merchants, and he offered each creditor 50 cents on the dollar. His reasoning was that if he went to bankruptcy court, the creditors would be lucky to get 10 cents on the dollar after three years. All they had to do was sign letters saying that Mondrian's debts were paid.

"A lot of restaurants just close the door; they don't go into bankruptcy," said Faison, which means the credit extended by farmers and suppliers would not be covered. "We were as happy as we could be—it was a lot better than a bankruptcy. Tom was forthcoming, and he didn't hide." All of his creditors accepted the deal happily, except for one. To this day, Tom will not do business with that company.

The experience at Mondrian convinced Bob Scott that Tom was a good bet, and they started discussions about opening another restaurant, this time downtown where rents were cheaper.

Beyond their business relationship, Bob Scott and Tom Colicchio were drawn together through their passion for fly-fishing, a passion shared by other chefs like Kerry Heffernan, and Tom Valenti of New York's Ouest restaurant, D'Artagnan co-owner George Faison, and architect Peter Bentel, many of whom would work with Tom over the years.

Bob Scott described the similarities between fly-fishing and cooking:

> When you are on the river and you are concentrating about casting flies, you are in a trance. When you are standing working on your *mise en place,* you are in a trance, and then you get to do it your own way, be creative. Same thing with tying flies: you sit at a vise, you have all these materials—I call it "needlepoint for guys"—you are totally into it, and you are creating these beautiful things. Then you are going to go out and combine that with this experience of standing in the river and you are going to catch a fish.
>
> In the case of fly-fishing, it's feathers and fur. In the case of cooking, it's fish, meat, and herbs, and you do something with it. In fishing you catch the fish. In cooking you serve it to your client: they enjoy it. You can get tons of feedback. It's very rewarding.

The concept of craftsmaning whether flies or food would grow on Tom's mind for several years, but first he needed the final class of his apprenticeship from a great restaurateur.

DANNY Meyer had discovered Tom at a charity event in 1991 and then come to know him a bit when the chef of his restaurant Union Square Café, Michael Romano, was also among the *Food & Wine* list of ten top chefs that same year. Meyer started coming to eat regularly at Mondrian and sent his chef and *sous chef* to eat there as well.

Meyer came from a well-to-do St. Louis family. His father was a tour operator, and Meyer spent youthful years in Rome leading tourists around and learning about food. He had opened Union Square Café in 1985 after a few years as a restaurant manager in New York. Union Square Café was part of a resurgence of more casual, bistro-style eateries. The restaurant featured an American menu and emphasized great service and hospitality. It was not an instant hit but it soon caught on, and by 1992 Union Square Café was rated 26 overall by *Zagat Survey.*

Shortly after Mondrian closed, Tom approached Danny Meyer at the annual *Food & Wine* Classic in Aspen to discuss a new restaurant with him. Meyer initially wasn't interested in working with Tom, but eventually they started meeting to talk about the business of running a restaurant and about where the industry was going.

They made a decision to travel to Italy together for ten days on the assumption that if they could travel together then they could work together. Meyer was fluent in Italian and Tom was eager to explore trattorias, so the trip went well. They decided to give it a go.

It took a year to find the location and then design and build the restaurant, a process new to Tom but one he enjoyed. The new restaurant was located above Union Square and closer to Gramercy Park, so in keeping with the local bistro concept, the partners called it Gramercy Tavern. They hired architects Bentel & Bentel, who had renovated Union Square Café under lead architect Peter Bentel.

The architectural concept of Gramercy Tavern was tavern as a community space. Bentel & Bentel founders Maria and Frederick had designed Motel on the Mountain for Restaurant Associates' Joe Baum in the 1950s. Their firm, however, was known primarily for their design of libraries, schools, and religious buildings. "Tom saw something in what we do and our attitude. We are extremely interested in the way things are made and how that is expressed in the way they look. Chefs are interested in the same thing," said son Peter, a partner in the firm.

Gramercy Tavern's partners believed that hospitality is easier to deliver in a well-designed restaurant. Peter and his brother and fellow partner Paul researched taverns in America. Then they researched a list from Danny Meyer of trattorias all over Italy.

What they discovered was that the most hospitable restaurants had rooms 21 feet across—the length of chestnut beams—which allowed for an arrangement of three tables across. Such restaurants were a series of rooms allowing for circulation between rooms and creating a sense of community within each room and within the restaurant as a whole. Bentel & Bentel added a further refinement when designing Gramercy by defining rooms not only by walls but also by ceiling treatments. Gramercy included a tavern or casual dining area and a fine dining area.

The original menu of Gramercy was based on dishes that Tom had cooked at Mondrian. As Gramercy Tavern evolved, however, the dishes became less three-dimensional or "architectural" *à la* Alfred Portale and simpler in terms of ingredients. Ruth Reichl, then restaurant critic of *The New York Times*, lauded the restaurant a year and a half after it opened:

Courtesy of Archphoto/Eduard Huber

INTERIOR OF GRAMERCY TAVERN

"From the light crisp rolls with sweet butter to the tarte Tatin of quince and apples with maple ice cream, there was not a single misstep. Mr. Colicchio's cooking has lost the tentative quality of the early days: he is now cooking with extraordinary confidence, creating dishes characterized by bold flavors and unusual harmonies."

Danny and Tom codified their ideas of good hospitality with the term "enlightened hospitality," a term that would be adopted in 1997 by Danny's Union Square Hospitality Group, the parent company of Union Square, Gramercy Tavern, and his future restaurants. Their secret ingredient: treat staff well. In the employee handbook it includes five tenets, "caring for each other, caring for our guests, caring for our community, caring for our suppliers, caring for our shareholders (our bottom line)."

Tom explained this philosophy from the kitchen's viewpoint: "You can't have someone coming into the kitchen afraid that the chef is going to scream at them and then put on a nice happy face and take care of the customer. Most of the time the waiter is getting screamed at because they are trying to get the customer something."

Danny explained this philosophy from the viewpoint of the front of the house:

> The only thing I really need to know about any of my restaurants or anyone else's is watch the staff as they walk into work. If it appears that they are by and large psyched to be there, you're going to have a good restaurant. So, the biggest thing I need to do to retain staff is to surround them with people whom they find really motivating to work with and to provide opportunities to grow. To the degree that I don't do either of those, why wouldn't they leave?

"The day Gramercy Tavern opened, it was on the cover of *New York* magazine—the cover!" Danny recalled. And it was packed. Like Danny Meyer's other restaurant, Union Square Café, it took a few years to hit a top-rating stride, but when it did, it kept moving up. Within two years, Gramercy Tavern rated among the top restaurants in *Zagat Survey;* by 2003 it had supplanted even Union Square Café as the most popular restaurant. Their emphasis on hospitality showed in reviews.

During the year that the restaurant was being built, Tom stayed home to care for his infant son Dante, with banker Kristen Johanson. By Gramercy's second year, however, Tom's relationship with Johanson was failing. He started dating Lori Silverbush, one of Gramercy's opening waitresses who had finished a film degree at New York University and was waiting tables to pay bills while she began working in the movie industry. She worked as a captain for a year after their relationship started and then quit to pursue film full-time. Lori and Tom eventually moved in together.

In the meantime, Danny and Tom started drifting apart.

Initially, Tom wanted to be a 50 percent partner with Danny but settled for 36 percent, which he held with Bob Scott. He also signed an employment agreement. Phil Colicchio, Tom's cousin and a commercial lawyer with Taylor, Colicchio & Silverman, later reviewed the agreements. "Tom, at the time, did not have the kind of leverage that an equal partner has at the outset, and he did sign an employment agreement as part of the deal that he did not have me review. I wish he had, as we might have been able to take care of some of that without bruising anyone's feelings later."

The employment agreement had a restrictive covenant in it: Tom agreed not to open a restaurant within a 20-block radius, a common term in contracts with chefs to discourage them from being poached by a rival restauranteur and cashing in on the fame and following they may have developed.

For Danny, Gramercy meant deepening his management skills. He had grown from one to two restaurants. To guide him, he went to Rich Melman of Lettuce Entertain You. As with Milliken and Feniger, Melman would often send David Swinghamer or other executives to help solve a problem.

Danny began planning two new restaurants. He and Tom had both taken a look at the Madison Square building that would later house Eleven Madison Park and Tabla. Then, Danny invited Richard Coraine to join his company Union Square Hospitality Group (USHG) as COO in 1996 and David Swinghamer as CFO in 1997. Coraine had previously worked with David and Ann Gingrass of Hawthorne Lane in San Francisco, and Swinghamer had worked with Rich Melman. USHG was incorporated at the end of 1997. Before the creation of USHG, Tom was offered a percentage of whatever entity was going to own the new restaurants. Sources close to the negotiation said the percentage was very small, 1–2 percent relative to Tom's position as a shareholder in Gramercy. Tom declined.

For Tom, Gramercy was his first ongoing success. Mondrian had gone out of business, and he had left the Quilted Giraffe, Rakel, and 40 Main, all of which later closed. Gramercy Tavern had only increased in popularity and success, yet his majority partner was adding new concepts without Tom's creative input. Also, unlike the other chefs at Meyer's restaurants, Tom came to the table at Gramercy Tavern with a major investor of his own, Bob Scott. In the years since Tom and Bob had first met, Bob Scott had been promoted several times—most recently from CFO to president and COO of Morgan Stanley (January 2001).

If restaurants are highly personal, people-oriented businesses, then partnerships can be likened to marriage. The growing distance between Tom and Danny led to disagreement over how each should be treated by the other. Tom (with Bob Scott) may have overstepped his bounds by assuming rights that may or may not have exceeded those granted by the Gramercy Tavern partnership. From Tom's point of view, however, it seemed that Danny may have considered him more of an employee than a partner.

Whatever the case, after Danny opened Eleven Madison and Tabla in 1998, Tom started thinking about opening a new restaurant of his own.

A landlord from a neighboring building asked Tom for advice about putting in a restaurant in his space. Tom expressed interest in the space himself and starting tossing around concepts. The proximity to Gramercy Tavern—the space was on the next block—made it possible for Tom to keep his hands on both places almost at once.

Lori added, "I think Tom's culinary style had been evolving for some time, moving from intricate to elemental, but he didn't want to make changes at Gramercy Tavern, since that was a menu that was working well." A new restaurant would give him an opportunity to create a more contemporary restaurant, to explore his evolution and play with it. The idea was to present the finest ingredients, each separately, so that the diner assembles the meal at the table. The point was to do a minimum amount of manipulation, so that the taste of the ingredients came through. The dishes would be served family style, shared among the diners. The new restaurant was born out of necessity: he couldn't do another Gramercy, especially not without the blessing (and participation) of Danny Meyer.

He went to Danny with the concept, and Danny expressed no interest. He kept Danny abreast of every major step; still Danny said nothing. Then, just as Tom was about to sign the lease, Danny refused his permission. Tom's employment agreement forbade him to open within 20 blocks of Gramercy Tavern.

The situation came to a head. Tom wondered why Danny was allowed to open two more restaurants essentially devoid of any participation by Tom, but Tom could not do the same without Danny's consent. Both of them had probably overstepped their obligations to each other by that time, but they decided to resolve matters quietly and amicably. With the help of lawyers on both sides, as well as Bob Scott, Danny acquiesced and an agreement was reached. Tom opened his restaurant unopposed. Both parties agreed that Gramercy Tavern was the property of the Gramercy Tavern investors and neither would take that concept further.

Still, the Meyer-Colicchio "marriage" had produced a child that neither wanted to lose. Both sensible adults, they came to a new arrangement and entered a new, limited relationship, so that Gramercy remained unharmed. They resolved that Tom would step aside as executive chef at Gramercy Tavern but become managing partner. John Schaefer, a longtime Colicchio protégé, would become executive chef. Otherwise, the commercial relationship was ended, and Danny and Tom went on their commercially separate ways, joined at the hip, as it were, by Gramercy Tavern, shared walls and all. They are still engaged socially: Danny came to Martha's Vineyard for Tom's wedding to Lori Silverbush just after 9/11.

Last word on the subject goes to Danny, and the matter is closed:

> We engineered a deal. It was challenging—people looked at us like we were crazy—where we are partners in Gramercy Tavern but we are actually competitors in other ventures. I know that nine out of ten people would have never done that, but—see that wall? That's Craft. It's only gotten busier [here at Gramercy] since Craft opened. He is known here as chef/partner, and John Schaefer is the executive chef. Tom is like a co-restaurateur with specialty in the kitchen; I'm co-restaurateur with specialty in the dining room.

TOM secured Bob Scott's interest in his solo restaurant. Bob Scott knows that the financial savvy he provides is often the difference between success and failure:

> The reason that most restaurants go out of business is that you've got a chef and his family. They put all their money on the table. That is enough to get the doors open, but they don't understand that you are going to operate for 6 months or a year or 18 months at a loss. It takes more money until you get established, until you get your clientele. Most restaurants open, operate for 6 months, and then go belly up. They haven't thought it through.

Tom already had a few investors lined up, like Tom Tuft, chairman of Equity Capital Markets at Goldman Sachs, while Scott brought in his boss at Morgan Stanley, former chairman Dick Fisher. All were enthusiastic restaurant-goers and looked at the investment as something fun as well as a financial vehicle for building wealth. They were also willing to ante up more money if the restaurant went overbudget.

Tom returned to Peter Bentel, the architect of Gramercy Tavern, to de-

Courtesy of Archphoto/Eduard Huber

INTERIOR OF CRAFT

sign his new restaurant, Craft. The restaurant space had been a copy shop, now derelict and abandoned. Tom provided only the barest of directions for Bentel. "We had to unpack his ideas," said the architect, while Tom described what he meant by cooking as a "craft" and his respect for ingredients. "The notion was that it should be a warm, inviting place and that you should feel like you are in someone's home."

Bentel slowed down entry, building up excitement by using the abandoned lobby off to the side to create an entrance for the restaurant. They broke up the large room without adding any walls, instead using existing terra-cotta columns and hanging chandeliers of bare amber bulbs that in effect lowered ceilings and created more intimate spaces. A curved, walnut and leather wall dominates one side, opposite a steel and bronze wine vault behind the bar. Artist Stephen Hannock designed a huge mural for the back wall that gave the sense of a window without being a bucolic landscape. The point was to present materials that contrasted with one another, that were handcrafted and would age with grace.

"We like to think of our work as turning nature into culture, viewed or tasted," Bentel explained. "We essentialize some aspect of natural things. That describes Tom's cooking quite well: he takes a morel and makes it taste more of morel than it did when it was growing."

Craft drew on Gramercy Tavern veterans for its staff, including two *sous chefs.* Tom recognized that one of Gramercy's assistant managers, Katie Grieco, a Cornell hotel school graduate, had business skills above her position at Gramercy. While Tom continued to oversee the kitchen at Gramercy, he put Grieco in charge of construction at his new restaurant.

Craft developed a similar kind of philosophy of hospitality to that of Gramercy. According to Grieco, "A lot of people confuse service and hospitality, and think they are one and the same. They are not the same. Service is a series of steps that take place. In our minds there are right and wrong ways to do service: you pour water from the right. We aim to do all those efficiently and properly, and in an unobtrusive way so that the guest doesn't even know it's happening. But hospitality is the intangible part of it, the warmth, the way the staff approaches the table and might go the extra mile. When someone says, I can't decide between these two wines by the glass, which should I have, the captain will take it upon himself to bring both bottles over and give a taste of each. So it's the little things like that, I think, that make a big difference."

Craft opened in March 2001, several months behind schedule because of construction problems. The lateness did not hurt too much, since after three nominations, Tom had finally won the James Beard Best Chef New York Award in the spring of 2000. That fall, his book, *Think Like a Chef,* had been published (and won a James Beard KitchenAid Cookbook Award in May 2001). *Think Like a Chef* was written during 1999 and finished in early 2000. Danny Meyer wrote a foreword for the book. Chef and cookbook author Catherine Young compiled the recipes of dishes Tom made at home. The text was written by Sean Fri and completed by Lori Silverbush.

Lori said, "I kept forcing Tom to tell me about a kid from Elizabeth, New Jersey, evolving into a great chef. I always felt that the learning process would be the key to the reader relating to him and trusting his creative process."

Think Like a Chef could be the slogan for Craft. Both represent the next step in his thinking about cuisine. Tom said, "I looked at what I was doing over the last ten years, between Mondrian and Gramercy. In most instances, it was the same dish that was pared down. I started to simplify, and there was a lot of talk about simple food and great products. That is where I got the idea. We are talking about great products and what is the best way to highlight these ingredients, to do as little as possible without combining them with a lot of other ingredients and just highlighting the ingredients. The difficult part was how do you do that."

What Tom came up with in 2001 was in part a return to the traditional menus from the turn of the nineteenth Century, when meat or fish and vegetable and starch were all ordered separately. Craft's menu listed dishes according to how they are cooked—braised or roasted—and by the ingredient—meat, fish, vegetables, mushrooms, potatoes, or grains.

"We had a *ton* of back-and-forth for at least a year," Lori said, "about whether people would go for family-style service coupled with *haute cuisine* and whether they would show up for food that seemed—at least on the surface—to be so 'simple.' I can remember at least one occasion when Tom, me, and my best friend Rachel stayed up almost all night debating this."

The original Craft menu did away with first and main courses, but that proved unpopular. Eventually the menu was divided along more traditional lines and even included a very un-Craft-like chef's tasting menu in which the diner had no choice at all. However, diners would continue to be served communal dishes from which they could help themselves family style.

The dishes were plain and white, Japanese-inspired dishware that most restaurants use. All this focuses on the ingredients. With only peas in a dish, they had to be perfect peas, cooked expertly. This emphasis on unadorned and uncomplicated superior ingredients could also be seen in Europe at Michel Bras and at Alain Ducasse's Spoons restaurants. "There is a big difference between buying Grade A sushi tuna and Grade C. It's all about the product," Tom said.

Service itself was also changed at Craft with the further demotion of the role of the waiter. Tom Colicchio's original design of the Craft menu is the ultimate expression of the diner designing his or her own food. As Bob Scott described in simple terms, "It's like a Chinese Restaurant with American food: Column A, Column B, Column C. You order the things you like. It comes family style, and everybody can share."

Actually, it is more like the Horn & Hardart Automat restaurant chain: the diner selects his or her own food. Of course, the difference between an Automat and Craft lies partially in the wait service but mostly in the quality of the food and preparation and the addition of fine wine. The food is all about the chef. At Craft, food is not made that morning to be stored in small compartments until diner selection; it is crafted on demand in the kitchen for final assembly by the diner. In effect, there is no more "plating" of food by the chef at all. Food is presented in communal dishes for final plating by the diner. Beyond the waiters' hospitality role, there was little for them to do but explain the customers' new role to them. As Adam Platt of *New York* magazine reported someone saying in Craft, "It's as if they've rearranged the way traffic works."

Was Tom consciously or unconsciously recalling the Automat concept? It seems that he had something like it in mind at inception. Craft's designer, Peter Bentel, said that one of the things Tom does not remember is his wanting for Craft "one room with a big refectory table." Bentel tried to retain that sense of "room" without breaking it up as had been done at Gramercy Tavern. Ultimately, Bentel compromised with lights and other space-creating tricks, to create intimacy. Otherwise, Craft would have been "too damned big"—like an Automat.

The verdict on Craft came back quickly. Five years earlier, Ruth Reichl had written about Tom at Gramercy for *The New York Times* that, "He seems to be trying to extract the essence of each ingredient, and he is fearless in following through." It is small wonder then that in April 2001, only one month after Craft opened, Reichl's successor William Grimes, wrote: "As the name artfully, or craftily, suggests, the cooking concentrates on fundamentals, with ingredients subjected to the bare minimum of manipulation. That's part of the idea. The other part is the job set aside for diners, who must throw aside their passive role and join Craft's chef and owner, Tom Colicchio, in the joyous job of building a meal . . . Mr. Colicchio, the chef and a part owner of Gramercy Tavern, breaks new ground at Craft." Two months later, Grimes weighed in rather fearlessly himself with three stars as his opening rating for Craft, which he christened "a vision of food heaven."

Another *New York Times* food journalist and prolific cookbook author, Marian Burros, also touted the Colicchio line on craftsmanship of simple, high-quality food rather the art of food transformation. She cited a chain of greatness, from Delmonico's a century earlier to Alice Waters and a group of top French chefs including Michel Bras, Jean-Michel Lorain, and Alain Ducasse. Unlike the rest, she noted, Tom "puts all the dishes in the center of the table, family style. Grazing is encouraged."

New York magazine's Adam Platt referred to Craft as "a palate-cleansing break from what my extremely chaste mother-in-law refers to as 'garbaged-up restaurant food.'" Still, Platt admitted, the menu might be a little too revolutionary: "This kind of culinary chaos may not put Craft in the pantheon of the city's great restaurants."

Grimes had also warned in his first review about Craft's menu, "It's more challenging than *The Weakest Link,* and at the moment there is no shortage of eager players. We'll see how many of them enjoy the game." By June 2001, while giving him three stars only three months after opening, Grimes further cautioned—almost addressing Tom directly with a fatherly (or patronizingly, depending on how one reads Grimes) tone, "In the abstract, freedom of choice is desirable. But the arts, including the culinary arts, function more efficiently as dictatorships. Down with interactivity. Readers do not really want to decide what happens in the next chapter of a novel, and diners are happiest submitting to the iron will of a good chef."

Other reviews were mixed, with some reviewers complaining about how expensive the restaurant was and how difficult it was to order. Tom admitted, "I didn't know if people paying this price point would say, 'Hey, I am not serving myself!' I don't think people were comfortable enough in a dining room 10 years ago for this to work."

Katie Grieco said that they took the criticism seriously and started to rethink the menu. They decided not to list the sauces and condiments separately. Tom reformatted the menu to indicate clearly what was a first or main course, relieving much of the customers' confusion.

Bob Scott's wife Karen was very dubious about the pricing, but Scott was confident that Tom would correct that pretty quickly. Waiters started to explain that each dish was large enough for sharing with other diners, encouraging people to order less.

Tom worked on a second cookbook published in October 2003, *Craft: Notes and Recipes from a Restaurant Kitchen,* again with Cathy Young and Lori, which sketches 24 hours in the life of Craft. Lori was responsible for the narrative. The recipes are largely from *chef de cuisine* Marco Canora.

WHEN Tom was negotiating the lease for Craft, he also looked at a lease for the space next door, which became vacant only eight months after Craft opened. Tom played with the idea of expanding Craft but decided against that and against a private dining space, popular in New York restaurants.

"What we really wanted was to make a fun place that we would want to go on our night off, if we didn't work there," said Katie Grieco. "I think Tom believes—and I think he is right—that one of the things that makes Gramercy Tavern a complete experience is that it has the front, casual part—the tavern, a more casual place—before the more formal place in the back. So, it was our attempt to have that part of the Craft concept. I think we are all really glad we did it." Grieco became the manager of Craftbar as well as Craft.

Tom opened Craftbar in January 2002, to warm welcome. Eric Asimov of *The New York Times* wrote in March 2002 that Craftbar is a place "where needs are joyfully met rather than challenged. In this way, Tom Colicchio, an owner and the chef of Craft and Gramercy Tavern, bridges the yawning divide between conceptually ambitious luxury restaurant and neighborhood hangout."

Craftbar's concept is similar to Charlie Palmer's Chefs & Cuisiniers Club of a dozen years earlier and lies only three blocks south (Craftbar is on 19th Street, the old CCC site on 22nd Street, now Charlie's Kitchen 22). Craft's *chef de cuisine* Marco Canora was given free rein to develop the simple bar menu, featuring sandwiches and a few entrées.

The restaurant was again designed by Bentel & Bentel and featured the same bare light bulbs and steel wine tower that were used in Craft. Sharing the kitchen with Craft, Craftbar didn't need a second liquor license.

Meanwhile, Tom was approached by a number of hotels and casinos in Las Vegas to build a Craft restaurant there. Gamal Aziz, the food and beverage director at Caesars, had courted him before Craft was built. Aziz moved to the Bellagio to work for hotel tycoon Steve Wynn and helped bring a number of America's best chefs to Las Vegas, including Jean-Georges Vongerichten, Todd English, Michael Mina, and Julian Serrano. Once Aziz became president of MGM Grand, he met Tom again at Gramercy Tavern while lunching with Julian Serrano.

Tom was convinced that Aziz did have the mandate to change the restaurants of the MGM Grand radically, and therefore the hotel's customers. He respected what Aziz had accomplished in the Bellagio and believed that the MGM Grand would attract chefs of his caliber. The MGM Grand built out the entire restaurant on the site of the old Brown Derby for $5 million. Tom supplied the menu, chef, and training for hotel-employed staff. The result was Craftsteak, opened in 2002.

Bentel & Bentel again handled design. Craftsteak shares much of the same elements as Craft, but it is much larger and in a new kind of space, namely the shopping mall and restaurant area of a world-class hotel. Lighting plays perhaps an even more significant role, aided by furniture design, to create warm, table-centered communities within large, otherwise plain rectangular rooms the size of halls.

Tom brought in veteran Chris Albrecht to run the show. Albrecht is a study in Colicchio: cool, smart, and hardworking. Still, Albrecht faced some tough odds in Vegas. The restaurant competed with earlier established chef-name or brand-name steakhouses on the Las Vegas Strip, including Charlie Palmer Steak, Emeril's Delmonico, Jean-Georges' Prime, Smith & Wollensky, Ruth's Chris, Fleming's, and others. To add to that burden, the restaurant also had average checks of $60 competing with hotel room rates as low as $79 at the MGM Grand itself.

"If you don't do serious volume, labor is expensive, since it's a union house," Tom said. "We need a certain level—250 seats sometime during the evening. We are not getting that early or late, but we still need the staff."

Tom lowered prices to appeal to the hotel guests. He marketed the

INTERIOR OF CRAFTBAR

Courtesy of New York Magazine

restaurant to locals as well as convention-goers. Thanks to the hotel, he can offer guests private shortcuts into the restaurant so they don't have to slog through the hordes milling about one of the world's largest hotel-casino-mall complexes (5,034 guestrooms alone). A year after Craftsteak opened, individual guests at the hotel were spending 15 percent more on average during their stay.

One consultant who watched the deal commented on all the challenges facing Tom. "I never believed in that deal in the first place. The MGM Grand has over 5,000 rooms. It's self-sufficient. It's not an easy hotel to get into. Locals don't go. The parking lot is a nightmare. The restaurant is far from the lobby." The hotel itself is in transition while Aziz buys all the restaurants in MGM Grand and puts in new concepts.

Despite these odds, Craftsteak received accolades from R. W. Apple Jr. in his end of 2003 review of Las Vegas steakhouses, "Craftsteak produces my best meal of this visit," beating out Jean Vongerichten's Prime and Charlie Palmer Steak.

Just as the Craftbar space had come available, so too another space next to Craftbar also came up. Sisha Ortuzar, a *sous chef* at Craft and former *sous chef* at Gramercy Tavern, was anxious to do something in that space that would take Craft into a new area. He wanted to make it a sandwich bar, which was the original plan for Craftbar. The sandwich bar concept became "Wichcraft."

Katie Grieco, by then acting COO for all Craft restaurants, was again put in charge of the project. "In some ways it's more difficult. It's a part of the business we have never done. We don't do takeout. We have ideas about the different margins business-wise, but I have no idea if we are going to do 100 or 400 covers a day. I have no idea how many people will walk in the door. That makes it particularly challenging. It's really unknown territory." The take-out restaurant with a few seats on an upper floor opened in May 2003, gaining coverage and praise from critics.

Wichcraft is in fact the possible roll-out vehicle. It's easily replicable and easily sellable. The MGM Grand in Las Vegas planned to open a Wichcraft by midyear 2004. Tom is also penning his third book based on the sandwiches served at Wichcraft.

Yet, Wichcraft lies outside the original Craft concept. Customers can't choose the ingredients they want in their sandwiches, nor can they choose to have them grilled or not. The menu is set as it is in Craftbar.

Still, the ingredients are up to the Craft standard, and quality is what Tom is finding at the heart of his Craft brand.

As Danny Meyer did with Union Square Hospitality Group, Tom and Bob Scott created Foodcraft, LLC, which acts both as holding company for Colicchio-Scott interests and as back-office management company.

To generate extra cash for both restaurants and staff, Tom consults. When he was planning Craft, an opportunity came to him to work on another restaurant, raising some cash and using his staff. Charles P. ("Buddy") Darby III and his family company was developing Kiawah Island, a private development off the coast of South Carolina that includes a world-class golf course. They invited Tom to fly down to Kiawah to discuss doing a restaurant for the club at about the same time that he was starting to build Craft. The clubhouse's restaurant was called Voysey's, after the English architect Charles F. A. Voysey, upon whose work the clubhouse is modeled. Independently, Darby had also hired architect Peter Bentel.

Tom gave Kiawah a copy of Craft's rather than Gramercy Tavern's cuisine. Doug Blair, a chef from Kiawah, trained at Craft and Gramercy. Tom, his *sous chef,* and sommelier all visit the restaurant often, lured as much by golfing and fly-fishing opportunities as by contractual responsibilities. Tom's title is consulting chef, and both he and his cuisine are mentioned in Kiawah literature.

Tom consulted for Bid, a restaurant at Sotheby's on the Upper East Side. He put a former *sous chef* from Gramercy Tavern and Tabla, Matt Seeber, in as executive chef and Chika Tillman as pastry chef, also a Gramercy veteran.

Tom consulted for the Core Club, a private club at 65 East 55th Street in Manhattan due for completion in the first half of 2004 and founded by Jennie Saunders, who helped create the Reebok Sports Club New York. The designer, Universal Design Studio, also designed Damien Hirst's restaurant Pharmacy as well as Stella McCartney's first store in New York and boutique in London. Again, an outside chef from the club trained at Craft and Gramercy.

These consultations generate extra income so that Tom can hire more back-office staff at Foodcraft, such as human relations and public relations people, while training more managers for future restaurants. "I will take those deals when they help me build infrastructure," Tom said.

On the wall of Tom's office above Craft is a huge framed poster of a boat with the name *Seacraft.* "We are talking about doing Seacraft, a seafood restaurant similar to what we are doing at Craft. I always wanted to do a seafood restaurant. I love fishing. I love the ocean. That is the last thing I will do in the Craft brand."

Bob Scott, who vacations in Palm Beach, Florida, is urging him to do a Seacraft there. Kiawah's Buddy Darby wants a Wichcraft and Seacraft on his island. Tom may also do a Seacraft in Manhattan or at a golf course in New Jersey. He is open to combining elements of all the Craft restaurants into new ventures in which he might mix a raw bar with a Wichcraft or a Craftbar.

One of Tom's investors, Tom Tuft, has proposed raising a $20 million fund to be spent over five years on various projects, including more Craft restaurants. That would put an end to raising funds for individual restaurants, as most restaurateurs do now. It would also mean coming up with a five-year expansion plan for Craft, Craftbar, Wichcraft, and Seacraft, consulting, branding and cobranding product lines, and growth of management-level staff. Tom is considering the idea seriously.

"If I had the right people I would do another long-distance restaurant, in L.A., or somewhere on the West Coast or in Scottsdale, Arizona, or overseas. Again, I will do it if it makes sense. L.A. would be a perfect place for Craft. We have tons of people who come in who work in L.A. If you are on any diet you can go to Craft and it works, it's so liberating it's great. We have a huge Hollywood following," said Tom.

ANOTHER component of Tom's empire is supporting other restaurants. Tom has said, "I want someone to come to me and say, I have an idea, I found a space, and my response will be: sit down and write a business plan with Katie. She will help you, but I want you to think it through. I want you to think about the business end of it. I want you to have some ideas. I don't want to have to say 'I want to do this' and hire this guy to do it. I want them to come to me and say, I have a passion and a desire. I want to do something."

The first experiment in backing other chefs in his organization is backing his most important chef, Marco Canora. Just as Tom himself wanted to do a restaurant on his own, without Danny Meyer, Canora wanted to come out from beneath the shadow of Tom Colicchio. Rather then sever his ties with Craft, which he helped build, Canora wanted to keep a relationship with Craft while going out on his own to build his own restaurant, Hearth, which opened in November 2003 in New York's East Village.

Canora and Gramercy's former general manager Paul Grieco, Katie's husband, approached Tom for help. He figured Craft would provide the back-office support, including public relations, in exchange for a management fee. This would add to the possible success of the new venture, since neither Canora nor Grieco has ever owned or managed a restaurant by themselves. The income from the management fee would help build infrastructure within Craft for future expansion.

The model that Tom has created has taken Charlie Palmer's business to a new level. His Foodcraft will service not only the back office for his own restaurant, but other chefs' as well. In addition, Canora can keep working with Craft in some capacity rather than cut his ties with the restaurant. Tom asked his investors if they were interested in backing Canora and Greico's new venture. Many opted in.

Tom said, "Paul and Marco came to me and said, we want some help with this, but we don't want this to be a Tom Colicchio restaurant. And I don't want it to be either: it's their restaurant."

Bob Scott recognized the benefit to the Craft brand of expanding it to embrace Canora's restaurant. "To his credit, Tom is recognizing in Marco the same feeling he had for Gramercy—I need to have something in my own name, try my own thing—and rather than see that as a challenge to his authority, Tom's interpretation of it is: here is a way for someone to be my protégé and my partner. It's an opportunity, not a problem, and therefore, let me be supportive. If Marco becomes visible and developed his skill at Craft, it's a different way of leveraging the brand. Marco becomes part of the brand: let's embrace that rather than feel that it has to end in divorce." Craft, no matter how loosely it is associated with Hearth, will benefit from the brand extension.

As the brand developed, the original partners in Craft, who were also partners in the other restaurants so far, had to take stock of who owns the brand. "The people who took the risk, the people who provided the financing," Bob Scott explained, "Tom is one of those people. He has a substantial financial stake. Me, a few other people, we collectively own the brand. I admire his instincts to leverage that. The market is waiting to see the new things you guys are going to do." But the choice of how to grow the brand clearly rests with Tom Colicchio, not his partners.

BASKETBALL. Michael Jordan is playing basketball. A Dr. Dre song plays in the background, What's the Difference, and Phish sings the refrain "What's the difference between me and you?" While a narrator explains that this is Michael Jordan, who won six NBA championships even though he missed half his shots, the scene shifts to a stocky white guy playing basketball. The narrator explains that this is Tom Colicchio and declares that in *his* competitive industry he can't afford to miss, even once.

So begins "Heat," an episode from the PBS series *Life 360.*

Tom had repeatedly said that he would not do television. "If they want 64 segments, I can't do it. You know, a two-week shoot where that is all I am doing—I can't do that right now. There is just too much going on."

While Craft was being built, however, Tom took the unusual step of allowing a film crew in to shoot the restaurant. The producer, Robe Imbriano, a veteran writer-producer from ABC News and CBS News, was initially going to film three different chefs and tie their experiences together, but eventually he settled on doing an episode only on Tom for *Life 360,* a collaboration between ABC's *Nightline* and PBS.

When Imbriano met Tom at Gramercy Tavern, he was excited. "We didn't want pressure: we wanted pressure *and* craftsmanship. Under pressure you would create something wonderful: swinging doors, celebration and peace and beauty on one side, and through the doors, chaos, pain, blood. We sat down with Tom at Gramercy and started talking about craftsmanship. He started laughing. I said, 'What is wrong with you?' and he said, 'I am actually opening a restaurant, and we are calling it Craft!' We knew it was supposed to happen."

Tom gave Imbriano and crew complete access to Craft as it was being built. The episode, which aired in October 2001, showed the great extent to which the whole project was in the hands of Katie Grieco. "He puts a lot of trust in very young people. His name is attached to it and his ability to deliver. They rise to the challenge, and he lets them know they are valued," said Imbriano. The episode also showed the first evening of Craft's new food and a restaurant full of Craft investors and their guests.

The opening basketball shots made Imbriano's point clear—that drive, natural and learned talent, and teamwork are as much admired and desired in chefs as in professional athletes. The same kind of celebrity that many athletes strive for to bring them monetary returns and accolades is what the chef looks to earn, too. Chefs and athletes just play in different courts.

Tom was no newcomer to television. The top-ten rating in 1991 from *Food & Wine* magazine provided his first media opportunity, a cooking spot on the *Regis & Kathy Lee Show.* Arriving as instructed for a shoot at 8:00 a.m., he found a producer furious with him for failing to show up for 6:30 a.m. rehearsal. By the time his segment came on, in which he prepared red snapper with roasted eggplant caviar, he was a nervous wreck.

"I had a whole eggplant that I had cut and scored, and I had another that was already cooked in the oven. The oven wasn't turned on. Regis turned and saw the oven wasn't on and started trying to turn it on. I looked at him and said, 'Come over here!' I started showing him what to do and took the eggplant out of the oven. He turned to me and said, 'I guess this is what happens when you miss rehearsal!' " Regis was not referring to Tom; he had also missed rehearsal and was talking about himself. "It was very funny. It was a great segment," Tom said.

The producer invited him to come back whenever he wanted, but he turned her down. Since then, he has done plenty of television appearances on daytime talk shows and food shows, but he has chosen not to do his own TV show.

Despite his protests, however, he *is* doing more TV than *Life 360* or the CBS *Early Show.* About the same time as he did *Life 360,* he participated in another documentary by Kostas Metaxas called *The Stylist: Kings of the Kitchen.* Bob Scott, however, is against any serious incursion into TV. "If that were his priority, then something would be happening to Tom the person that I would find unattractive."

Tom has already discussed further TV, albeit more limited than a series. "We have an idea to do *Think Like a Chef.* It's there. We know how to do it. We can put together a production crew. I don't know if I can shoot it," but Lori has experience in film and access to production staff.

Tom is tempted.

CONCLUSION

THE most talked about issue among chefs and Super Chefs today is branding. Many chefs with only one restaurant talk about building a brand. Yet personal brands even among movie stars and athletes are hard to measure compared to corporate brands like Coca-Cola or Nike. Brand experts disagree on what constitutes a personal brand and what does not.

David Falk, who has been Michael Jordan's business agent for almost two decades as well as a restaurant investor, said, "There are chefs with high visibility because of television, not cooking. Television has transformed those individuals into celebrities. Wolfgang—in very limited circles he may [have a brand], not on a wide consumer basis." In his opinion, most Super Chefs are celebrities and can endorse products, but they do not have personal brands.

"Michael Jordan is a brand," Falk said. "When they put his silhouette on a cologne bottle, they didn't put the name on: *that* is a brand. . . . If you turn on the NBA finals and see Shaq and Kobe playing, there is an audience worldwide of 500 million people watching it." Barely 5 million people watch a chef show, Falk estimated, and less than 5 percent of Americans would ever recognize any given chef's silhouette.

Wolfgang Puck Worldwide, which owns the Wolfgang Puck brand, has tried to create a mass-market brand by reinforcing brand elements. They use the "Live, Love, Eat" slogan everywhere. Wolfgang chants "Live, Love, Eat" relentlessly on his TV show. His latest cookbook is called *Live, Love, Eat: The Best of Wolfgang Puck.* "Live, Love, Eat" is slapped all over the Wolfgang Puck Express units. The Wolfgang Puck Coffee website has a page called "Live, Love, Eat" Coffee Break. A popup page greets new visitors to his home page with the banner "Live, Love, Eat with Wolfgang Puck!" and then invites visitors to sign up for e-mail.

Expert David Aaker, author of such books as *Brand Portfolio Strategy* (2004), *Brand Leadership* (2000), *Building Strong Brands* (1996), and *Managing Brand Equity* (1991), disagreed with Falk's definition. "A brand is anything that denotes who makes a thing or provides a service. When you get on TV, your awareness goes way up and so does your credibility," Aaker said. "A chef that gets his strength from a few restaurants won't have nearly the exposure of someone on TV." Still, creating awareness alone, through TV or otherwise, is not enough to strengthen a brand. Quality must be consistently maintained, or awareness simply spreads negative customer loyalty. Thus, not only must Wolfgang have a TV show, but it must be consistently good, expanding viewership, strengthening the brand, and so forth. This goes for his restaurants, his pots and pans, and all his other businesses.

Most chefs do not think long term, and they do not think of the discipline demanded in consistent branding. Consistency implies a long time and demands discipline—the discipline to say no to inappropriate income sources, no matter how attractive. Most chefs, however, opt to maximize immediate income and sign up for every half-reasonable-sounding deal that comes their way, rather than refuse short-term deals that may hurt whatever brand they have developed. David Falk refers to this kind of chef as a "flash in the pan." In general, Wolfgang, Todd, and Mary Sue and Susan have all fallen into the "flash in the pan" trap at one point or another. Charlie and Tom have managed largely to avoid it.

As for mass-market branding, Mary Sue and Susan are still undecided about their brand and hope to clarify it through a new TV show. They may have missed a golden opportunity to let others take over the corporate aspects of their empire, including branding, and let themselves concentrate on their own creative abilities. Tom Colicchio is toying with the idea of expanding brand awareness in Wichcraft but in no other areas. Charlie Palmer has toyed with food and kitchen products, but none of those efforts have brought big rewards. Lately, he has started potentially franchisable restaurant brands, such as the "Charlie Palmer Steak" and "Kitchen" concepts.

The only other chef among these Super Chefs who has heavily pursued mass-market restaurant concepts and branding is Todd English, and as his empire re-emerges from hard times, his new team is focusing on brand consistency based on quality in his restaurants. Priceline's Jord Poster, working with Todd to build his brand, believes that everyone has a brand. "Companies have brands. Restaurants have independent brands that we are happy to see are rolling up in the consumer's mind into a consistent message about the global brand." In searching for the essence of the Todd English brand, "All the things Todd does seem to reduce to Excitement, Quality, and Integrity. We are trying to figure out the priority of those." Poster is a firm believer in the one-liner brand proposition: "You have to stand for one thing." (Aaker is dead-set against this concept about brands: "They are very complicated, just like people. Most brands are not represented by three words.") Poster's three-term brand proposition is so generic that it could in fact apply to any Super Chef—as could Wolfgang Puck's three-term proposition Love, Love, Eat.

Todd's blurb in *People* magazine's 50 Most Beautiful People issue of May 2001 seems to be the starting point of Poster's branding for him:

> The square-jawed looks of celebrity chef Todd English are no happy accident. Like the interpretive Mediterranean-style cooking at the 13 Olives Group restaurants he owns across the U.S., they're all about technique and presentation: Vidal Sassoon haircuts every six weeks, daily 40-minute runs and regular eyebrow trims. English, 40, who lives in Brookline, Mass., with his wife, Olivia, 41, and their three children, is a self-confessed style "monster." Suit? Make it black and Armani. Shoes? Prada or Gucci. His "thin, stringy hair," he says, needs Kiehl's Extra-Strength Styling Gel ("I'm neurotic if I don't have it"). The routine works for his pal Martha Stewart, who says. "Oh, those deep sunken eyes, the high cheekbones, his big hands and broad shoulders." So enamored was one diner in his Boston restaurant that she strode up to English and handed him a rose. "I've been on a crazy ride lately," says the 6-foot 3-inch chef, who grew up in Atlanta and last November opened a Manhattan branch of his restaurant chain. "It's wild how chefs have become like rock stars."

There is not one description of food, only of those of his tailor, cobbler, and hair creamery. This is not Todd English, the chef: this is Todd English, the image.

Sid Feltenstein, former head of Long John Silver's, did not buy into Todd's image when he hired him as a consultant:

> We did *not* hire Todd because he is a celebrity: we hired him because I felt he was a great chef. I felt he was very creative. I felt he could do things for us that we could not do for ourselves. We haven't merchandised him in any way to the consumer, because the average consumer doesn't know who he is anyway. So it is not a question of celebrity chefs. In my opinion, the better question is, is there room for outside resources to bring greater culinary creativity to the quick service restaurant segment, and I think the answer to that is definitely yes. And it could be totally an unknown [chef].

Allan Hickok, restaurant industry analyst with Piper Jaffray, agreed: "Branding is sometimes so much mumbo-jumbo: you have to *deliver* at the end of the day."

Is branding even worth pursuing for chefs? From David Falk's viewpoint, the answer is no:

> If you walked into New York and asked 1,000 people who Nobu is, they might tell you he is a South American rugby player or a race car driver. I don't think most people know who he is. I am a sushi nut, so I know who he is, but a brand means that when you walk into an area of commerce that there is a widespread recognition of what the brand is and what it stands for. If you say "Timex," people would say, "It takes a licking and keeps on ticking," or "It's a moderately priced watch." If you say "Maytag," people would say "it's reliable." If you say "Rolls Royce" they would say "upper end"—every body knows what it means as a brand. If you say "Nobu," I guarantee you that most people in America have no idea who he is. The average person in Saint Louis or Chicago, has no idea who he is.

Falk's model of brand building is to move from celebrity to image to brand. Todd is in the process of moving from celebrity to image. Just as consumers no longer watch Michael Jordan play basketball, so they will no longer (only) eat Todd English's food. In which case, will Todd English be about food anymore? And if Todd is basing his brand on press reports about himself, does that mean his new image-based branding is really only so much distorted feedback—from *People* magazine?

Perhaps the problem of mass-market branding is even more fundamental. Think about it in TV terms. A spectator can revel in a basketball player's drive down court and spectacular shot, but once the spectator has watched a chef prepare a dish, there is no corresponding thrill in watching a chef or an audience eat the dish. The biggest thrill in food comes from eating, not watching others eat, and barely from preparation. At best, a cooking show incites spectators to participate themselves by either cooking for themselves or seeking out great food in restaurants. Ultimately, food is not a truly mass-market, spectator sport for television. In which case, television may never be the platform to launch a mass-market personal brand for chefs as it has been for athletes.

SUPER Chefs are here to stay—for as long as any major food trend ever stays. On the immediate horizon, their expansion seems to be curtailed. The 1980s were the time in which most of the Super Chefs in this book established their fine dining credentials and flagships. The 1990s were the time of expansion, most flamboyantly into luxury co-branding at resorts, either Las Vegas or golf courses or cruise ships.

Since the economic downturn of the new millennium, exacerbated by 9/11, it seems that the early 2000s are witnessing a period of consolidation. Las Vegas continues to attract great chefs, currently the *crème de la crème:* Daniel Boulud, Alain Ducasse, and Thomas Keller. Cruise lines continue to add chef names and cobranding differentiators like Seabourn's Chef's Circle and Crystal Cruises hybrid Chinois at Jade.

Cunard seems unable to cobrand enough. In addition to the Todd English restaurant, the QM2 launched with a Veuve Cliquot champagne bar, Harrod's store, a Dunhill's shop, Wedgwood china, Waterford crystal, ad nauseam. Crystal Cruises has added Berlitz language classes, a Barnes & Noble reading club, Yamaha piano classes, and Cleveland Clinic health seminars in addition to Nobu menus to its Sushi Bar and Silk Road restaurant. "Times may change, though," speculated *The Miami Herald.* "Years ago, you never saw chain stores and restaurants in airports. So perhaps the day is not far off when cruise ships may raise a flag with yellow arches." Wolfgang Puck Express, anyone?

The impact of Super Chefs on the food, restaurant, and newly encompassed industries is more profound then these glitzy, ephemeral events. The impact is better seen over the course of the past century. Of the Super Chefs profiled, Tom Colicchio comes closest to encompassing this impact with his original concept for Craft. In one sense, Craft was supposed to engage the diner as chef: choosing each ingredient, creating the dish, and sharing it with other diners. More subtly, the process by which diner approaches chef further removed the last traces of wait service in fine dining restaurants, so that fine dining approaches fast food in terms of table service.

How could this have evolved? Master chef Jacques Pépin explained:

> When I was in France, the people who were important were the *maître d*'s. They had contact with the customers so they could get money. That is what happened with Escoffier and Ritz, and they could get investors and they could get into business. The perfect example is [Henri] Soulé. When he came here, you turn around and you are a chef—and you had no respect . . . There was a big *maître d'* Oscar in Maxime in the twenties with Soulé when he opened the Pavillon. It was great cinema. The carving in the dining room was very important.
>
> Then all of a sudden with *nouvelle cuisine,* the chef decided to divide all of the different vegetables and arrange them on each individual plate—one step further. The dining room became irrelevant [to preparation]; the waiter was just a gofer who goes and gets the plate and puts it there.
>
> Maybe Sirio [Maccioni], Danny [Meyer], and Drew [Nieporent], a few restaurateurs remain, [but] there are no more important *maître d*'s. It was a big switch that comes from *nouvelle cuisine.* From Carême certainly and Urbain Dubois [1818–1901], who started doing *service à la russe,* we have sequential service rather than *service à la française.* From that time on there were big trays being carved in the dining room even though they were sequential.
>
> So the big jump was to move from those trays to put everything on a plate. So all of a sudden there was no more for the dining room in a sense [in terms of food preparation]. All of a sudden, with Bocuse and Dumaine, La Mere Brazier, and Ferdinand Point, all of them created a theory, with Les Troisgros. They spread the gospel: the chef was in the dining room.

Wolfgang Puck agreed with Pépin. As he recalled, Michael McCarty and Patrick Terrail thought that as *restaurateur* as well as *maître d'* that they were the most important people in the restaurant. "They thought that people come to see the *maître d'*. Now, it's great to have a *maître d'* who knows everybody and everything. I'm not saying that that job is not important, but at the end of the day, if you don't have somebody who runs your kitchen really well, then, culinarily speaking, you're going to be in the weeds. And this is a business where you don't want to get in the weeds!"

Pépin and Puck have envisioned the general change in food and restaurants up to the point of *nouvelle cuisine* chefs, but Super Chefs and in particular Tom Colicchio have taken this process another step forward. Tom's original Craft concept reduced wait service almost completely to the level found in a diner: they just bring the food. The demand on the diner was a bit too radical for the times, but that Tom presented it at all and that he won the ravest reviews from the toughest critics at *The New York Times* shows that the general public was nearly ready for this trend.

What is the next step, beyond Craft? Diners picking up their own plates at a kitchen window, with no wait staff at all? What about food preparation? After Craft, will diners enter the kitchen and prepare their own food? Unlikely, said William Grimes: "Diners are happiest submitting to the iron will of a good chef."

Is this so unlikely? A "chef's table" is typically inside the kitchen, where diners share not only food directly from chefs but also watch and learn. What about fine dining food kits, in which all the ingredients are shipped to a diner's home and the diner gets to "cook" the mostly prepared food according to instructions? Over the past century, the chef has assumed two roles, that of restaurateur and that of wait staff who finalize food preparation, but Tom is suggesting that chefs surrender the newly won wait staff function directly to the diner.

Where wait staff can still make a difference is in hospitality, and so hospitality is highly prized by Charlie Palmer, Wolfgang Puck, and Tom Colicchio, hearkening back to César Ritz and Auguste Escoffier in the grand hotels and restaurants in Europe and America. As Michel Escoffier, Auguste Escoffier's great-grandson, said, "Both Ritz and Escoffier created the modern luxury hotel system, which is still in practice today. Obviously, there have been technical changes but not in terms of hospitality or quality of service." The "enlightened hospitality" developed by Tom Colicchio and Danny Meyer at Gramercy Tavern and the hospitality of Charlie Palmer and Wolfgang Puck strive to match great cuisine with great hospitality.

As Patrick Terrail wrote of Ma Maison:

> We became *the* place to be seen. Why did this happen to Ma Maison and not some other restaurant? If I had the answer, I would package it and sell it. But I can tell you what I think contributed to the restaurant's success: at Ma Maison, we created a pleasant environment that had great food, great service, and an atmosphere where the guests were always comfortable.

FEW of the Super Chefs planned to build empires when they started their careers. "I can't believe that any of these people . . . had ideas 20 years ago," said Tom Colicchio. "I can't believe that Todd English said to himself 20 years ago, 'I want to own 20 restaurants': none of us did. We didn't have a model to do that, until Wolfgang Puck. When I started cooking when I was 15 years old, I had no idea—I didn't know what a chef was!"

While Super Chefs had no models, the challenge to the young chefs of today is no longer whether to venture into uncharted territory but whether they want to stay the more traditional course of an André Soltner or move into the newly charted territories of Super Chefs, either as their rivals or as teammates. The decisions they are making today are made more complicated by the successes of Super Chefs, who have helped make the marketplace more attractive and competitive. A little help from friends, advisors, schools, and partners never hurts in the decision-making process, but there is little science in any of this, only art and accumulated experience.

Each of these choices has its good points: remaining a one-shop chef, expanding into a few restaurants or into many, maintaining and refining fine dining food and service, or extending those into casual dining and on down, teaching on television or creating the interest to learn cooking through TV entertainment, selling superior food and cooking products, and writing insightful cookbooks. Super Chefs have expanded the horizons for all chefs and even expanded the field of study at culinary schools. One can only hope that each and every new chef cherishes and treasures these choices—and chooses well, so that the accumulated experience and knowledge of centuries continues to be handed down, generation upon generation.

Glossary

Amuse Bouche: Small dish served before a meal begins to whet the appetite, literally "amuse (the) mouth."

Casual Dining Restaurant: Casual or homey décor restaurant with full service, bar or wine service, and signature food menus, at less expensive prices than a Fine Dining restaurant.

Chef (de cuisine): The chief (of the kitchen), to whom reports the *sous chef*. As kitchens have grown larger, there may be more than one *sous chef*. When chefs or restaurateurs expand, there may be an executive or corporate chef over several *chefs (de cuisine)*.

Coquilles St. Jacques: Scallops or "shells of St. James," so called in French because the scallop shell was the symbol of the crusader Order of Saint James.

Crostini: Thin slices of lightly toasted bread, with a variety of spreadable toppings.

Cuisine Bourgeois: Food cooked homestyle.

Cuisine de Grand-mère: Food cooked according to traditional recipes transmitted from mother to daughter, literally "grandmother's cooking."

En Papillote: Food baked inside a wrapping of parchment paper.

Fast Casual Restaurant: Casual décor restaurant with limited wait service, some wine or beer offerings, and more upscale menu offerings than a Fast Food restaurant.

Fast Food Restaurant: Minimal décor restaurant with very limited or no wait service offering inexpensive food.

Fine Dining Restaurant: Formal décor and full wait service restaurant with extensive signature menus, wine lists, and high prices.

Front of the House: The diners' (waiters') section of a restaurant, as opposed to the kitchen, which is the cooks' section.

Garde Manger: Cook responsible for the the pantry.

Grains of Paradise: Medieval European pepper substitute undercut by pepper from India, also known in English as guinea grains, alligator pepper, and Meleguetta pepper, which gave its name to the West African "Pepper" or "Malaguetta Coast" (present-day Liberia). Not to be confused with *capsicum fructesens malagueta* or Malagueta chili of Brazil.

Haute Cuisine: Food prepared in an elaborate or refined manner, usually cited as starting with LaVarenne (1615–1678), literally "High Cooking" (like High Fashion).

Hobo Pack: foil-wrapped packet of food cooked on coals.

Hoisin Sauce: A rich, dark, sweet barbecue sauce made of soybeans and seasonings, used in Chinese cooking.

Nouvelle Cuisine: This French movement of the early 1970s encouraging simpler sauces with less butter and cream, seasonal ingredients, and more regional dishes than in haute cuisine.

Paillard: A thin slice of beef or veal that is quickly grilled.

Parchment Paper: A heavy grease- and moisture-resistant paper.

Plating: Arranging food on a plate that will be served to the diner.

Quick Service Restaurant: Industry term for Fast Food Restaurant (q.v.).

Service à la Russe: The practice of serving dishes sequentially at a formal meal so that food would not lose flavor and hot dishes would be eaten as hot as possible. It largely replaced *service à la française* in which many dishes were displayed at the same time in a great show of abundance and choice, often sacrificing flavor for show.

Shabu Shabu: Literally "swish, swish" in Japanese, a dish prepared at the table by the diner who cooks thin slices of beef or other meat and vegetables in flavored broth and then dips the slices in various sauces. The broth is then eaten with noodles.

Shelf-stable Product: Packaged food that stays fresh without refrigeration, such as bottled or canned products.

Stage/Stagier(e): Cook who is granted a *stage*, which is temporary work in a kitchen for little or no money for the purpose of learning a chef's techniques.

Turns: Number of times each meal that seats are filled with diners.

Sources

These are people and organizations that have helped in the writing of this book, providing interviews, information, or other assistance:

Wolfgang Puck: Barbara Lazaroff; Klaus Puck; Tom Kaplan, Bella Lantsman, Jannis Swermann, Irving Feintech, and Pam Korman; Maggie Boone, Kay Collins, and Madeline Benito; Jennifer Naylor and David Robins; Joe Essa; Carl Schuster, Kevin Charbonneau and Clare Britell; Rob Kautz, Don Karas, Irv Siegel, Steve Gratz, Rebecca Miranda, Jason Budow, Andrew Muñoz, Norm Kolpas, and Barbara Westfield; Sydney Silverman; Tom Moats, and Lee Magnes.

Charlie Palmer: Lisa Palmer; Craig Fuller; Kathy Perretta, Karen Chamberlain, and Judy Lederman; Spero Plavoukos, Randy Scott, Robert Belcher, and Tim Bartley; Andrew Bradbury; Joe Romano, Megan Romano, Dante Boccuzzi, Bryan Voltaggio, Mark Purdy, and Dan Shannon.

Todd English: Todd's mother, Wendy English; Gina Gargano; Jord Poster, Ken Cox, and Sam Slattery; Joe Brenner, Steve Mannino, Clay Conley, Victor LaPlaca, Chris Ainsworth, Todd Winer; Michael Ilic and Tony Cochones.

Mary Sue Milliken and Susan Feniger: Josh Schweitzer; Carollyn Bartosh; Chris Mortenson (and author-wife Laura Kopelke) and Randy St.-Clair.

Tom Colicchio: Lori Silverbush; Phil Colicchio; Bob Scott; Katie Mautner Grieco; Marco Canora and Chris Albrecht; Jason Lapin; Jocelyn Morse.

Other Super Chefs and Chefs: Roy Yamaguchi of Roy's; Alan Wong of Alan Wong's Restaurant; Joachim and Christine Splichal, and

Octavio Becerra of the Patina Group; Nobu Matsuhisa, Gregorio Stephenson, Yukari Hirata-Elston and Ritchie Notar of Matsuhisa International; Mark Peel and Nancy Silverton of Campanile; Suzanne Goin of Lucques and A.O.C.; Marc Orfaly of Pigalle; Martin Yan of Yan Can Cook; Bradley Ogden of Lark Creek Group; Michael Mina of The MinaGroup; Debbi Puccinelli of Aqua Development Corporation; Ann Gingrass of Desiree Café; Justine Miner of RNM; Thomas Keller of The French Laundry; Hiro Sone and Lissa Doumani of Terra; Mark Miller and Javier Escalera of Coyote Café; Kerry Simon of Simon Kitchen & Bar; Jennifer Jasinski of Panzano; Robert Del Grande of Schiller Del Grande Restaurant Group; Paul Prudhomme and Shawn McBride of K-Paul; Robert Kirchoff; Barbara Lynch of No. 9 Park; Brad Stevens of Food Project Youth; Sara Moulton of the Food Network and *Gourmet;* Lidia Bastianich of Felidia; Alfred Portale of Gotham Bar & Grill; Rick Moonen of rm; David Burke of Park Avenue Café; Gerry Hayden of Amuse; Kerry Heffernan of Eleven Madison Park; Daniel Boulud, Georgette Farkhas, Joel Smilow, and Lili Linton of DINEX Group; Alain Ducasse, Michelle Bouillet-Escale, and Marianne Walsh of ADG; Larry Forgione and Justin Rashid of American Spoon Food; Jean-Georges Vongericthen of Jean-Georges Enterprises; Bobby Flay of Mesa Grill; Bill Rogers of NoHo Star; Douglas Rodriguez of O.L.A.; Scott Linquist of Dos Caminos Mexican Kitchen; Dennis Foy of Dennis Foy's; Luke Palladino of Specchio; Masaharu Morimoto and Don Fellner of Moridon; Jerry Bryan of Coastal Grill; Norman Van Aken and Carl Burggemeier of Norman's; Jean-André Charial of l'Oustau de Baumanière; Kajsa Dilger of Carlyle; Tinker Boe of Mood Food.

RESTAURATEURS: Atsuyuki Tsukikawi of SOHO's Hospitality Group; Michael McCarty of Michael's; Piero Selvaggio of Valentino; Mickey Kanolzer of Palace Entertainment; Barbara McReynolds of L.A. Eyeworks; Kevin Finch of Dish; Deann Bayless of Frontera Foods; Rich Melman of Lettuce Entertain You Enterprises; Gerald Centioli of Icon LLC; Sid Feltenstein (retired) of Yorkshire Global Restaurants (now Yum! Brands); Michela Larson of Sapphire Restaurant Group; Steve Hanson of B. R. Guest, Inc.; Danny Meyers, David Swinghamer, Jenny Zinman, and Cathy Clausing of Union Square Hospitality Group; Drew Nieporent and Tracy Nieporent of Myriad Restaurant Group; Buzzy O'Keeffe and Joe Delissio of River Café; Phil Suarez of Suarez Restaurant Group; Steve Tzolis of Periyali.

Culinary Schoolmasters: André Soltner, Jacques Pépin, and Dorothy Hamilton of the French Culinary Institute; Frederick Metz, Tim Ryan, and Ginny Mure of the Culinary Institute of America; Rick Smilow and Steve Zagor of the Institute of Culinary Education; Florence Berger and Kathy Dedrick of Cornell University's Stattler School of Hospitality.

Experts on Food & Restaurants: Julia Child; Anne Willan and Janis McLean of La Varenne; Julie Duran of Fondation Auguste Escoffier; Michele Escoffier; Chuck Williams of Williams-Sonoma; Len Pickell and Caroline Stuart of the James Beard Foundation; Judy Gethers; Catherine Young; Tori Rogers Klein of Fork in the Road Marketing; Rick DeMarco of Zyng Noodlery; Charles Baum of The Bartiste Group; Elizabeth Blau and Lisa Hoyt of Elizabeth Blau Associates; Bob Sutcliffe, Esq., of Digital Gene Technologies; David Rosengarten of *The Rosengarten Report;* Ariane Daguin and George Faison of D'Artagnan; Jim Koch and Michele Burchfield of Boston Beer Company; Elizabeth Carovilliano of Whole Foods; Nick Valenti of Restaurant Associates; Frank Guidara of Au Bon Pain; Timothy McMahon of ConAgra; Alice Elliot of Elliot Associates; Dolf Berle of House of Blues; Allan Hickok of Piper Jaffray; Richard K. Miller of Richard K. Miller & Associates; Joe Chabus of Darden Restaurants; Walter Dunn (retired) of Coca-Cola; Barry Wine; Helene Siegel; Tom Warner; Martha Wright of Scott Paul Wines; Colette Rossant.

Media & Entertainment: Ken Hertz and Niki Johnson of Goldring, Hertz & Lichtenstein LLP; David Jackel of Gelfand, Rennert & Feldman LLP; Tom Ryder and Ellen Barker of Reader's Digest; George Lois of Lois/USA; Eric Ober of Global Information Group; Gary Grossman, Rob Weller, Debbie Supnik, Steven Lange, and Christine Cavalieri of Weller/Grossman Productions; Reese Schonfeld and Pat O'Gorman of Beauchamp Communications; Carrie Welch and Sangeeta Rao of the Food Network; Lou and Leslie Ekus of AirTimeCorp; Holly Jacobs of Buena Vista TV; Risa Saslow and David Roberson of *The Wayne Brady Show;* Laurel Lambert of KCET; Elise Bromberg of UPN; John Bard Manulis and Lulu Zezza of Visionbox Media; Meyer Gottlieb of Samuel Goldwyn Company; Hector Elizondo, Jacqueline Obradors, and Mark Teitelbaum of Teitelbaum Artists Group; Robe Imbriano of Crystal Staircase Productions; Bruce Camber of Small Business School with Hattie Bryant; Kostas Metaxas of Exero Media; John Shoup of *Great Chefs;* Shep

Gordon of Alive Entertainment; Rob Kenneally of Creative Artists Agency; Carl Bressler of Montana Artists Agency; Perry Rogers of Agassi Enterprises; David Falk of SFX Sports Group; John Steinbach of TaylorMade; Neal Lenarsky, Adam Bauman, and Stacey Normandie of Strategic Transitions, Inc.; Arnold Peter of Little Mendelson PC; Jonathan Fisher of Urban Angler; Angel Gil-Ordóñez of the Post-Classical Ensemble; Tim Zagat of Zagat Surveys.

Hospitality & Hotels: Gamal Aziz, Chuck Bowling, and Jenn Michaels of MGM Mirage; Kevin Stuessi of Wynn Resorts; Hal Kolker of Pendragon Development LLC; Philip Kendall of Meadowood Napa Valley; Marc Ricci of Starwood Hotels & Resorts; Brian Yost of Marriott International; Menze Heroian of Disney's Swan and Dolphin Hotel; Charles P. "Buddy" Darby and Ronnie Musselwhite at Kiawah Development Partners; Ainsley Wintrip of The Four Seasons; Michael Wilkings of MagiCorp Entertainment; Edie Bornstein of Cunard; Richard Meadows of Seabourn; Ramsey Mankarious of Kingdom Holding; Paolo Patrone of Terraved Management; Tom La Tour of Kimpton Group; Larry Meltzer of LSG Sky Chef; Marco Degl'Innocenti of National Hall; John Assumma of Waccabuc Country Club; Cinda Poulsen of the International College of Hospitality Management "César Ritz."

Architects & Designers: Eddie Sotto of SOTTO Inc Studios; Mark Fuller of Wet Design; Peter Bentel and Rob Costello of Bentel & Bentel Archtitects; Joan MacKeith of Rockwell Group; Eric Engstrom of Engstrom Design Group; Paul Vega of Vega P. Architecture; Tony Chi and Tammy Chou of Tony Chi Design; Adam Tihany and Adriana Gelves of Adam Tihany Design International; James Rossant of James Rossant Architects; Tomas Rossant of Polshek Partnership Architects.

Business Experts: David A. Aaker; Bruce Stein of Westridge Consulting LLC; Ichak Adizes of the Adizes Institute; Bruce Hodes of Contextual Management Institute; Selwyn Joffe of Motorcar Parts & Accessories; Dr. Robert Koblin; Don Stone of Stonekelly; Charles Cohen of Cohen Brothers Realty; Bryan Earl of American Woodworks.

Charity: Pam Korman of the American Wine & Food Festival, Maryanne Bloomfield of City Meals on Wheels; and Gail Margolis and Charles Spaulding of Scleroderma Research Foundation.

Press: Michael and Arianne Batterberry of *Food Arts;* Dana Cowin, Susan Choung, Melissa Lynch, Elizabeth Curtis, Elisa Shevitz, Salma Abdelnour, and Kate Heddings of *Food & Wine;* Ruth Reichl and Jocelyn Zuckerman at *Gourmet;* Barbara Fairchild of *Bon Appétit;* Richard Martin of *Nation's Restaurant News;* Peter Elliott of Bloomberg; Charles Perry of *Los Angeles Times;* Laurie Ochoa of *LA Weekly;* Alison Arnett of *The Boston Globe;* Tom Sietsema of *The Washington Post;* Susan Radlauer of *People;* Annie Post of *Slammed;* Bruce Shenitz and Eric Chandler of *Out* magazine; Donna Fenn of *INC* magazine; Arthur Lubow of *The New Yorker.*

PR & Events: Jennifer Baum and Susan Gross of Bullfrog & Baum; Melissa Fields and Ariane Yazdan of Yazdan & Fields; Julie Fox and Alyssa Holzman of Julie Fox Consulting; Elaine Driscoll of Regan Communications; Mimi Gorin of R/A Performance Group; Alan Segan and Holly Fussell of Rubenstein PR; Amy Voll and Sharon Bowers of First Name Media; Stephanie Wilson of Kirvin Communications; Sam Folsom of Welles Folsom; Christine Ziccardi Schwartz of Magnet Communications; Michael Weisberg; Sharon Cook of Cook PR; Frank Flynn of Verité Communications.

Books: Some of these books were sources, while others inspired—Timothy Shaw, *The World of Escoffier;* Anne Willan, *Great Cooks and Their Recipes: From Taillevent to Escoffier;* Patric Kuh, *Last Days of Haute Cuisine;* William Echikson, *Burgundy Stars;* Felipe Fernández-Armesto, *Near a Thousand Tables;* Eric Schlosser, *Fast Food Nation;* Patrick Terrail, *A Taste of Hollywood.*

Libraries and Bookstores: The Los Angeles Public Library system for both books and online services, particularly the in-depth online *Los Angeles Times* database; Dartmouth College Digital Library for Alumni; Myra Weinberg of National Restaurant Association Library; Cook Books by Janet Jarvits (Pasadena, CA); Cook's Library (West Los Angeles); and Kitchen Arts & Letters (New York).

Special mention goes to Jacques Pèpin, David Falk, Joachim Splichal, Christine Splichal, Octavio Becerra, Daniel Boulud, Georgette Forkas, and Len Pickell for their insight and comments, as well as Michael and Ariane Batterberry for covering these chefs so well for so many years, first in *Food & Wine* and then at *Food Arts.*

INDEX

AUTHOR BIOGRAPHY: JULIETTE ROSSANT

JULIETTE ROSSANT is an author and journalist raised in New York City. After co-founding *The Stonefence Review* at Dartmouth, she was stationed in Istanbul, Moscow, Paris, and Jeddah, where she wrote as much on food and travel as on business and politics. At *Forbes* magazine she wrote the Celebrity Chefs column in the *Forbes* annual "Celebrity 100" issue as well as the Middle East section of the annual "Billionaires List." Now based in Washington, D.C., Juliette is working on her second book as well as consulting to the media and food industries.